How
Breakthroughs
Happen

How Breakthroughs Happen

The Surprising Truth About
How Companies Innovate

———

ANDREW HARGADON

Harvard Business School Press

Boston, Massachusetts

978-1-57851-904-0 (ISBN 13)
Library of Congress Cataloging-in-Publication Data
Hargadon, Andrew.
    How breakthroughs happen : the surprising truth about how companies innovate / Andrew Hargadon.
       p. cm.
Includes bibliographical references and index.
    ISBN 1-57851-904-7 (alk. paper)
  1. Technological innovations—Management. 2. Technological innovations—Management—Case studies. 3. New products. 4. New products—Case studies. I. Title.
    HD45.H336 2003
    658.4'063--dc21

                      2003006393

Contents

Part Three: How Firms Pursue Innovation Through Technology Brokering

Foreword

Can Innovation Really Be Routine?

Strategy answers two fundamental questions: where to go and how to get there. Yet although most executives give a perfunctory nod to the importance of how to get there, they spend their time on where to go. The emphasis of strategic thinking in many corporations is on debating a particular position strategy, such as low cost, or a specific competence strategy, such as exploiting a unique logistics capability. As a result, executives focus on picking markets and competencies rather than on coming to grips with how they can discover, shape, and execute strategies more effectively.

Nowhere is the folly of neglecting how to get there more striking than in markets where strategy relies on repeated innovation. In these markets, positions are fragile and competencies are often short-lived, making where to go challenging to figure out. At the same time, the required innovation is inherently serendipitous and almost impossible to predict, making how to get there essential to understand.

This focus on how to get there is, in brief, the breakthrough of Andrew Hargadon's book. Andrew has uncovered insights into how innovation really happens. The book moves past examining emergent innovations from a 50,000-foot perspective to passionately caring about how they occur—up close and in gritty detail. It dismantles the myths of innovation to reveal how some executives, engineers, and scientists make breakthrough innovations almost routine.

While *How Breakthroughs Happen* is replete with insights, from my vantage point two observations are crucial. The first is the idea that innovation is the result of synthesizing, or "bridging," ideas from different domains. As Andrew observes, Henry Ford and colleagues created the assembly line from an unlikely blend of observations drawn from Singer sewing machines, meatpacking, and Campbell Soup. Elvis mixed gospel music with rhythm and blues, while growing up between the black and white communities. The engineering firm Design Continuum pulled together ideas from medical devices to develop the breakthrough Reebok Pump shoe. These and other extraordinary innovations are the result of simultaneously thinking in multiple boxes, not of the oft-prescribed "thinking outside the box." In short, extraordinary innovations are often the result of recombinant invention.

The concept of bridging reveals a couple of counterintuitive points. First, whereas it may be appealing to focus on the future, breakthrough innovation depends on exploiting the *past*. Combining often well-known insights from diverse settings creates novel ideas that can, in turn, evolve into innovations. This kind of evolutionary approach is how biology, in some ways the most innovative science, works. Moreover, innovations that rely on the past are pragmatic. They save developers and their managers time and money, even as they lower risk. In contrast, innovative attempts that focus on developing fundamentally new visions from entirely novel knowledge very often fail. This path is too slow, too challenging, and too risky.

A second counterintuitive point is that organizing *structure* can dominate individual creativity. Most of us buy into the myth that breakthrough innovation is the product of individual creative genius. Yet years of academic research suggest that, beyond some fairly low threshold, successful innovators are not really more gifted or creative than the rest of us. Rather, they simply better exploit the networked structure of ideas within unique organizational frameworks.

The other crucial observation is that breakthrough innovations depend on "building" communities. Of course, the substance of the innovation has to be there. But the ideas that go on to become breakthrough innovations rely on fundamentally rearranging established networks of suppliers, buyers, and complementers into new networks or ecosystems. Otherwise, hoped-for innovations never develop. The initial innovation is the starting line of the race, not the finish.

This observation underscores yet another counterintuitive point: Innovation is as much *social* as it is technical. Resistance must be met, and alliances forged, because people often cannot understand innovations, or cannot see how they would benefit if the innovations were adopted. Breakthrough innovations must often be cloaked with references to existing activity. For example, Amazon.com's managers and engineers disguised their Internet technology with the trappings of the retailer around the corner, such as "shopping carts" and "checkout." eBay's founders developed a cozy myth about Pez dispensers to attract early, nontechnical customers who wanted to trade their collectibles. Thomas Edison even capped his electric lightbulb with a useless lamp shade that nonetheless provided customers with a comforting reminder of their old gaslights. In contrast, attempts to bring digital film technology to Hollywood have been thwarted by the resistance of the established network.

The example of Edison brings up a final counterintuitive insight. Although myth portrays Edison as a lone creative genius, he actually worked in a *collective*. He depended especially on a close collaboration with about fifteen other people at his own Menlo Park lab. Ironically, as that lab dispersed, Edison's "genius" ebbed. So whereas innovators may often feed the romantic myth of the lone inventor, breakthrough innovations are more likely the products of groups.

When Andrew asked me to write this foreword, I was more than a little surprised. Of course, I was familiar with some of his ideas from working with him at Stanford, but I did not realize how much Andrew had become his own "technology broker." Most books that set out to describe innovation rely on the lens of either the wizened business veteran or the dispassionate academic scholar. In contrast, Andrew synthesizes his experience as an engineer charged with creating innovations and his practiced, disciplined eye as a thoughtful social science researcher. He blends real-world experience with smart concepts from networks and, more broadly, complexity theory, such as small worlds, weak ties, and structural holes. He uses a backdrop of Schumpeterian economics blended with a clever dose of quirky stories and genuine passion about how innovation really happens. He banishes the myths about the creative loner with the futuristic vision; they are replaced with a much more accurate and actionable view that is at once both startling and comforting. Breakthrough innovations depend on ordinary people, bridging their expertise and building communities around their insights. They can be managed. Breakthrough innovations may never become routine, but they certainly can become more likely. As I mentioned earlier, strategy too often neglects the question of how to get there. Yet, especially when innovation matters, the strategy *is* the organization.

—Kathleen Eisenhardt
Stanford, California

Preface

Perhaps the most important question about innovation is whether to pursue it at all. From the strategic choices of the executive management team to the decisions of managers in the trenches of new product and process development, organizations continually face this choice. Ultimately, it comes down to a trade-off between exploiting existing technologies to survive today and developing revolutionary new technologies to thrive tomorrow, between exploiting existing advantages and exploring for new ones.[1]

In boom times, firms often ignore this trade-off by throwing money at both. In tough times, however, R&D investments get cut like everything else, and projects focused on breakthrough technologies are shelved to devote resources to the more certain returns of incremental extensions to existing product lines. This is a mistake. Not in the choices firms make—hard times are hard times—but in the assumption that such a trade-off must be made.

This book is about the strategies and work practices of groups and firms that have built an enduring capacity for breakthrough innovations. It describes ten years of research on a set of firms that found a way to avoid the trade-off between exploitation and exploration and to circumvent the years, if not decades, it usually takes to move from invention to commercial exploitation of a new technology. Theirs is not a strategy of large or long-term investments in developing revolutionary breakthroughs, yet somehow that's what they produce—in many cases, time and again. Instead, these organizations have figured out a way to explore and develop innovative new technologies by exploiting existing ones. They show us that the pursuit of innovation need not require big bets on uncertain futures.

Along the way, these organizations also show us another way of thinking about, and organizing for, the innovation process. The notion of the lone genius laboring away in the basement laboratory to invent a future is, by now, one we should all be safely free of. And yet its vestiges remain in the way organizations pursue innovations: We've exchanged basement laboratories for isolated R&D centers, eccentric geniuses for newly minted M.B.A.'s and Ph.D.'s, and the "Eureka" moment for patent filings. Even in the trenches of new-product development, we reward people for coming up with new ideas and, in the process, create "not invented here" cultures that refuse to pursue ideas they didn't come up with themselves.

Moving between historical accounts of the labs, workshops, offices, and factory floors where past technological revolutions originated and field studies of similar processes at work in today's organizations, this book provides a framework for understanding how the innovative efforts of a few people, working with already developed ideas and objects, can piece together revolutions. In short, this book describes how innovative firms can succeed not by breaking free from the constraints of the past but instead by harnessing the past in powerful new ways.

The result is an innovation process that thrives by making smaller bets, by building the future from what's already at hand. It's not about a cheap way to get secondhand innovations—some of the most profound technological revolutions in history emerged in this way. Indeed, I will argue that such humble origins are a requirement of truly revolutionary innovations.

Nor are these firms all that rare, although this side of their story seldom comes out. To many, for example, Thomas Edison was a creative genius. Indeed, Edison did more than perhaps anyone else to fix in our minds the notion that innovation is the province of the creative genius and his or her inventions. Yet those who worked alongside him tell a different story, as does closer examination of the technological marvels that emerged from his Menlo Park lab. Instead, Edison owed his success to his ability to build his inventions from the previous work of others—work that spanned markets, continents, and decades. Edison took elements of these existing technologies and recombined them in ways that had never existed before and for markets that had never seen them before. The origins of other technological revolutions—the development of mass production, the transistor, the personal computer—reveal similar hidden histories. These backstage stories do not detract from the revolutionary impact of these technologies, but they do require dramatic changes in how we perceive and, in turn, pursue the innovation process.

To capture this process, this book develops a networked perspective of innovation, a perspective that is shared by fields as diverse as network theory, cognitive psychology, microsociology, and the social studies of technology. Recent work in these fields has, either explicitly or implicitly, sought to explain the complex dynamics that take place between individuals and the larger systems in which they are embedded. Individual thought and action are powerfully shaped by their surroundings and yet, at the same time, individuals remain capable of using these very surroundings to create new and profound changes. From this perspective, an insight becomes an innovation becomes a revolution, through its relation to the larger network from which it comes and which, ultimately, it reshapes. Edison and others were capable of generating breakthrough innovations because they understood and exploited this larger landscape—they pursued an innovation strategy of *technology brokering* that enabled them to exploit the past in creating the future.

This book establishes the theoretical framework for such an innovation strategy, links this theoretical framework to the psychological and sociological mechanisms that underlie the innovation process, and considers its implications for managing innovation in organizations. The book is divided into three parts. Part I introduces the strategy of technology brokering. Part II describes the networked perspective of innovation and how this strategy influences the innovation process within organizations. Part III, the majority of the book, is devoted to providing specific and practical examples of how firms have chosen to implement technology brokering strategies.

In the research and writing of this book, business, history, and science all came together—quite literally. The original insights that spurred this book took place while I was conducting fieldwork as a doctoral student with Professor Robert I. Sutton at Stanford University. We were studying IDEO, a highly successful engineering design firm located in Palo Alto, California: hanging around, talking to the designers, watching them at work and at play. We did not go to IDEO looking for the firm's innovation secrets. I had worked there part-time as a mechanical engineer while I was a graduate student in Stanford's Product Design Program and had been struck by the culture of the place. We went there as researchers to consider how that culture shaped the risks engineers were willing to take every day in pursuit of new ideas. At the same time, however, I was reading George Basalla's wonderful book *The Evolution of Technology*, which traces the neglected but decidedly continuous origins of revolutionary innovations. I recognized in his accounts of the historical origins of the steam engine, for instance, the same process that was at work in IDEO as engineers designed new medical devices, computers, and toys. To be sure, the steam engine triggered the first industrial revolution, while the others did not. But the process was the same—an accumulation and recombination of existing ideas rather than a flash of inspiration and unprecedented invention.

It occurred to us that one of the critical conditions that made IDEO so innovative was how the firm organized around this process of recombination rather than invention. As a firm, it bridged multiple industries. Its innovative new designs brought together many of the interesting ideas its engineers had seen at work in these different settings. The firm's culture and work practices, such as brainstorming, did not so much make the engineers creative as it made them able to exploit these connections to other industries. As I looked deeper into other histories of innovations and looked past the initial accounts of individual heroes and their inventions, I found more supporting evidence suggesting the same process was at work.

We called IDEO a *technology broker* because as a firm it profited by spanning industries and moving ideas from where they were known to where they were not, and published our findings in two articles in *Administrative Science Quarterly*, the top journal for organizational scholars. I then spent the next five years pushing this line of inquiry further. What other organizations acted in this way? How did the work practices of these firms interact with their larger strategies? And how did these strategies interact with the larger network? What effects did this process have on individual learning and creativity? I have since published some fifteen academic articles on various aspects of this work—ranging from academic volumes to more practical outlets such as *California Management Review* and *Harvard Business Review*.

Academic studies of organizations are often derided as lacking practical value for managers, but I have always believed, as the eminent psychologist Kurt Lewin once said, that there is nothing more practical than a good theory. As such, this book represents the next logical step in the process that moves from research to practice. Having developed these ideas within the give and take of the academic community, I turned to the writing of this book and the introduction of these ideas to the mainstream management audience.

The primary audience for this book is managers who, in their own work and in the work of their organizations, are engaged in the pursuit of innovation. My goal was to combine and translate past academic research into practical and valuable lessons for anyone attempting to build the innovative capabilities of his or her organization. The major findings in this book place the creative work of individuals and groups within the larger context of organizational strategy, and place that within the larger context of ongoing patterns of technological change across industries. As a result, I've tried to make the ideas of this book useful both for managers looking to increase innovation within their teams and for executives constructing the innovation strategies of divisions and firms.

But the history of this book, the paths that brought it to this point, required that it be written for an academic audience as well. For historians of business and technology, I have foremost tried to demonstrate the enormous potential of their ideas in providing both context and guidance in managing innovation in the modern enterprise. Space prohibits me from doing justice to the depth of their research that underlies the histories presented in this book. It is my hope, however, that these accounts point the way toward more efforts to bridge the divide between the historian's account of what happened and the manager's need to understand what happens.

Finally, this book is for management researchers and consultants. I have tried to build a view of the innovation process that highlights connections between such previously diverse fields as economic history, sociology, and psychology. The meticulous scholarship of historians of technology, the solid and growing work in social networks, and the vast literature on creativity have each, alone, provided valuable insights into the innovation process. But even more valuable insights will come from the combination of these theories and methods and their application to practical problems in the management of innovation.

PART ONE

Technology Brokering and the Pursuit of Innovation

1

The Business of Innovation

In 1877, on a single workbench, sat a small collection of objects that would in the next few years profoundly change the technological landscape of America and, in short order, the rest of the world. The workbench ran the length of Thomas Edison's laboratory in Menlo Park, New Jersey. From 1876 to 1881, that lab produced innovations in high-speed, automatic, and repeating telegraphs; telephones; phonographs; generators; voltmeters; mimeographs; lightbulbs and filaments; and vacuum pumps. To be fair, during that time the lab also produced many promising but ultimately fruitless innovations in iron mining, electric railroads, thermal sensors, ink for the blind, electric sewing machines, and vacuum storage of food.

Edison built the laboratory, in his own words, for the "rapid and cheap development of an invention" and promised "a minor invention every ten days and a big thing every six months or so."[1] And he delivered. In six years of operation, the laboratory generated over 400 patents and was known worldwide as an invention factory. It was Edison's most prolific period as an inventor; on leaving Menlo Park, he turned his efforts to exploiting a number of the business opportunities the lab had created.

The Menlo Park laboratory represented the first dedicated research and development facility and showed the industrial world the power of organized innovation. Over a hundred years later, it still provides valuable insights into the innovation process for modern managers and researchers.

Thomas Edison, for example, remains the prototypical inventive genius. Countless books and articles have tracked his every move since childhood: He was born in 1847 in Milan, Ohio, the youngest of seven children. He was a poor student, with less interest in schooling than in the agricultural and industrial machinery that lay about the town. He sold newspapers and candy on the Grand Trunk Railroad to Detroit. He was a constant experimenter. He disrespected authority. He took a lot of naps. He invented a lot of things.

We know a great deal about the man, but, for all that we know, we've learned very little about how to manage modern companies in the pursuit of innovation. Historians and journalists alike provide a clear picture of Edison's childhood and his work habits but really tell us little about how to replicate his success. All of this knowledge, told and retold countless times, tells us more about our assumptions concerning the innovation process than about Edison's success—that innovation is about the invention of revolutions, carried out by individuals capable of abandoning the past and embracing the future. Gary Hamel, for instance, writes in *Leading the Revolution* that those of us incapable of escaping the pull of the past will be lost to the future. In Hamel's words, and building on the ideas of Charles Handy, entrepreneurs (like Edison and his laboratory) must be able to "produce something out of nothing. They struggle not against Nature but against the hegemony of established practice."[2] In such deep-seated beliefs, the notion remains that innovation is best undertaken by those gifted few who are capable of ignoring established practice.

Edison certainly exploited this image of the inventor as a heroic genius fighting against the misguided ways of the existing markets and technologies. Indeed, when the group at Menlo Park realized the value of Edison's growing image in the press, they all took to the process of mythmaking, as one of the engineers at Menlo Park recalled. Edison's worldwide search for the "most perfect" fiber for his lightbulb filament, for example, took place largely as a publicity campaign to advertise his lightbulb and his invention process—Edison had already found a perfectly acceptable material in bamboo fibers pulled from a fan lying about.[3] The image of inventive genius served Edison well by drawing potential investors, the media, and ultimately customers to his innovations and influencing the inevitable patent disputes with other inventors.[4] When Edison died in 1931, the *New York Times* said of him:

> No figure so completely satisfied the popular conception of what an inventor should be. Here was a solitary genius revolutionizing the world and making an invisible force do his bidding—a genius that conquered conservatism, garlanded cities in light, and created wonders that transcended the predictions of utopian poets.[5]

Edison's lone genius tapped into the American dream that anyone with an idea and energy could make it big. But while that image of solitary genius may have helped Edison, it doesn't help—and may even hurt—those of us trying to understand and replicate his laboratory's success.

Networks of Innovation

This book is about Edison and others who have shown they are capable of producing breakthrough innovations time and again. It is also about clearing away the smoke, looking behind the mirrors, and seeing how the innovation process *actually* took place in Edison's Menlo Park laboratory, in Henry Ford's Highland Park factory, and in so many garages and on so many workbenches throughout the past century.

Getting past the smoke and mirrors requires a new perspective on the innovation process, a networked perspective. The networks we are interested in are not the clean and simple notions of networks that dominate the headlines, such as those that wire us into one global village, where communication is instantaneous and connections abound; not the networks that corporations use to build virtual organizations, manage distributed project teams, or form global alliances; not the networks that made up our rolodexes yesterday and make up our Palm Pilots today; not even the networks that link ant colonies, beehives, and other complex communities—though all of these do have their effects. The networks we are interested in are much messier. But if we are willing to tolerate their ambiguity, we'll see that their influence on our beliefs and actions is more profound.

The networks we are interested in are those that link people, ideas, and objects together in ways that form effective and lasting communities and technologies. Max Weber, the father of modern sociology, once said that man is suspended in webs of significance he himself has spun. These webs form the networks we're interested in because they give order to the infinite number of people, ideas, and objects that surround us. You won't find these networks listed on an organization chart, in some root directory, or in the assembly instructions of your computer. Yet we confront their reality daily.

The network that surrounded the electric lightbulb in the 1870s, for example, connected Edison to Moses Farmer, whose own incandescent bulb Edison had seen in 1859 in a shop window in Boston. It connected Edison to Joseph Swann, a contemporary working in Newcastle, whose experiments in the 1850s and again in the 1870s with the incandescent bulb may have led Edison to this design as well. And it connected to the intriguingly elusive J. W. Starr, who had filed a caveat for a U.S. patent on the incandescent bulb in 1845, but who died on his return trip from England, where he had filed a similar patent. Edison's original patent application for the electric light was rejected, it was reported in the January 18, 1879, issue of *Scientific American,* because "Edison's invention was an infringement upon that of John W. Starr, of Cincinnati, who filed a caveat for a divisible light in 1845."[6] The web of innovation that surrounded Edison's electric light involved others as well. Most of the time in Menlo Park, between five and fifteen engineers all worked in relatively tight quarters upstairs, in a single long room where the workbenches, technical apparatus, books, and raw materials were kept. Working so near to one another meant that each was intimately involved in the projects and experiments of the others. In the words of one engineer who was lucky enough to work there, "we were all interested in what we were doing and what the others were doing."[7]

But the network that surrounded Edison was more than simply other people. Edison learned much by using, building, and tinkering with the objects of the emerging telegraph industry and elsewhere. He learned from the wiring that connected telegraph lines across the city, so dense in places that it darkened the skies. He learned from the circuits that allowed two, then four, and then eight telegraph signals to use a single line. He learned from the generators and other artifacts being built around arc lighting. And he shared in the rapidly changing ideas about electricity both in the scientific community and in industry.

To single Edison out from this growing web is to record one truth—that Edison was quite remarkable—and in the process experience many lies: Edison neither invented the lightbulb nor acted alone in improving upon it. The web around Edison was thick with ties to other people, ideas, and objects that together made up his particular "invention." Who Edison knew, what he and his engineers learned from the existing technologies of the day, what they believed possible, and who they convinced to join in their ventures all created the landscape in which his innovations took shape. Ignoring these connections hides central insights into how innovations unfold, because this web shapes the behavior of individuals and organizations in profound ways.

The price we pay for a networked perspective, for abandoning the simplicity of individual inventors and their inventions, is significant. Established facts need to be revisited, old assumptions questioned, and traditional stories retold. Reading so many modern business tomes, it seems as though we have, in the words of one student of technology, John Law, "lost the capacity to apprehend complexity."[8] Of course, there is as little value in finding out that "it's all very complicated." But those who stay with this book until the end will find the value of a more nuanced view of the innovation process itself.

Technologies as People, Ideas, and Objects

We tend to think about technologies as hardware or software—nuts and bolts, bits and bytes—the purely physical objects that come to mind easily. But these objects are themselves deeply enmeshed in particular networks of people, ideas, and other objects. To work as intended, they need skilled people and appropriate ideas. The twenty-two-ounce hammer on my desk right now is fundamentally different in the hands of a skilled framer, who knows how (and why) to drive a tenpenny nail home in two blows. More complex technologies involve more complex objects, but also more complex links to particular people and ideas.

From a networked perspective, these relationships among people, ideas, and objects *are* the technology. More formally, *technology* is defined here as the arrangement of people, ideas, and objects for the accomplishment of a particular goal. Such a perspective provides a way for us to consider the relationships among these three elements of technology. Existing technologies are unique combinations of these three elements. The objects are hardware and software, the physical objects that are tangible and relatively unchanging. The ideas are understandings of how to interact with those objects. And the people are those who know the ideas and objects. Their experiences have given them the tacit knowledge that makes the ideas and objects work effectively together.

Take a low-tech example: the guitar. As an object, it is a body, neck, headstock, and strings. As an instrument for producing music we can call it a technology—just as a milling machine cuts steel or a software accounting system keeps books, a guitar produces music. But it remains just an object. The idea of music varies across cultures, as do the ways that people use those ideas. To say a flamenco guitarist and a classical guitarist are using the same technology is to recognize what's common but deny some very valuable differences. Consider Bo Diddley, Dick Dale, John Lennon, and Pete Townshend. Each used a guitar, but in fundamentally different ways, for different audiences, and for different purposes: to sing the blues, ride the waves, spread the word, or just vent. Changes in any of these three elements—the people, the ideas, or the objects—can have profound changes on the overall system.

Now consider the telegraph. It has been called the "Victorian Internet," and its impact on the structure of business and society in the nineteenth century was rapid and revolutionary.[9] Its emergence as a technology describes the coming together of a particular set of people, ideas, and objects. The first telegraph, in 1774, was a set of twenty-six conductors (one for each letter of the alphabet), though neither electricity nor wiring was well understood at the time. Over time, new ideas about generating electricity and insulating wires were added. But arguably the most important addition was Samuel Morse's 1837 idea of conveying text messages through a series of dots and dashes over a single wire (Morse code). The next important addition to the emerging telegraph network was the telegraph operator, who learned to hear, and speak, in Morse code fluently. The technology continued to evolve throughout the nineteenth century, as people like Thomas Edison and others developed new objects and ideas that allowed the sending of more signals, faster and farther, over the network of wires spanning the globe.

Ever more complex technical systems emerge from combinations of smaller technologies. The Internet grew out of an initial combination of computers, networking technologies, and communication protocols, to which optical fiber, network servers, local networks, mail servers, modems, personal computers, desktop applications such as e-mail and Web browsers, Internet portals such as AOL, retailers such as Amazon.com, Web site designers, Java programmers, and many other elements have been added. Organizations similarly represent the accumulated combination of people, ideas, and objects, typically bundled into smaller components ranging from research and development to manufacturing to order processing to sales and service. Markets and industries describe larger networks that relate firms, complex systems, and customers to one another. As we ascend the hierarchy, each larger network describes the arrangement of elements that were themselves arrangements of elements.

How Breakthroughs Happen

Breakthrough innovations cause these networks to shift dramatically. Whole groups of people, ideas, and objects form new relationships seemingly overnight. New technologies obsolete not just old objects, but also the people and ideas linked to them and, in a chain reaction, the complex organizations and markets that grew up around these combinations. Edison's system of electric light sent the existing gas lighting companies scrambling to find their place in new markets in the same way that the personal computer reshaped the typewriter and mainframe industries. The same dramas unfold within organizations: New people, new ideas, and new objects overthrow traditional priorities in organizations. Peripheral upstarts, like Intel's microprocessor group in the 1970s or Hewlett-Packard's inkjet printer division in the 1990s, for instance, suddenly become central elements of their organization's strategies.

Physicists studying complexity theory call these sudden shifts from one network structure to another *phase transitions*. Seemingly small changes in the links between just a few nodes—in our case, small changes in the relationships among people, ideas, and objects—rapidly trigger other changes until the networked landscape suddenly looks completely different. Malcolm Gladwell suggests these phase transitions in his book *The Tipping Point* when he describes how everything from smoking to fashion to crime can be seen as social movements that spread with surprising rapidity through otherwise stable networks. In these moments, old traditions suddenly seem irrelevant, new relationships need to be defined, and new opportunities and old markets evolve rapidly.

Understanding these networks and their underlying dynamics is critical to understanding the innovation process. These networks, the webs of significance we ourselves have spun, shape who we are and what we think. Each of us sees these networks differently, depending on our past experiences, what Allan Newell and Herbert Simon called our "network of possible wanderings."[10] The worlds we've experienced in the past shape how we act in the future by giving us the raw materials—the choices for how to act—for the future. The new possibilities we imagine are built from pieces of the realities we've seen; the constraints we feel are the tug of those same ties binding us to those realities. These worlds are the boxes we think in, and the boxes we insist others must think outside of.

The idea of the heroic inventor treats Edison and other inventors as individuals overturning established worlds, tearing apart old networks—thinking outside the box. Success is a matter of individual genius, courage, tenacity, and rebellion. But this perspective strips away the networks that locate these individuals in their own place and time.

This book puts forth a counterintuitive proposition: that these entrepreneurs and inventors are no smarter, no more courageous, tenacious, or rebellious than the rest of us—they are simply better connected. Sure, some people are smarter, braver, and bolder than others, but fifty years of creativity research has failed to find a significant impact of any one of these traits on creative success once people get past a relatively minor threshold. Isaac Newton once said, "If I have seen farther than other men, it is because I have stood on the shoulders of giants."[11] The same argument holds for organizations. Beyond relatively standard distinctions in size or bureaucratic structure (mechanistic versus organic), there is little evidence that innovative behavior is an innate quality in some elite set of organizations. In the words of one review, the only consistent finding in innovation research is the inconsistency of the findings.[12] This book assumes that most individuals and organizations can see the same distance but, depending on their past wanderings through the networked landscape, look out across vastly different views.

Some organizations have found ways to exploit the networked landscape; as a result, they are able to continuously innovate by seeing and making connections between people, ideas, and objects from across the broader landscape. By focusing on their networks, rather than their solitary genius, we can learn a great deal about the innovation process.

The network that surrounded Edison, for example, explains a great deal about the continuous stream of innovations that emerged from his Menlo Park laboratory. The classic story—of a heroic genius working alone to build an electric future with nothing but his "imagination and a pile of junk"—may have elements of the truth, but it is misleading. Edison was neither that heroic, that imaginative, nor that alone. By studying entrepreneurs like Edison outside of their natural environment, we risk setting down one truth and, in the process, many lies. If we focus on the collective efforts of the team in Menlo Park, if we look at how the laboratory was embedded in the networked world of its time, and if we look at how Edison changed that network, we find a whole different set of truths about the innovation process.

Technology Brokering

One such truth is that the secrets of Edison and others are not to be found in their solitary genius and capacity for invention. Instead, Edison, like his modern counterparts, was capable of creating one breakthrough after another because his organization was built around *technology brokering,* a strategy for exploiting the networked nature of the innovation process. Rather than producing fundamentally novel advances in any one technology or dominating any one industry, technology brokering involves combining existing objects, ideas, and people in ways that, nevertheless, spark technological revolutions.

Such an innovation strategy relies not on breaking from the past but instead on *exploiting* it by harnessing the knowledge and efficiencies that reside in elements of existing technologies. Such recombinant innovations can have profound impacts: Robert Fulton, for example, combined the steam engine and sailing ship to radically alter global commerce. He didn't invent the steamship so much as bring together the right technical components, business ideas, and people to make it work. To the extent that it is more effective to modify an existing and already well-developed technology than to invent a wholly new one, technology brokering offers an advantage in the pursuit of innovation.

Technology brokering describes a strategy that firms have developed to expressly pursue such recombinant innovations. This strategy involves *bridging* distant worlds. By working in a range of different industries or markets, firms are in a better position to see when the people, ideas, and objects of one world can be combined in new ways to solve the problems of another. For these companies, innovation isn't a process of thinking outside of the box so much as one of thinking in boxes that others haven't seen before. Edison didn't invent the electric light, but he brought together previously disparate people, ideas, and objects from his network of past wanderings in a way that launched a revolution.

That's just the first step. Technology brokering also involves *building* new communities around those innovative recombinations. Rather than rebelling against the old social order, technology brokering focuses on building new networks around emerging ideas. Elias Howe, for example, didn't invent the sewing machine, but rather pulled together (and improved upon) the existing machines of his time—that he made any money at all from his work was the result of the combination of businessmen he joined with, and of the rapidly growing community of sewing machine manufacturers that pooled their various patents. Had he insisted on going it alone, he would likely have lost—as he almost did—the necessary community that forms around and advances new ideas.

This book looks backstage at historic places and events, like Edison's Menlo Park lab and Ford's Highland Park factory (the birthplace of mass production), and at current organizations that pursue technology brokering strategies. These examples show that the innovation process depends less on the solitary genius of individuals and organizations than on how such individuals exploit the network dynamics that make up the process.

Edison Revisited: Edison as a Technology Broker

Thomas A. Edison got his start in the emerging telegraph industry of the 1860s, working as an itinerant telegraph operator across much of the Midwest before ultimately landing in Boston. There his constant tinkering with the artifacts of telegraphy—transmitters, receivers, batteries—fit right in with the independent inventors and machinists who inhabited the local machine shops. His earliest products brought the ideas and objects of this industry to new markets. His electric fire and police alarm consisted of a dedicated telegraph line from house to police station. His gold-price indicator used the telegraph and an automatic recorder to transmit gold prices from the stock market to nearby offices. His electric mimeograph pen borrowed from a perforating device in automatic telegraphy that punched holes in paper to record the dots and dashes of incoming signals.[13] After selling patents for his work on an improved quadruplex telegraph and seeing market success with his mimeograph and electric pen, Edison became a consultant to many of the large firms (and a number of smaller ones) hoping to exploit the newly emerging potential of the telegraph industry.

In 1876, he moved his operations from Newark, New Jersey, to a small farming community twelve miles to the south called Menlo Park. There he built a laboratory and put together a team that worked with a wide range of organizations on an equally wide range of projects, both inside the telegraph industry and elsewhere. Built to Edison's specifications, the laboratory was 100 feet long and 30 feet wide. The upstairs was devoted to the engineers, or "muckers" as they called themselves, and was a single room with workbenches through the center and shelves of materials, chemicals, and books along the walls. The muckers would work for days straight in pursuit of a solution, then punctuate their work with late-night breaks of pie, tobacco, and bawdy songs around the giant organ that dominated one end of the laboratory.

Edison's Menlo Park lab offers valuable insights into the process of technology brokering. There, Edison created the ideal conditions for the continuous generation of innovations. In the words of one historian, those five years Edison spent at Menlo Park represented "[t]he most concentrated outpouring of invention in history."[14] But what enabled Edison to develop new products that would shape features into the technological landscape for at least the next century?

Setting aside the notion of Edison as an inventive genius allows us to look at how the Menlo Park lab was shaped by and, in turn, shaped the networked landscape of its time and place. Edison's success came less from what he learned while selling newspapers on the Grand Trunk Line as a child than from what his team learned while working on last month's projects. The incandescent lightbulb had been around for twenty years before Edison made his fame "inventing" it (in fact, one of Moses Farmer's platinum incandescent bulbs hung in the machine shop where Edison spent his time). And while his improvements to the telegraph and telephone were dramatic, so too were his races to the patent office to beat competitors with similar ideas. Edison's advantage lay not in his ability to build something out of nothing but rather in his ability to exploit the network. As we'll see, he implicitly, but certainly actively, pursued a strategy of technology brokering.

The organization at Menlo Park divided its time between doing engineering work for clients in the telegraph, electric light, railroad, and mining industries and conducting its own experiments. By working for a range of clients and in a range of industries, Edison was able to move among the worlds that made up each of these industries—using his work for different clients to bridge these different worlds when he and his team saw ideas in one that showed promise elsewhere. As Andre Millard notes in *Edison and the Business of Innovation*, "Edison quietly blurred the line between the experiments he did for others and those he did for himself. Who was to know if a result from contract research was applied to another project or if experimental equipment built for one customer was used in work for another?"[15]

Edison borrowed often from the ideas of other industries. And the laboratory's range of clients from many different industries meant that any one development project offered valuable information that Edison could exploit in other projects.

Popular history has credited Edison, the individual, with the outpouring of invention from Menlo Park, but personal accounts describe the intimate collaboration between Edison and his fellow muckers. Edison built a community at Menlo Park that was deeply committed to the innovation process. The group at Menlo Park numbered approximately fourteen, including Edison. Of these, five had prominent roles working closely with Edison: Charles Batchelor, John Adams, John Kruesi, John Ott, and Charles Wurth.[16] Edison worked most closely with Charles Batchelor, an Englishman whose training as both a mechanic and a draftsman complemented (and grounded) Edison's more flighty visions.[17] The relationship between Edison and Batchelor was demonstrated by their agreement to split profits 50-50 for all inventions and to receive stock in all resulting companies.

Edison modeled the laboratory after the machine shops from which he and many of the others emerged, where mechanics and independent entrepreneurs would work side by side, sharing machines, telling stories, and passing along promising ideas or opportunities. According to Francis Jehl, one of Edison's assistants, the lab's culture was, like these earlier shops, "a little community of kindred spirits, all in young manhood, enthusiastic about their work, expectant of great results," for whom work and play were indistinguishable.[18] Many of the breakthroughs on the electric light, the telegraph, or the phonograph are attributable to insights achieved by Batchelor, Adams, or one of the others who were working on the projects while Edison was dealing with clients or scrambling for investors. When an experiment looked promising, Edison would not hesitate to incorporate a new company and build a team to pursue it.[19]

All the while, Edison and others worked hard to perpetuate the myth of the lone genius building something out of nothing. For example, Edison has famously insisted that his inventive abilities came by ignoring the existing knowledge: "When I start in to experiment with anything, I do not read the books; I don't want to know what has been done."[20] Yet at the same time, he described his methodology in his notes as follows: "1st. Study the present construction. 2nd. Ask for all past experiences . . . study and read everything you can on the subject."[21]

Onstage, Edison abandoned the past in his search for the future. Backstage, he worked hard to create that future from the best pieces of the past that he could find and use. Pursuing a strategy of technology brokering, Edison bridged old worlds and built new ones around the innovations that he saw as a result. Much of Edison's work combined existing ideas in new ways; in spite of such humble origins, those innovations revolutionized industries.

What set Edison's laboratory apart was not the ability to shut itself off from the rest of the world, to create something from nothing, to think outside of the box. Exactly the opposite: It was the ability to *connect* that made the lab so innovative. If Edison ignored anything, it was the belief that innovation was about the solitary pursuit of invention. Edison was able to continuously innovate because he knew how to exploit the networked landscape of his time.

Edison is not alone in pursuing such an innovation strategy. William Gibson, the science-fiction author who crafted some of the earliest visions of the Internet in his novel *Neuromancer* (and coined the phrase *cyberspace*), was once asked how he got his fantastic yet prescient ideas about the future. His answer: "The future is already here, it's just unevenly distributed."[22] Had Edison heard that sentiment, he would have agreed. Edison built his organization and structured his work to redistribute the ideas emerging first from the telegraph industry and then from wherever electricity was being applied. His innovations had major impacts by bringing these ideas to other industries that had not yet adopted them.

Edison's strategy at the Menlo Park lab was focused on innovation, not on any particular markets. Had he attempted to dominate any one particular market, his ability to find good ideas in one area and redistribute them would have taken second priority to perfecting the same ideas for the same market. By creating first teams and ultimately entire companies dedicated to exploiting innovations that came out of his lab, Edison built the new networks that would bring his group of muckers, and then investors, technicians, scientists, and manufacturers together around innovations like his system for electric lighting.

Like the Menlo Park laboratory, today's technology brokers seek strategic advantage by bridging a wide variety of industries. They exploit this position to build new combinations from the existing objects, ideas, and people they find in these different worlds. Few reach the levels of success that Edison did, but their ability to consistently generate innovative new products and processes still provides valuable insights.

Design Continuum: A Modern Technology Broker

Design Continuum is a full-service product design firm that provides industrial, electronic, and mechanical design solutions for clients. It has designed products ranging from surgical devices to squirt guns, and from computers to tape dispensers. Located in a single two-story building in Newton, Massachusetts, a suburb of Boston, the engineers and industrial designers fill the second floor in an open layout with cubicles clustered around open spaces. Design Continuum was founded in 1983 by Gianfranco Zaccai and Jerrold Zindler and has consistently won honors for its innovative product design. It is regularly praised in the design literature and has won thirty-five *Business Week* Industrial Design Excellence Awards, six in 2002 alone. Its products range from nursery monitors to ultrasonic toothbrushes to modular (and adjustable) bathrooms, from a joystick for video game consoles to a laparoscopic device for surgeons, and from rollerblades to silicon wafer–handling robots.

Design Continuum's client list includes over a hundred companies working in a range of industries, including computers, office equipment, communication systems, consumer electronics, appliances, consumer nondurable goods (e.g., diapers), sporting goods, industrial products (e.g., robotics), medical instrumentation, and health care products. The CEO, Gian Zaccai, describes the firm as follows:

> We enjoy working in diverse industries, and it brings great benefits to our clients. We design medical products, both direct patient care devices and also diagnostic instruments. . . . We design quite a bit of office equipment, with an emphasis on totally new forms of display and interface. We also have a tradition of designing "home life" products, ranging from windows to faucets to appliances, but even in a traditional product category we can provide innovation, if it is appropriate. Making new products, and applying new technologies, is only worthwhile if they are the right products. Sometimes a technology, brought in from the most unlikely source, can revolutionize a product. However, that technology must be integrated in ways that serve users rather than burden them.[23]

Design Continuum currently employs around 110 people, with approximately seventy-five engineers and industrial designers. While the bulk of its work is product design, the firm also has groups specializing in interior design and graphic design. Clients come to Design Continuum for help with new product designs. This help ranges from early conceptual work (aligning technologies and business strategies to potential product lines) to engineering and design work and to analysis and improvement of existing designs. In this way, client projects can be described as ranging from "What should we do?" to "Have we done this right?"

In 1988, Reebok approached Design Continuum to engineer a response to Nike's recently introduced Air technology, an "active energy return" system in the form of a balloon that cushioned the heel of a shoe. After several weeks of study, the Design Continuum project team came to the conclusion that designing another energy return system would not have the market impact Reebok was looking for. They decided to look for other ideas. One idea was that an inflatable shoe might create a custom fit for each customer and help prevent ankle injuries.

The Reebok Pump concept first emerged during the user studies that Design Continuum engages in at the start of each project to learn as much as possible about the existing market. One of the designers, who had previously designed an inflatable splint, recognized how such splints might *prevent* injuries by building ankle support into a basketball shoe. In talking with another member of the team, who had worked on hospital equipment before, the two saw how medical IV bags could be modified to provide the oddly shaped air bladders that would make this "splint-in-a-shoe" concept work. During a subsequent brainstorming meeting with several other designers, who had worked with diagnostic instruments (and the little pumps, tubing, and valve components that made up those products), a solution emerged for how to inflate and deflate the shoe easily.

These ideas came together because of the creativity of Design Continuum's project team. But the story is incomplete if we only give credit to these engineers and ignore how their work emerged from within the network of relationships that is Design Continuum's world. Design Continuum has worked for hundreds of clients in dozens of industries. Like Edison, the firm is in the position of pursuing strategies of technology brokering—spanning multiple markets and using ideas it sees in one or more areas to solve the problems of clients that do not have access or experience in those other places. As one Design Continuum manager involved in the project recalled, "The idea of putting an air system into a shoe seemed like magic to Reebok and to us it seemed like, well, you weld together some film and you put in a little pump and some check valves and some tubing, what's the big deal? We know how to do this stuff."

Sure, Design Continuum's engineers—or Reebok's, for that matter—could have spontaneously come up with the idea of putting an inflatable splint in a shoe. Or of using the technologies (and existing materials and manufacturers) of an IV bag to make the air bladder. Or of piecing together and then ultimately integrating valves and pumps into a tiny dome that fits on the tongue of a shoe. But these ideas all came easier to Design Continuum's engineers because they had already, in vastly different conditions, worked with all of these different ideas. As a result, they were quite comfortable with using them again in a new place:

> It was innovative, it wasn't invention. And we knew that we didn't have to invent anything. We knew you could call up this company and get little check valves and call up this company and get little molded rubber parts and on and on. And these welded things, all these things that the shoe industry had no connections to.

It is one thing to know *of* a technology; it's something different to know how to apply it, what else it can do, and how to adapt it to new settings. Those skills only come through use, if only just once or twice (and maybe, as we'll discuss later, only *because* the designers have used those ideas once or twice).

Thus, Design Continuum's engineers could come up with the Reebok Pump because they had seen many of the components in vastly different uses. With this prior experience—from their vantage point spanning multiple industries and markets—they were able to design a revolutionary sneaker and do it faster than anyone expected. Beginning with the green light from Reebok, it took only six months to design the shoe and another six months to ramp up for its manufacture. The maker of the IV bags that Design Continuum had worked with before became a supplier of the inflatable inserts. The whole project cost less than $250,000. In the year that the Reebok Pump shoe was introduced to the market, it accounted for over $1 billion in revenue in the highly competitive athletic shoe market and gained wide praise in the business press for its creativity.

Imagine what would have happened if Reebok's engineers, or Design Continuum's, for that matter, had tried to invent the Pump from scratch. Imagine going from zero to over a million new shoes, each with tiny pumps and bladders that a sneaker company had never made before, and not being crippled by the failures, manufacturing bugs, poor yields, or worse, product recalls that plague many new innovations. Reebok was able to avoid all that because Design Continuum already had experience designing these components and, moreover, because the firm already had vendors who knew what they were doing. Design Continuum was able to recombine the objects, ideas, and people of the world it knew in ways that shook Reebok and its world of athletic shoes.

Technology Brokering and the Organized Pursuit of Innovation

Few companies can claim, like Edison or Design Continuum, that their sole business is innovation. For most, manufacturing and sales remain essential activities that rely heavily on established processes and tightly linked relationships. Economies of scale, customer and supplier linkages, and organizational competencies all grow through repetition and learning. So even the most "innovation-driven" large firms recognize that their strategies must move them toward central positions in their markets. Take General Electric, for example, whose stunning growth and innovation was propelled by Jack Welch's ruthless desire to dominate any market in which GE played. Be number one or two in your market, or get out. Getting to number one or two takes much more than innovation, it also takes six-sigma quality control (another of Welch's corporate philosophies) and strong connections to customers and suppliers alike. Breakthrough innovations don't usually mix well with the pursuit of six-sigma quality control, nor with those customers who just purchased your last generation of products.

Yet successful companies will have to master the process of continuous innovation if they want to compete in markets where new technologies can rapidly shift the existing landscape, overturning old ideas about efficiency, disrupting established customer relationships, and turning old competencies from assets into liabilities.

To study Edison's lab and others like it is to study an innovation process and an organizational design stripped for creativity and speed. These are the companies that have developed effective organizational structures and work practices centered on the process of technology brokering, and thus offer lessons for other organizations hoping to exploit the network dynamics of innovation. Looking at these firms, we see a set of strategies and work practices that are aligned and focused on generating many small inventions every week and a big invention every month or so. The lessons we can learn from these firms are invaluable because they reveal aspects of the innovation process that can be exploited by small and large firms alike.

This book describes the network dynamics that underlie many breakthrough innovations, and draws lessons from those organizations that are able to use these dynamics to their advantage in pursuing innovation. These dynamics constrain most efforts at change, and yet, to those who can see and exploit them, they provide the raw materials for revolutionary breakthroughs. The next chapter looks in more detail at the recombinant nature of innovation. Part II of this book describes the the resulting advantages in the innovation process that come from bridging multiple worlds, and the subsequent necessities of building new worlds around emerging innovations. Part III looks at how organizations have developed successful technology brokering strategies for exploiting these dynamics. These strategies range from the full-time pursuit of innovation through dedicated technology brokering strategies, to the construction of internal groups committed to bridging the disparate divisions and building new innovations within the organization, to firms that know how to successfully respond to unexpected opportunities for technology brokering.

Recombinant Innovation

In many organizations, and in the design of many research and development laboratories, the pursuit of innovation is synonymous with the pursuit of invention. The performance of divisions, laboratories, and individuals is measured in terms of patents generated, and breakthrough products become the stuff of legends. Just as Edison invented the lightbulb, so Art Fry of 3M invented the Post-it Note, Doug Engelbart of SRI invented the computer mouse, and William Schockley at Bell Labs invented the transistor. Such a focus on individuals and the novelty of their inventions undermines the very process of pursuing breakthrough innovations.

While innovations are new in some ways, they are old in others. Abbot Payton Usher, a historian of technology, wrote in 1929 that "Invention finds its distinctive feature in the constructive assimilation of pre-existing elements into new syntheses, new patterns, or new configurations of behavior."[24] So while we might marvel at Edison's "inventions," we can learn a lot more by asking where those ideas came from. Edison's system of electric lighting combined elements of the telegraph, the arc light, and even the existing gas lighting industry. Edison's mimeograph pen borrowed the mechanics of the high-speed telegraph repeaters from which it was taken. The Pump air bladder was novel to everyone but Design Continuum's engineers and, of course, the IV bag manufacturer that had already made millions just like it. Innovations that recombine objects, ideas, and people that have emerged and evolved elsewhere have a singular advantage in that they hit the ground running. Edison succeeded in large part because he didn't have to invent the lightbulb, let alone the batteries, generators, wiring, insulation, engineers, and even market need that were all necessary pieces of his breakthrough technology.

The pursuit of innovation changes dramatically when the goal shifts from invention to inventive recombination, from pushing people to think outside of the box to helping them think in other boxes. Chapter 2 describes the recombinant process behind most innovations, where existing technologies—as combinations of people, ideas, and objects—are disassembled and reassembled in ways that spawn revolutions, and discusses the implications of this approach for rethinking organizational innovation strategies.

The Networks of Innovation

The network dynamics that empower recombinant innovation create opportunities for organizations that can exploit these dynamics through technology brokering. That's because technology brokering involves seeking out those positions in the larger network that make the actions of bridging and building possible, and it involves crafting the organization's structure and work practices to take full advantage of this network position.

The network positions link organizations to multiple worlds rather than embedding them deeply within any one. Technology brokers are characterized by their connections to multiple small worlds and, further, by their connections to worlds that otherwise share few connections between them. Network theorists use the concept of *range* to describe the breadth of connections any one person may have in a network, as measured by the number of non-redundant ties (meaning I know Bill in accounting and Carol in manufacturing, but Bill and Carol don't know each other, nor do Bill and Carol's colleagues know each other, and so on). In essence, range presumes there are costs associated with each connection that people have to others, such as the costs of keeping in touch and of keeping up to date on what's going on. The greater someone's range, the more of the larger network territory he or she is able to cover for the least cost. Technology brokers attempt to maximize their range of connections because by doing so they are in a better position to be the first to see how the people, ideas, and objects of one world may provide valuable solutions in another.

Chapter 3 describes the strategic opportunities for technology brokering within a fragmented network. To technology brokers, the ideas they see, the objects they run across, and the people they meet rarely know, or are known to, each other. In this way, technology brokers connect otherwise disconnected worlds. Rather than being strongly tied to a single community, these brokers are weakly tied to a number of different ones. This not only ensures that they are the first to see new opportunities, but also that they are usually the last to be caught in the webs of established practices and embedded interests that constrain inhabitants of individual worlds. Chapter 3 outlines these fundamental advantages that technology brokering strategies provide in the pursuit of innovation.

Bridging the Small Worlds of a Networked Landscape

It is sometimes difficult to imagine how piecing together bits of existing technologies can create revolutionary change—after all, by definition these pieces have been around for a while. What makes recombinant innovation so difficult, however, is that the elements that make up existing technologies do not come apart, nor come together again, very easily. Most recombinant innovations bring together people, ideas, and objects from the many different worlds that make up the networked landscape, and that means taking apart and building anew the myriad webs that connected these pieces to their own small worlds. Albert Szent-Györgyi, the Nobel laureate credited with discovering vitamin C, once said, "Discovery is seeing what everybody else has seen, but thinking what nobody else has thought." [25] From a network perspective, this means seeing the same elements of a technology but recognizing different connections (or the potential for different connections) between them. For Edison, it meant seeing the potential of the lightbulb when combined with a distribution system like that of gas. For Design Continuum's engineers, it meant seeing the connections between an inflatable splint, an IV bag manufacturer, and a basketball shoe. Technology brokering entails bridging these different worlds and recognizing how the people, ideas, and objects found in one world can be useful in others.

Much of the literature on managing creativity is about getting people to think differently by loosening up their notions of the *right* thing to do, to challenge the authority of traditions, to think outside of the box. But this advice misses a critical ingredient: People need other ways to think before they abandon the old ways. The very networked landscape we inhabit—the connections that make up our small worlds—prevents us from seeing the new connections that are required to "think what nobody else has thought." As Don Cohen and Laurence Prusak point out in *In Good Company: How Social Capital Makes Organizations Work,* the ties that bind are also the ties that blind. Which colleagues we talk to, which events we notice, which articles we read, which phone calls we return, and countless other daily activities all shape how we think. Breakthrough innovations require seeing many of those same things but thinking about them differently.

Chapter 4 discusses the network dynamics that create small worlds and shape how we see and think about our surroundings. The individuals and organizations who move among these worlds are no smarter or more visionary than the rest of us, but they are capable of thinking differently about the people, the ideas, and the objects they see. As we'll discuss, these differences, when nurtured, can have effects that go far beyond those of brainstorming, creativity workshops, or casual Fridays in managing the pursuit of innovation.

Building New Worlds

Too often people believe that good ideas will sell themselves. But having a good idea, to borrow a phrase from Winston Churchill, is not the end; it's not the beginning of the end; it is the end of the beginning. The pursuit of innovation requires patiently and humbly building a new network of people, ideas, and objects around the original innovation. That's why technology brokering entails not just the ability to bridge small worlds, but also the ability to build new worlds from the best pieces of the old ones.

Innovation requires collective action because, at the beginning, the power of these groups provides the conditions for generating truly novel recombinations. The act of innovation is, in its early stages, just another act of deviance. Until it succeeds, the established community frowns upon it, feels threatened by it, and in turn threatens it. Sure, there may be individuals out there who are capable of going it alone. But look closely at almost every innovation and you will find a group working closely together. Edison had Charles Batchelor, Francis Upton, John Kruesi, and the rest of the muckers. There were Steve Jobs and Steve Wozniak, Bill Gates and Paul Allen, Gilbert and Sullivan, Lennon and McCartney (and their producer, George Martin), and Watson and Crick (and their anonymous lab assistant). Groups are critical to the innovation process because they can convince themselves of the value of their ideas, the rightness of their cause, and the possibilities of their success.

Later, the growing community attracts others, who bring with them still more ideas and objects and continue the evolution of the system. Edison's electric system grew because the community that crystallized around it grew. Advances in the production and distribution of electricity and in the uses for such increasingly available power began to make Edison's original efforts look revolutionary. Take the development of alternating current, an alternative standard for generating and distributing electricity. Edison fought the idea, yet it extended the impact of the new technology where Edison's own ideas and equipment could not. Indeed, the electrified future Edison envisioned didn't really become a reality until General Electric promoted the development of the electric refrigerator and other appliances in the 1920s.[26]

Chapter 5 describes how, from a network perspective, the pursuit of innovation relies on the web of people, ideas, and objects that emerges around the original innovations. New ventures often fail because too little attention is given to building these networks— ideas are instead expected to sell themselves, or "inventors" want all the credit and profit. In contrast to lone inventors, communities draw other actors, objects, and ideas together into tightly knit networks, where people's roles become clear and interdependent, where objects adapt to fit their new applications, and where ideas become shared organizing principles.

How Firms Pursue Innovation Through Technology Brokering

Many organizations can benefit from the insights into the nature and effective pursuit of innovation that the study of technology brokers provides. Chapter 6 considers the range of organizations that exploit strategies of technology brokering, from engineering entrepreneurs to law firms, and from multidivisional firms to component suppliers.

The remaining chapters focus on the three predominant ways that organizations can pursue innovation through technology brokering. Chapter 7 describes those firms that, like Edison's Menlo Park lab, are built for the sole purpose of innovating, and the organizational structure, work practices, and cultures that make them successful. Although these firms have relatively extreme strategies, they nonetheless offer valuable insights into how these internal characteristics support or discourage efforts to bridge distant worlds and build new ventures.

Chapter 8 develops a set of lessons from large organizations whose disparate divisions are focused on developing their own markets and technologies. Several have successfully created internal technology brokering groups that are able to span the small worlds experienced by each division. These internal groups innovate by combining the people, ideas, and objects that emerge within one division but have potential value in others. Like firms with dedicated technology brokering strategies, these internal groups are able to develop unique structures, cultures, and work practices that enable them to innovate where inhabitants of particular divisions cannot. These groups often gain broader perspectives on the organization's knowledge and resources, and are less embedded in any one place with its particular people, ideas, and objects.

Chapter 9 looks at organizations that have successfully exploited one-time opportunities for technology brokering. These are typical organizations that are focused on succeeding within a single market yet come across opportunities to either export their technologies to another market or import existing technologies from the outside and combine them with the organization's existing resources in powerful new ways. These organizations cannot dedicate their resources to the full-time pursuit of innovation. Nevertheless, the lessons of successful technology brokering provide a set of guidelines for how to respond quickly and effectively when opportunities do arise.

Chapter 10 offers some general principles that have emerged from the study of individuals and organizations that act as technology brokers. These principles can be used to guide the pursuit of innovation—whether you are a manager attempting to foster innovation within your group, division, or organization, or an entrepreneur pursuing a new venture, or both.

• • •

The strategy of technology brokering takes advantage of a relatively simple but consistently overlooked characteristic of many breakthrough innovations—that innovations are the recombination of old people, objects, and ideas in new ways. So before we consider the ways in which technology brokering works in organizations, let's first explore the recombinant nature of innovation in more detail.

2

Recombinant Innovation and the Sources of Invention

This book is fundamentally about the advantages that a strategy of technology brokering provides established organizations and entrepreneurs alike in the pursuit of innovation. However, underlying this argument are two central ideas about the innovation process that deserve particular attention. The first, described in chapter 1, is that technologies are formed of tightly coupled arrangements of people, ideas, and objects; the second is that innovation is a process of taking apart and reassembling these elements in new combinations. These ideas are simultaneously obvious yet deeply significant. Together, they organize our insights into technology brokering and the pursuit of innovation.

The notion that innovations can be seen as recombinations of existing ideas is not itself new. Joseph Schumpeter recognized that most innovations were the result of recombinations of existing ideas: "To produce other things, or the same things by a different method, means to combine these materials and forces differently."[1] More recently, Nelson and Winter, who changed our thinking about the strategic resources of the firm, argued that "innovation in the economic system—and indeed the creation of any sort of novelty in art, science, or practical life—consists to a substantial extent of a recombination of conceptual and physical materials that were previously in existence."[2] However, this perspective has yet to generate practical insights into managing the innovation process.

In part, this is because innovations tend to be described with terms like *evolutionary* versus *revolutionary, incremental* versus *radical, continuous* versus *discontinuous*. These terms don't distinguish an innovation's origins from its impacts, and sometimes even confuse them. Labeling something *evolutionary, incremental,* and *continuous* suggests disappointing, even paralyzing, ties to what has existed before; *revolutionary, radical,* and *discontinuous* suggest the bold leaps forward that trigger dramatic shifts in the market. But do revolutionary impacts require such bold leaps?

All innovations represent some break from the past—the lightbulb replaced the gas lamp, the automobile replaced the horse and cart, the steamship replaced the sailing ship. By the same token, however, all innovations are built from pieces of the past—Edison's system drew its organizing principles from the gas industry, the early automobiles were built by cart makers, and the first steamships added steam engines to existing sailing ships. Robert Fulton's 1807 steamship, for example, had profound impacts on the shipping industry, but his ideas were decidedly evolutionary in their origins. The original idea for a steamship had first been proposed in 1543, and commercial efforts had been under way since 1707. The components of both the steam engine and the ship's design drew from a continuous and incremental line of technological predecessors, each improving on the last.[3]

In 1972, Ray Tomlinson wrote one of the first killer apps, electronic mail, for the Internet (which at that time was still the ARPAnet) by combining the code of an existing *intra*computer messaging application with an *inter*computer file transfer protocol. As Tomlinson himself describes:

> It seemed like an interesting hack to tie these two together. To use the file-transfer protocol to send the email to the other

machine. So that's what I did. I spent not a whole lot of time,
maybe two or three weeks, putting that together and it worked.[4]

Tomlinson's e-mail program was included in the next release of
the operating system and had an immediate impact on how the
ARPAnet was used and viewed. The ARPAnet was originally intended to provide access to archival information all over the world—
more like the Internet of today. But Tomlinson's innovation made
fast, simple communication and file exchange possible and, in the
beginning, became the dominant use of the emerging technology.

And of course, we could not understand the history of innovation at Microsoft without seeing how its ideas built firmly on past
people, ideas, and objects.[5] One of Bill Gates and Paul Allen's first
commercial efforts was BASIC for the Altair, a programming language that allowed others to write applications software. This program borrowed from the existing versions of BASIC (written for
mainframes and minicomputers) and from prior work done by
DEC. As Paul Ceruzzi writes in *A History of Modern Computing,*
"with its skillful combination of features taken from Dartmouth and
from the Digital Equipment Corporation, [BASIC] was the key to
Gates' and Allen's success in establishing a personal computer software industry."[6] MS-DOS, Microsoft's operating system for the IBM
PC, was acquired for $75,000 from the tiny Seattle Computer Com-
pany. Microsoft Word was originally written by Xerox PARC engineers as Bravo (but never marketed); it became a Microsoft product
when Microsoft hired one of its original authors, Charles Simonyi,
away from PARC. Excel was derived from Visicalc by Software Arts,
and from Lotus. Internet Explorer built on the ideas of Netscape
Navigator. And the graphical user environment that is Windows first
appeared at PARC in the Alto personal computer, and then in the
Apple Macintosh, before becoming Microsoft's flagship product.

Finally, today's TiVo digital video recorder—now threatening
to upset the television industry—is an innovative combination of
video recorder, *TV Guide,* and personal computer (complete with
motherboard, hard drive, and Linux operating system).

Many of the examples that we'll discuss in this chapter focus on mechanical technologies and the recombination of physical objects and ideas concerning their use. But there are as many different resources to be combined as there are unmet needs to be solved. Many new software applications combine functions, if not whole sections of code, from a range of existing programs. And some of the fundamental leaps forward in the design of integrated circuits came from the development of design components that performed specific yet relatively general functions, like addition or multiplication, that could then be easily used in new combinations to create ever more complex chips.

Recombinant innovations can also be seen in many places where the technology is not so clear at first glance. Wherever close-linked networks of people, ideas, and objects come together and perform effectively, they become the raw materials for others to later exploit in their own pursuit of innovation. Such a perspective is useful, for example, in understanding social changes. Rock and roll is an example. To many, it's nothing more than a popularized version of rhythm and blues (R&B), a musical tradition in the black community for at least fifty years before its introduction to a market of white kids. Indeed, a citizen's group in New Orleans in the 1950s responded to the rising popularity of rock and roll by imploring the youth of America to not buy Negro records, not offer them in jukeboxes, and not play them on the radio. But it was too late. Artists were learning the powerful benefits that came from combining rhythm and blues with lyrics and vocals tailored for a new audience. Rock's impact on the marketplace and, as a number of historians have argued, on society, is undeniable.[7]

Little Richard was one of the earliest artists credited with pioneering rock and roll. Little Richard grew up playing rhythm and blues, getting his start in traveling circuses and exotic dance clubs. This was the early 1950s, and the musical genres of Country & Western and R&B were distinct and different worlds. Little Richard crossed over to the larger market of white teenagers with his 1955 rendition of "Tutti Frutti." For him, it was the same music—just a different audience. For America, it was much more.

Another artist, Elvis Presley, grew up poor, living in mixed neighborhoods where country and gospel music existed side by side. He played country, but often hung out as a kid by the back doors of R&B clubs. During his first recording session at Sun Studio, in 1953, he was placed with two local Western swing musicians. After several months of rehearsal, they released a 45 with a country song on one side and an R&B song on the other. The blues song, "That's Alright Momma," was a hit but also possibly a fluke. The next song they released, "Blue Moon of Kentucky," sealed Elvis's fate. It was a bluegrass standard, written by Bill Munroe, that through a series of recorded rehearsals can be heard transforming itself, combining with R&B rhythms to become a hybrid hillbilly tune with a rocking beat.

To the musicians caught in the moment, the process of recombination was well understood, as indicated by the confluence of music that, in the 1950s and 1960s, defined rock and roll. The Beatles learned rhythm and blues from records brought into Liverpool by merchant ships, and made their start covering American R&B and rockabilly tunes in Liverpool and Hamburg, Germany. Lennon imitated the rockabilly menace of American rockabilly artist Gene Vincent; McCartney worked on his "Little Richard screams."

David Crosby, of the Byrds and later of Crosby, Stills, Nash, and Young, described what the Beatles brought to rock and roll as a recombination of what had come before:

> I heard folk sort of [chord] changes with rock and roll sort of
> beat [in the Beatles music]. Now, most new musical forms are
> created that way, the synthesis takes place by two disparate
> streams of stuff hitherto unrelated being mushed together.[8]

When the Beatles arrived in the United States, they were unsure of their reception—after all, they were bringing American music to America. But the combination of British musicians playing American rock music with folk influences and looking European somehow clicked. The rest was history.

The same recombinant process can be seen in art. The artist Nathan Oliveira once ascribed his success to the belief that originality is an end rather than a point of departure.[9] Oliveira typically begins his paintings with concrete images, but in the process of repainting produces markedly original works. Similarly, Picasso's notes and preliminary sketches reveal that his famous mural *Guernica* was pieced together from images drawn from newspaper photographs and etchings. The final painting was clearly his, but he used those original images unmistakably as a point of departure.[10]

Even Hollywood relies on recombination, ranging from remaking foreign films with American actors (*Three Men and a Baby* first succeeded as a French film, *Swept Away* as an Italian film, and *The Magnificent Seven* as the Japanese *The Seven Samurai*) to placing the stories of William Shakespeare and Jane Austen in more contemporary settings (*The Taming of the Shrew* became *10 Things I Hate About You; Emma* became *Clueless*). Combining an established storyline with name-brand actors and a popular genre may not guarantee box-office success, but it reduces many of the uncertainties that typically surround and inhibit big-budget filmmaking.

To see how networks of innovation come together by taking apart and reassembling the elements of existing technologies, we'll revisit another of the prototypical stories of innovation, Henry Ford's development of mass production. From this story, we can understand the potential for revolution inherent in recombinant innovations and begin the search for valuable lessons for today's managers and entrepreneurs.

The Birth of Mass Production: Ford Motor Company, 1908–1914

In 1900, the automobile industry was in its infancy.[11] There were fifty-seven firms devoted to building cars in the United States, and those firms built 1,681 steam-powered, 1,575 electric-powered, and 936 gasoline-powered vehicles. At the time, owning a car was an extravagance afforded mainly by the rich. By 1905, however, the industry was taking shape, offering glimpses of what it might look like when it matured. In those five years, for example, the design

standardized around the internal combustion engine, reducing uncertainty on the part of entrepreneurs, investors, and potential owners alike. And by 1906, Henry Ford knew the direction the market
was going:

> [The] greatest need today is a light, low-priced car with an
> up-to-date engine of ample horsepower, and built of the very
> best material. . . . It must be powerful enough for American
> roads and capable of carrying its passengers anywhere that a
> horse-drawn vehicle will go without the driver being afraid
> of ruining his car.[12]

He wasn't the only one with that vision. The idea of a low-cost car
was no different than the idea of a low-cost computer today. The
problem, like today, was building one.

Ford set his engineers to the task, and by 1908 they had developed
the Model T, a car that met Ford's goals for strength and performance
and sold for $850. Based on the design alone, sales agents ordered
15,000 cars before production had even begun. So began a seven-
year engineering feat that, when the dust settled, not only changed
the automobile industry and the countryside but also the way the
world thought about manufacturing. In 1908, the Ford Motor Company built close to 6,000 Model T's. The next year, it more than dou-
bled production to almost 14,000; production then rose to 20,000,
then 53,000, then 82,000, then 189,000. In 1914, it was 230,000. During that time the price dropped steadily from $850 to $490, while
Ford's market share rose from under 10 percent to 46 percent.

The development of mass production at Ford Motor Company
took shape almost completely between 1908, when Ford introduced
the Model T, and 1914, when the final pieces of the production
process were in place. Henry Ford became an industrial success
story. *Encyclopaedia Britannica* commissioned Ford to write the ar-
ticle on mass production, which was also published as a Sunday feature in the *New York Times*. Famous already as an automaker, Henry
Ford became the father of mass production, and his Model T became the symbol of American industrial growth and of the bound-
less opportunities that awaited a world embracing mass production.

A closer look at the origins of mass production reveals the role of recombinant innovation at the Ford Motor Company. Ford invented neither the automobile nor the techniques he used to mass produce it, but he did bring these ideas together in a way no one else had before.

The early years of the automotive industry were filled with entrepreneurial automakers designing and building cars in small numbers of anywhere from one to several hundred. Parts were built in machine shops, each according to the latest design, and assembled on the spot or shipped to another factory for final assembly. The Ford Motor Company built most of its early cars this way, outsourcing most parts from local suppliers. All this would change with the Model T. The events that came to be known as the birth of mass production took place first in Ford's Piquette Avenue factory in Detroit and then in its Highland Park factory. There, Ford's engineers brought together three manufacturing technologies that had evolved over the last hundred years and one that was relatively new: interchangeable parts, continuous work flow, the assembly line, and the electric motor.

Interchangeable Parts

As the Ford Motor Company began producing the Model T, a brochure introducing the new car proudly announced, "We are making 40,000 cylinders, 10,000 engines, 40,000 wheels, 20,000 axles, 10,000 bodies, 10,000 of every part that goes into the car . . . *all exactly alike.*" At Ford—and the rest of the automobile industry— ideas about interchangeability were exciting and new. But the idea of interchangeable parts had been in the public domain since 1801, when Eli Whitney first presented ten identical horse pistols to Congress. To the Army, interchangeable parts promised that working pistols could be assembled from the functioning locks, stocks, and barrels of broken ones. To manufacturers, interchangeable parts promised to reduce their dependence on skilled craftsmen—if all the pieces could be built to fit perfectly together, there was no need for costly and time-consuming filing.

These promises were good, but reality had to wait for the development of machine tools—milling machines, lathes, punch presses, and drill presses—capable of producing consistent results in high volumes. This in turn had to wait until the advances in metallurgy and design that took place in the late 1800s. By the turn of the twentieth century, however, that reality had arrived, and machines were producing watch assemblies, sewing machines, and other small, high-volume consumer items accurately and reliably.

To car companies making only a few thousand cars a year, though, the ability of machine tools to turn out thousands of identical parts did not seem relevant. Few of the engineers and entrepreneurs were familiar with, or cared to explore, the potential of machine tools for producing cars. Henry Ford, however, with his dreams of a car for the masses, was interested.

Ford first learned about interchangeability and the machine tool industry when he tooled up for production of the Model T's predecessor, the Model N. It was then he met Walter Flanders, a machine tool salesman. Flanders had worked previously at the Singer Manufacturing Company, maker of Singer sewing machines and an early pioneer of interchangeability, and before that he built machine tools at the Landis Tool Company. Few men knew machine tools and volume manufacturing like Flanders. Flanders introduced Ford to Max Wollering, who had worked as a tool builder for International Harvester and for the Hoffman Hinge and Foundry Company. Ford hired Wollering as superintendent of the new Highland Park factory Ford was opening and, a few months later, hired Flanders as overall production manager at Ford.

Together over the next two years, Flanders and Wollering oversaw the design, development, and installation of machine tools, fixtures, and gauges for the production of automobile engines. Drawing on their experience in the machine tool industry and in the use of machine tools for everything from sewing machines to harvesters to foundries, Flanders and Wollering created for Ford what they called "farmer tools." These were single-purpose machine tools dedicated to producing one type of part or performing one particular operation on one part—drilling, cutting, or grinding. The idea was that a farm boy using these tools could turn out work as good as that of a first-class mechanic: Each piece had the necessary accuracy to fit together with the other parts being produced.

With these tools, Ford exploited over a century of development within the machine tool industry. To outsiders—and to many within Ford—these tools were revolutionary, but to others, they were explicitly built from the pieces of past technologies. As Max Wollering once said, "There was nothing new [about interchangeability] to me, but it might have been new to the Ford Motor Company because they were not in a position to have much experience along that line." [13]

Continuous-Flow Production

When Ford was building the Model N, production looked like that of all the other car manufacturers at the time. Batches of parts and subassemblies would arrive at the final assembly plant on Piquette Avenue, and the major subassemblies (such as the engine or the drive train) would take shape on a stationary assembly horse, or stand, around which a team of assemblers would gather to piece together the necessary parts from bins surrounding them. The work stayed still, while the people moved around. Parts departments, such as those devoted to engine blocks, crankcases, axles, and bushings and small parts, each put together their subassemblies; these were then brought together into larger and larger assemblies until they reached final assembly.

When Henry Ford tooled up a new factory in Highland Park, however, and dedicated it to producing only the Model T, he abandoned these old notions. He reorganized the production process around the flow of work, placing operations such as casting an engine block or boring a cylinder head on the factory floor in the order they occurred. He invested in machine tools that were dedicated to one operation, such as drilling locating holes in six engine blocks at one time. And he built conveyor belts and gravity slides that moved the work from one machine to the next. By doing so, he reduced the amount of inventory that could pile up in between each operation (preempting the just-in-time movement by seventy-five years) and created a continuous flow of materials from inputs to outputs. At its peak, production of the Model T involved unloading iron ore, wood, and coal at one end of the factory and driving Model T's out the other.

How new were the ideas and objects (and people) of continuous-flow production? Decades before Ford first began building cars, other industries had already developed a continuous, rather than batch, flow of product through the factory. In 1882, for example, a cigarette-making machine was patented by James Bonsack that produced 120,000 cigarettes a day. At the time, handworkers could at best produce 3,000 a day. Fifteen of the new machines could supply the world's demand.[14] Continuous processing techniques and equipment were also being developed and used in the production of cereals and flour, particularly in the form of the automatic all-roller, gradual-reduction mill, which was described as "the first in the world to maintain under one roof operations to grade, clean, hull, cut, package, and ship oatmeal to interstate markets in a continuous process."[15] These manufacturing techniques were also emerging in the canning industries, where produce, condensed milk, and canned meats were packaged for shipment across the United States. The firms that first adopted these techniques remain household brands today: H.J. Heinz, the Campbell Soup Company, and the Borden Milk Company.

By the time Henry Ford brought continuous-flow manufacturing techniques into the automobile industry, they were already well developed in a range of other industries. Oscar Bornholdt had the job of tooling up the Highland Park factory for the Model T. Bornholdt had seen the layout and machine tools of canning operations and other similar continuous-flow factories, and readily admitted that these existing lines were the source of the continuous-flow innovations at Ford: "At the Ford Plant, the machines are arranged [sequentially] very much like the tin-can machines."[16] Like Wollering before him, Bornholdt did not have to create a new system from scratch—instead, he could combine the people, ideas, and objects already in use in other industries. The Ford Motor Company did not have to invent the machines, train engineers in how to design them, or teach the mechanics to service them. And while Ford's engineers challenged these machines to solve problems specific to building automobiles, most of the hard work had already been done in the cigarette industry, the canning industry, watchmaking, and the breweries.

Assembly Line Production

The third technological innovation that characterized Ford's mass production was the assembly line. Having achieved interchangeability in parts (reducing the need for skilled craftsmen in the process) and having invested in dedicated machine tools arranged to produce a continuous flow of work, the only source of troubling variation that remained in Ford's system was the worker. In putting together the various parts of the car using the previous system, roving teams would move down a line of assembly stations, performing a specific set of tasks. Around this assembly process, a complex ballet of parts suppliers ran between subassemblies and storage to ensure everyone had the necessary parts when they needed them. When the workers were at their best, the complex movements ran smoothly; trouble happened when parts deliveries were delayed, or when assembly gangs got in each other's way.

The assembly line solved all of this. Ford and his engineers arranged the workers in a line; each worker was given a simple task to do and would then move the work piece down to the next man, who would perform his simple task and move the work along as well. Rather than keeping the work on assembly stands and moving the men past it, the assembly line kept the men still and moved the work. The results were immediate and obvious. The first experiments with an assembly line were done in Ford's magneto assembly room, where workers had traditionally assembled magnetos individually and had, on average, produced roughly one every twenty minutes. The first day of the experiment, workers averaged one every thirteen minutes. Within a year they would have that down to five minutes each. Few experiments with innovation prove themselves on the first day—the assembly line at Ford did. Within a year, most of the other departments at Ford had changed over to an assembly line process.[17]

The assembly line was revolutionary in its impact at Ford, but again, was it new? Henry Ford credits the "disassembly" lines of the Chicago meatpackers for the original idea of the assembly line. The 1906 publication of Upton Sinclair's *The Jungle* made public the details of work in the slaughterhouses of the time, as whole pigs and cows came in one end and cuts and parts went out the other. The workers stayed in place while the carcasses moved past them on a chain. William Klann, head of the engine department at Ford, recalled touring Swift's Chicago plant thinking, "If they can kill pigs and cows that way, we can build cars that way."[18]

There were other problems that the assembly line needed to solve, however, before the workers could build cars that way. In particular, two problems dominated the assembly line: the pile-ups that happened either when one team slowed everyone behind them or when suppliers showed up late or got in the way of the assemblers. To make the assembly line work at Ford, these two crucial problems needed to be solved. The solutions, of course, lay elsewhere.

The Westinghouse Airbrake Company had by 1890 developed a system for casting iron parts that involved moving a mold carrier on a conveyor past molding machines and under a ladle built for the continuous pouring of molten iron into the molds. After this it was moved to where the molds were broken down, the parts removed, and the sand moved back, by another conveyor, to where the molds were made again. The system eliminated practically all wheelbarrows and shoveling. Ford adopted this technique for use in the Highland Park factory. This foundry system moved the work past the men and, just as important, moved all the necessary materials to exactly where they were needed when they were needed.

Ford's engineers also adopted ideas and equipment that granaries and breweries had been using for over a century. Before working for Ford, Klann had worked repairing grain elevators and other conveyors for the Huetteman & Cramer Machine Company of Detroit. Breweries and granaries used many of the same hoppers and conveyors to move materials around, and another Ford employee who had worked at Huetteman & Cramer had showed Ford a catalog of foundry and brewing conveyor systems. As Klann once said, "We combined our ideas on the Huetteman & Cramer grain [conveying] machine[ry], and the brewing experience and the Chicago Stockyard. They all gave us ideas for our own conveyors." [19]

Bringing It All Together

The ability of Ford's engineers to capitalize on the well-developed ideas of the machine tool industry, the granaries and breweries, and the meatpacking industry all hinged on another emerging technology that had developed elsewhere but was ripe for introduction into manufacturing: the electric motor. In the early 1880s, Edison was one of the first to introduce a commercial electric motor and to see all of the possibilities it presented. The first commercial uses were in streetcars, and then as replacements for steam engines as single power sources within factories.

But steam engines and electric motors were different beasts entirely. There were tremendous economies of scale in steam engines: The larger the engine, the more efficient. Entire factories in the nineteenth century were built around the steam engine, which powered machinery throughout the plant through a complex system of shafts and belts. Central shafts powered local ones, which in turn powered individual machines—all connected by belts. Breaking belts, which shut down whole lines and sometimes even the entire plant, were a common problem (sometimes costing as much as 25 percent of the plant's productivity).

Electric motors did not share these economies of scale: Small motors were no less efficient than large ones. Brent Goldfarb, an economist at the University of Maryland, tracked the diffusion of electric motors throughout American manufacturing from 1880 to 1930. [20]

He found that although the electric motor enabled changes in almost every industry, those changes were hampered by the established practices and objects within each industry and even within each plant. At first, electric motors replaced central steam engines, where they did not require changes in the elaborate systems of shafts and belts—but where they also did not show much improvement in performance. Then came "group-drive" motors, which powered multiple machines but within only a single department. Finally, as Ford was tooling up his Highland factory, the electric motor was being used for "unit drives," which powered individual machinery.

Ford was the first automobile manufacturer to grasp the potential of this new technology and to use it to the fullest. As late as 1919, Goldfarb shows, 50 percent of all automobiles were manufactured using electric motors—all of them by the Ford Motor Company. These changes were truly revolutionary because they allowed Ford to experiment with continuous-flow production lines. His engineers could move machines without having to redesign the shafts that powered them, and they could try running them at different speeds. The factory could be built around the flow of work rather than around a central power plant. Finally, the overhead space could be cleared of all the shafts and belts, allowing Ford's engineers to install overhead cranes, conveyors, and other means of moving the components to the workers and finished assemblies down the line.

• • •

Ford was aware that he neither invented the automobile (which was first demonstrated over a century before) nor the components of mass production that he used to build his Model T. In a patent dispute over the true inventor of the automobile, he once testified:

> I invented nothing new. I simply assembled into a car the discoveries of other men behind whom were centuries of work.
> . . . Had I worked fifty or ten or even five years before, I would have failed. So it is with every new thing. Progress happens

when all the factors that make for it are ready, and then it is inevitable. To teach that a comparatively few men are responsible for the greatest forward steps of mankind is the worst sort of nonsense." [21]

The Ford Motor Company succeeded instead by bridging a wide range of industries and building from the pieces of those different worlds an organization that combined the best people, ideas, and objects it could find to build a car. Ford's system was revolutionary in its impact on the automobile industry, on manufacturing, and on society, but it was revolutionary *because* its origins drew on existing technologies. Eli Whitney's ten interchangeable horse pistols precipitated a machine tool industry that produced accurate machines. James Bonsack's cigarette machine, along with countless nameless engineers constantly tinkering with the equipment to process cigarettes, cereals, and flour, continued to evolve the ideas and objects of continuous-flow production. The ideas and machines of the Westinghouse foundry (themselves built on previous ones), Swift's meatpacking disassembly lines, and Huetteman & Cramer's conveyors and hoppers made up the assembly line. And finally, Ford relied on people like Walter Flanders and Max Wollering, who knew about machine tools and how they were being used in each of these different worlds. All of these pieces provided the raw materials for constructing the innovation that was mass production.

A Modern Tale of Recombination, Revolution, and Mass Production

Recombinant innovation can also be found in a central technology powering the biotechnology revolution: PCR, or polymerase chain reaction. PCR is the biochemical process by which single strands of DNA can be replicated in great quantities—allowing both the study of particular DNA strands and also their insertion into the DNA of other biological hosts, which in turn enables the production of organic compounds. Developed in the early 1980s, this technology triggered the great leaps forward in the biotechnology revolution that we are experiencing today.

PCR is to molecular biology what Ford's mass production was to the modern factory—a chance for individual laboratories to mass-produce DNA for use first in their experiments and later, as entrepreneurs, in developing and producing genetically modified organisms. In the words of Paul Rabinow, the critical contribution of PCR as a technology was to "make abundant what was once scarce."[22]

Was PCR an invention? To the committee selecting the Nobel Prize winners in 1993 it was, and they recognized Kary Mullis, a scientist working at Cetus Corporation, for his conception of the process back in 1983. And as far as the courts were concerned, PCR was an invention; they upheld the Cetus patents despite countless lawsuits.

Beyond that, the story becomes muddy. Kary Mullis once described his achievement in the following way:

> In a sense, I put together elements that were already there, but that's what inventors always do. You can't make up new elements, usually. The new element, if any, was the combination, the way they were used. . . . The fact that I would do it over and over again, and the fact that I would do it in just the way I did, that made it an invention. . . . The legal wording is "presents an unanticipated solution to a long-standing problem," that's an invention and that was clearly PCR."[23]

What Mullis did was bring together already-existing techniques for making oligonucleotides (particular fragments of DNA), for separating those strands from others by gel electrophoresis, and for transferring and detecting them on a membrane. Each of these techniques was relatively well understood in biochemistry, and new techniques and technologies were rapidly improving their performance. But identifying, isolating, and replicating particular fragments of DNA was still a laborious and time-consuming process. In fact, it was precisely the laborious nature of these tasks that led Mullis to explore how he might speed the process up. Mullis's innovation was to recognize that these techniques could be combined in a way that produced a (polymerase) chain reaction—a feedback loop by which the DNA fragments that were produced would then be used to produce even more such fragments. The result was an exponential production process, in which each loop through the process produced twice as many fragments as the step before. Thanks to Mullis's recombinant process, the time and money needed to produce a workable quantity of any fragment of genetic code plummeted.

Was PCR a revolution? Yes. But this isn't saying much. The better question to ask is whether the revolution came from what made PCR an invention (Mullis's insight to combine the existing elements in the way that he did) or from those existing elements themselves. The full impact of Mullis's "invention" has yet to be felt, but the process of PCR has already triggered discontinuous changes in the development and manufacture of new medications in the pharmaceutical industry. However, Mullis's contribution, by his own admission, was not the invention of wholly new ideas or techniques but rather the inventive recombination of existing ideas. The discontinuous changes wreaked by Mullis's work were the result of a continuity in the ideas Mullis used to construct his new biochemical manufacturing technique.

Managing for Recombinant Innovation

We tend to think that the ideas that spawn revolutions must themselves be revolutionary. Few people involved in the process of generating and selling "revolutionary ideas" stand to gain anything by saying otherwise. It's in everyone's best interest to suppress or in other ways neglect the ways in which radical innovations are obligated to those ideas that have come before them, and from which they have drawn—often quite heavily. But understanding breakthrough innovations like Ford's mass production, like PCR, like the Reebok Pump shoe, like electronic mail, and like the Beatles depends on understanding where the ideas behind the innovations came from and how they came together in the ways that they did.

It's one thing to dress an innovation up like an invention by hiding the true origins of the central ideas. That's just good marketing. (As Picasso once said, "Good artists borrow, great artists steal.") Problems arise, however, when the organized pursuit of innovation begins with the assumption that revolutionary impacts require revolutionary origins, and that embracing the future requires abandoning the past. The phrase "not invented here," or NIH, is one with which all organizations are (or should be) familiar. It is the natural response that emerges as people gain experience with a particular project or problem. They come to think that their deep experiences give them an understanding of the problem that no outsider could have and, as a result, a greater ability to generate novel solutions than anyone else. That they never invent anything themselves only reaffirms the value of their existing ideas.

Most organizations embed these notions of innovation-as-invention into their very structures. Research and development labs, ensconced in corporate headquarters, invent their company's future safe from the distractions of the present. Surprisingly, Edison's Menlo Park laboratory is considered the prototypical corporate research lab. It certainly generated a lot of patents—the ideal measure of any corporate research lab. But it was also a laboratory in the wild—with ties to many different industries, clients, investors, and business ventures. Trying to replicate the Menlo Park phenomenon inside a firm has meant, metaphorically, building the same building and everything in it. Most R&D labs ignore the fact that they have severed just about every tie Edison's lab had to its environment—the source of its inventiveness.

When individuals and organizations pursue innovation by pursuing inventions, they are cutting off the very raw materials from which successful innovations are quickly built. A strategy of technology brokering, on the other hand, targets the inherent potential of recombinant innovation. Bridging the old networks of distant worlds brings access to the established resources of different worlds; building new networks creates the ties needed to attract and hold these previously disparate resources together.

Conversely, the more an innovation is built from scratch, the more effort is required to develop and market it. Take the zipper, for example, which historian Robert Friedel describes so well in *Zipper: An Exploration in Novelty*. Whitcomb Judson, of Chicago, first applied for a patent on the idea of the zipper in 1891. His idea for "A Clasp Locker or Unlocker for Shoes" had, by Friedel's account, few precedents to draw from. Unfortunately for Judson and his investors, this meant they not only had to design all the elements of the new device, but also the machinery to manufacture it. It took two more decades of continuous development before Gideon Sundback, working for Judson's investors, developed a model that worked smoothly and could be manufactured cheaply, the Hookless #2. It took another two decades before the public fully embraced the product.

It's important that an innovation appears new to its intended market, but it's also important that it draws on the past. Ford's willingness to give almost carte blanche to a group of engineers with little to no experience in the automobile industry suggests that experience, specialized training, and advanced degrees in a single field may not be the best way to pursue innovation. Large-scale investments in research and development, built on a model of the internal development of scientific advances that break from everything that has come before, have sent a great many creative geniuses into their laboratories with implicit instructions to ignore the most fruitful source of innovations—what has already been done. Hiring the best and the brightest and then asking them to think outside of the boxes in which they've been raised may simply be unrealistic if the goal is creating breakthrough innovations.

• • •

The revolutions sparked by Henry Ford's system for mass producing automobiles and Kary Mullis's mass production of genetic material were both products of a recombinant process. The immediacy of Ford's successes, sometimes evident on the first day his engineers introduced changes to the factory floor, came from Ford's exploitation of existing technologies borrowed from other industries. Similarly, Mullis's PCR process could only have come about because the laboratory techniques and objects involved, such as electrophoresis, had already been well developed. Recombining existing but previously disparate elements often creates a whole that is greater by far than the sum of its parts because the process enables innovators to pull the best people, ideas, and objects from different worlds.

The recombination of existing elements into novel and powerful new technologies, scientific theories, and social movements is a process that depends critically on the individuals and organizations involved. But hiring smart people, building flat organizations and cross-functional teams, and engaging in brainstorming and rapid prototyping are not enough to make organizations innovative. It's not about free pinball, beer busts, casual Fridays, or whack-upside-the-head management techniques. To those in the automobile industry in 1910, Ford's engineers were thinking outside of the box, but to those same engineers, they were just thinking in different boxes.

Organizations pursuing innovation often unconsciously select individuals, organizational structures, and innovation strategies that will put them on the leading—some say bleeding—edge of their current markets and technologies. Research and development efforts look like races into the future. All the while, however, some of the most profound technological revolutions will be found not in front of rivals, but to the side, in other worlds where potentially valuable but unknown technologies have already emerged. Those who are too focused on inventing the future, like those who are too focused on holding on to the past, will miss the many valuable clues they pass by along the way.

We can learn a lot by applying a recombinant perspective to our old and familiar stories. Foremost, we can learn how to structure the innovation process to build from existing ideas rather then to invent new ones—what this book refers to as technology brokering strategies. Part II of this book talks about the value of moving across a wide range of industries and technologies rather than pursuing deep expertise within just a few. It also discusses the value of the collective pursuit of recombinant innovations rather than the individual pursuit of invention, and the role of communities in turning deviant ideas into dominant technologies.

Part III considers ways to organize around the pursuit of recombinant innovation through technology brokering. This section is about choosing markets, designing organizations, and developing work practices that enable firms to bridge multiple worlds, gaining access to the many different people, ideas, and objects within each, and to build new combinations of these resources to support new ventures elsewhere.

PART TWO

The Networks of Innovation

3

The Social Side of Innovation

Chapter 2 described the revolutionary potential of recombining existing people, ideas, and objects in novel ways. But if the elements of new innovations are lying about already, why doesn't this process happen more often? There are plenty of examples of innovations that were discovered by accident: the playful experiment that exposed nylon's potential, the telltale stain that created waterproof spray, the failed glue that led to Post-it Notes, the failed clinical trials that revealed Viagra. Like the surprise of meeting someone new in a café in Florence and discovering common friends, part of what makes stories of such accidental innovation so enjoyable is two seemingly different and distant worlds turning out to be related in unexpected and valuable ways.

In the pursuit of innovation, technology brokering entails not simply exploiting these fortunate accidents, but actually *triggering* them. By moving among worlds, technology brokering firms increase their chances of seeing how the people, ideas, and objects of one world might be useful in another. This chapter lays out the strategy of technology brokering, and how it exploits the network dynamics that give recombinant innovation its revolutionary potential.

To Louis Pasteur, who not only discovered germs but also the processes of vaccination and pasteurization, we owe the wonderful insight that "In the field of observation, chance favors only the pre-pared mind." This insight, now called *Pasteur's dictum,* has framed many subsequent scientific discoveries and technological innova-tions—the coincidences of failed experiments, accidental meetings, and other serendipitous events in the history of technological inno-vations.[1] Columbus discovered the Americas while looking for the East Indies, Nobel discovered the stability of dynamite when a leak from bottled nitroglycerin was absorbed by its surrounding packing material,[2] and Fleming discovered penicillin when he noticed that mold in one of his culture plates inhibited growth of *Staphylococci* bacteria. More recently, Art Fry discovered the potential for Post-it Notes during a failed attempt by another 3M scientist to make a stronger glue, and James Wright dropped boric acid into silicone oil and discovered silly putty. Indeed, chance has played such a large role in so many innovations that it begins to look like a critical step in any successful process.

These stories leave us with a choice: Either chance is the necessary step in the innovation process, which therefore, by definition, is un-manageable, or there is a common thread to these chance discover-ies that can be extracted, understood, and formalized. Many of these stories recount the moment when ideas from different worlds sud-denly come together, with the recognition—the Eureka moment—that there is great value to be had in this new combination. The stories are like the old commercials for Reese's peanut butter cups:

> "You got peanut butter in my chocolate!"
> "You got chocolate in my peanut butter!"
> (voiceover) Two great tastes that taste great together . . .

At 3M, Art Fry's need for a reusable paper tab to mark pages in a songbook ran into a glue developed by his colleague down the hall, Dr. Spencer Silver, that left no residue after removal.

At first glance, Pasteur's dictum promises a means for harnessing chance events—the prepared mind. But this approach doesn't in-crease the likelihood that such events will happen. Worse, a pre-pared mind can sometimes be the last one to recognize the value of a novel recombination. As the novelist Robertson Davies once said, knowledge "makes you wise in some ways, but it can make you a blindfolded fool in others."[3]

A British Parliamentary Committee of Inquiry in 1878 concluded that Edison demonstrated "the most airy ignorance of the fundamental principles both of electricity and dynamics." American scientists were no better; one responded to Edison's plans by declaring it would be "almost a public calamity if Mr. Edison should employ his great talent on such puerility."[4] Similarly, IBM famously passed on early chances to develop first the computer, then the microcomputer, and then the personal computer (and its race to catch up in the PC market precipitated the company's decision to give away the rights to its operating system). AT&T passed on building the infrastructure of the Internet. Proponents of Pasteur's dictum, then, must recognize its limitations.

Within stories of accidental innovation, however, we find two key mechanisms at work: moments when people, ideas, and objects from different worlds come in contact, and minds prepared to exploit these moments. Both must be managed with care and understanding. This chapter describes how technology brokering, by exploiting the networked landscape, stacks the game of chance in a firm's favor by creating moments and preparing minds to exploit the variety of resources available already in nearby, but seemingly distant, worlds.

Technology Brokering and the Network

In the language of social network theory, brokers link otherwise disconnected communities within the larger network. These can be project teams within a division, divisions within a firm, firms within an industry, or separate industries—wherever there are dense ties among a limited set of people, objects, and ideas and relatively few ties linking these elements to others. Within these communities, information flows easily, which, in turn, allows greater communication and coordination. The inhabitants of any one community become increasingly supportive of, and reliant on, their interactions with each other. Roles become clarified, practices interdependent, and interests aligned, and new technologies emerge that both reflect and reinforce these interactions.

These communities become, in essence, their own small worlds and by doing so fragment the larger networked landscape. These characteristics hold whether we're talking about product development teams, manufacturing plants, geographically dispersed markets, or different industries. The dense interactions within each community become the focus of attention and efforts and, as a result, create a fragmented landscape in which each community interacts less with other communities. As a result, fewer interactions take place between these small worlds. To answer the question with which this chapter began, the reason recombinant innovations are relatively rare is that the flow of people, ideas, and objects among these small worlds is relatively rare. Few people are in a position to see how the resources of one world might benefit another; fewer still are prepared to act on what they see.

Brokers are individuals, groups, and organizations that move among these small worlds. They have an advantage because they are often in a position to see how the resources of one world could be used to solve problems in another. Beginning in the early 1970s, sociologists have studied the advantages that go to those who connect otherwise disconnected areas of the larger social network. Three social network scholars in particular have shaped our understanding of the phenomenon of brokering.

The Strength of Weak Ties

The first scholar is Mark Granovetter, a sociologist at Stanford University, who was one of the first to document the advantages of making connections across a fragmented network when he asked, from a network perspective, how individuals found new jobs, apartments, and other valuable resources.[5] Most people assume, quite correctly, that information flows easily among those people with whom we interact regularly, with whom we share *strong* ties: the friends, nearby coworkers, and colleagues we talk to on a daily basis. If someone brings cookies into the office, has a birthday, or has a baby, we all learn about it quickly. Unfortunately, the value of this information tends to be marginal as far as innovation goes; because we know and interact with these same people on a regular basis, there is soon very little they know that we don't also know. So we are more likely to find valuable and novel information, such as an apartment becoming vacant or a new job opening up, from those with whom we have *weak* ties.

The difference between strong and weak ties is relatively simple and deserves a brief digression. In the language of social network theory, strong and weak ties do not describe the intensity of a particular relationship between two people but instead the social structure that surrounds them. Two people share a *strong* tie when the people they know, know each other; they share a *weak* tie when the people they know are not connected. I am strongly tied to my colleagues in my school because they also know and talk to each other. I am weakly tied to the barista at my local coffee shop, even though I may see her more often than some colleagues, because she travels in a distinctly different world of body piercings, tattoos, and day jobs. Strong ties are strong because information flows easily within the resulting communities, as we have all experienced from time to time. My incentive to overcharge, shirk, or in any way challenge the norms of the community is low because any negative repercussions are likely to come from people to whom I am close. These ties are strong because they bring strong social forces to bear.

We are all strongly tied to some and weakly tied to others, and, returning to Granovetter's findings, we are more likely to find useful (i.e., novel) information from those to whom we are weakly tied: casual acquaintances, the friends of brothers, the sisters of neighbors. Take Corrine, a hypothetical programmer on a software team. Corrine is strongly tied to the four others on her team because they all know each other well. She and her teammates represent a strongly tied group, but each also has weak ties to others outside the group: Corrine's manager interacts regularly with his own manager, and Corrine also spends time with Rusty over in customer support. It is this second group of connections that can provide the team with much of the novel and valuable information they seek—maybe about a competing project or a particularly valuable customer's problem. This is because these more distant people inhabit their *own* worlds, where they learn about more distant opportunities and can pass them along. Granovetter called this phenomenon the *strength of weak ties* in recognition of the novel and valuable information that often comes from these happenstance connections.

Structural Holes

Although we all rely on our weak ties to some degree, Ron Burt extended this notion by recognizing that some individuals and firms seek out and exploit these relatively weak connections.[6] He coined the term *structural holes* to identify the gaps in the larger network that individuals and organizations could exploit by moving resources between groups that were otherwise disconnected. For Burt, the power of this brokerage position lies in the lack of other, redundant, connections: Brokers seek to hold, and defend, their positions as the sole link between groups.

This theory is a powerful view that can be used to describe the advantages (and incentives) of financial brokers, realtors, and others who control the flow of relatively finished goods such as money, stocks, bonds, apartments, and jobs that emerge within one group and are valued in another. It can also describe the advantages that underlie traditional strategies of gaining control of a strategic resource and making a profit by controlling who gets access to it. From selling oil to selling software, the brokering advantage lies in being the only one through whom all resources must flow to get to the market.

Innovation rarely flourishes under these conditions, however, because such brokers will fight hard to maintain their unique advantages and to keep the networked landscape exactly as it is. They may innovate, but only to the extent needed to prevent others from forming connections around them. When ideas come along that threaten the flow of resources through the central broker, the broker will use every possible advantage to prevent those ideas from taking hold.

From a network perspective, for example, Microsoft's strategic advantage lies in its position between the user's computer experience and the world of computing, whether that's hardware, software, or access to the Internet. Over 90 percent of the market sees the digital world through Microsoft-tinted windows. When new technologies came along that threatened to bypass Microsoft's brokerage position, the company reacted in ways that preserved the status quo, the federal courts found.[7] Netscape Navigator's browser offered users a way onto the Internet that was largely independent of the user's operating system, and thus was an attempt to build a link between the digital world and customers that did not flow through Microsoft. The folks in Redmond responded by first developing their own browser, Explorer, and then embedding it into the Windows operating system. When RealPlayer developed a means to stream audio and video into computers, Microsoft reacted by developing and embedding its own media streaming technology. When Sun developed the Java programming language, enabling the creation of Web-based applications that could operate independent of the user's operating system, Microsoft altered the standard until only its version would work on Windows. Currently, Microsoft sees a threat in Sony, whose PlayStations outnumber computers in the home. Once again, Microsoft's unique position between the user and the digital world is at risk. Yet its response, the Xbox, has met a formidable enemy in Sony and its already established ties to the market, and the outcome is far from certain.[8]

Firms often exploit and defend their brokerage positions in this way and, in the process, actively suppress alternative innovations that threaten to dramatically change the technological landscape. But it's important to recognize that the advantages these established firms have came from originally finding and establishing that position as a broker. So although Bill Gates and crew now defend the status quo, early on they created a revolution using the people, ideas, and code of previous operating systems and applications.

Bridging and Building

If we are interested in how new innovations and new ventures form between worlds, rather than within any single world, and how they reshape the networked landscape as a result, then Burt's view of brokers remains an incomplete story. The third influential network scholar, Paul DiMaggio, a sociologist from Princeton, recognized that brokers can use their connections to distant networks to recognize and bring combinations of people, ideas, and objects from these different worlds together to create something of value that did not exist before.[9] Rather than simply moving resources from one locale to another, these brokers use their unique perspectives to envision and create novel combinations of these resources, and sometimes even novel industries. As a result, these brokers change the very structure of the network by building new ties between worlds.

For example, DiMaggio described how Paul Sachs constructed the Museum of Modern Art in the face of resistance from the entrenched community that surrounded the existing art museums. MOMA, as it has become known, was founded in 1929 with the mission of bringing contemporary art to the public. At the time of its founding, this was an innovation bordering on heresy, as the established art community believed—to grossly oversimplify—that an artist had to be dead before he or she could be good. The idea that a museum should display contemporary works of art, before time could test what was good and what was not, faced considerable resistance in the established world of art museums.

What made MOMA possible was the work of one man, Paul Sachs, who had connections across a range of different communities within which there was scattered interest, or at least open minds and open wallets, for developing such a museum. He knew society matrons, he knew academics, he knew museum curators, and he knew artists. But most important of all, he knew how to bring these people together in ways that pooled their complementary resources and overcame the resistance of the established art museums. As DiMaggio points out, Sachs's advantage was as a broker between these different worlds. Rather than being central in any one, his power derived from being well connected across the range of different small worlds in which isolated but potentially valuable resources sat unused. While Sachs's original advantage was as the sole link between otherwise disconnected worlds, he succeeded by building redundant ties between those he alone had previously bridged (eliminating his advantage as a broker in the process).

Here the value to a broker of finding and filling any one structural hole, any one gap in the flow of information among worlds, is temporary because as brokers build new connections they soon render their unique position redundant. But the likelihood of building successful ventures increases because of the resulting communities, in which more people can gain by the new bridges they build to others. For every successful Microsoft, countless entrepreneurs failed because they were unwilling or unable to create the opportunities—the strong ties—that would attract others to the new venture.

Most of the scholarly work on brokers and brokering has focused on *social* networks, on the interactions between people, and not on those networks that link people to the ideas and objects that they interact with as often as they do with people, if not more so. Yet we conduct our searches for novel and valuable ideas in many ways, which include but are not limited to our social networks. I am usually content listening to the music I heard growing up, but when I do learn about new music, it's usually from a friend who follows the industry closely by buying compact discs, reading trade journals, and scanning for online reviews. My first link is social, to a friend, but *his* links are to the objects of that world: compact discs, *Rolling Stone* magazine, and online reviews. This last object reflects one of the greatest virtues of the Internet (and its rapidly evolving search engines)—the ability it provides anyone to search far and wide. The Internet is like searching the library on speed. But we learn a great deal in other places and other ways as well: Engineers study competitors' products to learn about new design and manufacturing capabilities; store managers walk the aisles of other stores; mainstream musicians listen to alternative music; novelists read widely. All of these actions represent searches that link people facing problems to other ideas and objects that reside outside their own small worlds.

Edison, for example, held a brokerage position between the telegraph industry and emerging markets in fire and police alarms, in stock tickers, in mimeograph machines, in iron mining, and many others. During the Menlo Park years, at the height of his inventive career, he profited not by being central within any one of these industries, but rather by moving relatively freely among them—by connecting these otherwise small worlds and the people, objects, and ideas within each that might hold value elsewhere. The connections he identified and exploited were enormously valuable because, in many cases, they enabled the flow of electromechanical technologies into a range of industries that had little or no previous knowledge of them.

• • •

This chapter laid out the advantages to finding network positions that connect different worlds. The first advantages are those that brokers, by bridging different worlds, have in being the first to see how disparate ideas, objects, and people can be used to create innovative and valuable combinations. The second are the network connections that make it possible to build communities around a new venture from the previously disparate people of different worlds. Chapter 4 explores the implications of bridging distant worlds. Chapter 5 explores the importance of building new worlds from the pieces found in those old worlds.

4

Bridging Small Worlds

The strategy of technology brokering can take many forms in practice, as we'll see in part III, but two central activities remain the same: *bridging* distant worlds in order to see new ways of combining existing but previously distant people, ideas, and objects, and *building* new networks between and around these new combinations. This chapter considers the nature of bridging distant worlds; the next chapter looks closely at the nature of building new ones.

Bridging distant worlds overcomes two central obstacles in the pursuit of innovation. First, bridging offers a way to avoid the competency traps that, by making even changes for the better too costly in the short run, keep existing groups, organizations, and industries locked into the old ways of doing things. Bridging activities overcome these competency traps by bringing organizations into contact with the wide variety of already well-developed technologies that exist in other worlds. Recombinations of these existing resources, as described in chapter 2, can bypass much of the time, effort, uncertainty, and cost of inventing and developing wholly new technologies. Bridging activities also provide another critical advantage that can easily be overlooked. The act of bridging distant worlds actually changes the way people see and think about the worlds they inhabit. In this way, bridging activities overcome the parochialism that hinders individuals, groups, organizations, and even industries from seeing the value of people, ideas, and objects that reside outside their traditional boundaries. This chapter explores each of these advantages and describes some of the activities that firms engage in to bridge distant worlds. First, however, we need to understand how the many small worlds of the networked landscape constrain the innovation process for those who reside within any one.

Small Worlds and Their Constraints on Innovation

The communities that surround existing technologies reflect dense networks of interactions among the people, ideas, and objects that make up those technologies. In the larger landscape, they show up as many small worlds only loosely connected to each other. We should view them as small worlds for two reasons. First, this is the way they are experienced. To those who have cast their fortunes with the new electric light, with athletic shoes, personal computers, or the Internet, the world often shrinks to encompass only those with whom they interact on a daily and weekly basis, who belong in the same network and share the same ideas. Early industries are characterized by this single-mindedness. To Edison's muckers, Menlo Park, New Jersey, was the center of the universe; Edison and his muckers had little interaction with the tight-knit groups that were leading dramatic changes in the railroad industry at the same time. The same was true for those who were revolutionizing steelmaking or automobiles (although as a young man, Henry Ford financed his first prototype automobile, built in his garage at night, by working for Edison Electric). To the early developers of personal computers, it was Silicon Valley; to the early auto manufacturers, Detroit. The long nights, the weekends, devoted to building an enterprise leave little room for anything else.

The second reason these are small worlds is because, to network theorists, the label *small world* describes the surprisingly short distances that connect these many isolated pockets of dense interactions. We are, on average, somewhere between three and five degrees, or acquaintances, away from anyone else in the world. That means everyone knows someone (one link) who knows someone (two links) who knows anybody else (three links) in the world. We seldom know, and can't easily predict, who those two people are who stand between us and anyone else and we are continually surprised to discover in meeting strangers that we share common friends. We are continually surprised, that is, to discover just how small is the world that extends beyond our own local communities.

What's so important about the phenomenon of small worlds when it comes to the pursuit of innovation? Chances are, the paths that link us to everyone else in the world will pass through only a few people—brokers (also called hubs), who have a wide range of ties across many different parts of the larger network. Most of us are, instead, deeply embedded within our own small worlds, where the people, ideas, and objects with which we interact are all tightly connected to one another. These small worlds shape both the actions and understandings of their inhabitants—the individuals and organizations that reside within them.

The Competency Trap

Small worlds both enable and constrain action. The dense connections give any single world its structure and stability and, as a result, enable a complex set of people, ideas, and objects to work smoothly together as a single, coherent system. But these same dense ties also make it extremely difficult to change any one part of that system without affecting the rest. Consider what happened to the world that Ford built.

The development of mass production at the Ford Motor Company shows the breakthrough potential of finding new ways to use old technologies. It also shows how Ford managed to create an organization capable of pulling the best people, ideas, and objects from a range of otherwise distant and disconnected worlds. But in the decade after Ford had established mass production of the Model T, General Motors began a systematic strategy of dividing and conquering Ford's mass market by introducing a range of mid- to low-cost models.

Compared with the bold and experimental approach Ford took in manufacturing the Model T, his response to this new threat was stunning for its defense of the status quo. Rather than adopt the new marketing practices, Ford focused on what he knew already—lowering the cost of the Model T further. In his defense, he had few options. In the River Rouge factory, he had constructed such a tightly linked manufacturing operation that any changes in the design of a part or process cascaded painfully through the entire organization. The tight-knit relations between people, ideas, and objects that Henry Ford constructed around mass production and the Model T made it almost impossible to respond to General Motors's introduction of multiple models and annual design changes. Ultimately, the River Rouge plant, the pinnacle of Ford's system, had to shut down completely for nine months to abandon the Model T and convert to a new model. In short, Ford's success in piecing together a complex system of mass production sowed the very seeds of its failure—the inability to easily accommodate changes in particular elements.

These two periods of the Ford Motor Company, back to back, demonstrate both the revolutionary potential of innovations—as the recombination of elements of existing technologies—and the cause of this potential—the inability of most established systems to readily accept such changes. From 1908 to 1914, Ford succeeded in bridging multiple worlds and building a new world around these new combinations. The world he built, however, quickly became a small world of its own, with its inhabitants unable to change their actions in response to the new and valuable possibilities emerging just past its own boundaries.

A similar story, in an industry known for creative risk taking, is unfolding right now, quite literally as we watch. It's been going on for the last decade, and the outcome will shape the way we perceive entertainment and experience movies.

Lucas, Digital Film, and the World That Is Hollywood

George Lucas, one of the reigning kings of moviemaking, filmed *Star Wars: Episode II* using digital technology from start to finish. This was the first major feature film to be shot, edited, and distributed in digital format, never once becoming the traditional 35-millimeter print that we have all come to know and love for its frames, dust specks, and off-color character.[1] The unfolding innovation is quite compelling. Recent advances in digital video technology have made it possible to capture high-definition video with a fidelity imperceptibly similar to 35-millimeter film stock. And new developments in digital projectors have eliminated some of the earlier hurdles in achieving true blacks and saturated colors. *Star Wars: Episode II* represents an unusually cooperative breakthrough from the powers that be in Hollywood, a breakthrough that could fundamentally change the way we experience movies.

In the first place, the shift to digital filming threatens to change the network that is Hollywood—from its power structure all the way down to the daily practices of individual inhabitants. Directors can see the final quality of each shoot immediately—no more waiting for "dailies," prints of the day's shooting, to be developed and reviewed. If the scene looks good, it's a wrap. If not, they can do it again right then and there. In post-production, the footage can be edited using the high-powered computers that have been helping filmmakers for the last decade. Now, however, filmmakers can avoid the costly process of converting film stock into digital files, editing them, and converting the finished product back to film. What goes in digital stays digital. Finally, for filmgoers (and theaters), every showing of the movie has the same quality and crisp colors of the first showing. No more worn film stock, dirt, or scratches, which often compromised the average print after even a few showings.

But the impact of digital film will go far beyond enhancing the traditional ways we experience film. If theaters use digital projectors, the difference between showing movies and other forms of entertainment will blur. We may be able to watch a live Broadway performance in our local theater. Or, by bypassing the costs of creating film stock, the new technologies may make it possible for theater owners to show independent and locally produced films as shorts or double features, or to fill in off hours.

With some of the interactive systems that have been considered, the audience could participate in interactive video experiences. Imagine a theater audience competing with other theaters across the country for prizes. And of course, as digital filmmaking and projection technologies increase in quality and come down in cost—as is the experience of any technology once it becomes adopted—other venues may be able to offer video experiences. First-run digital movies may be projected in bars, museums, and other gatherings—for a premium—in "private screenings." Independent filmmakers have a better chance of distributing their own digital films to a wider audience in this way, thus escaping what Ben Affleck called the "horizontal monopoly" that studios hold over the distribution of films.

The media are excited about the potential revolution of digital filmmaking. Various Hollywood associations and volunteers from the Society of Motion Picture and Television Engineers have been meeting as the Digital Cinema Technology Committee to set industry-wide specifications for digital cinema systems. Technicolor has taken the lead in helping finance the installation of digital projectors in theaters.

But is all of this collaboration and reciprocal innovation the sign of a healthy community—the Hollywood that business writers love to describe as one of the success stories of networked worlds? Not quite. George Lucas has been pushing for digital filmmaking since the early 1990s. "Hollywood could be a winner," Lucas said, "if studios cough up the vital research and development funds. Technology could help to dramatically reduce the spiraling costs of making films, while offering the promise of making them more exciting."[2]

But despite his power at the time, he could not move the vast, tightly integrated Hollywood network in a new direction. In fact, to begin working in digital, he had to work outside the film industry—attempting to do in television, with the series *The Young Indiana Jones Chronicles,* what he could not in Hollywood: work in digital film, and exploit the savings in film and editing while exploring the possibilities of the new technology. Using digital editing, he could turn a few people into a crowd and construct digital towns, all at roughly 10 percent the cost of traditional shoots. "We did a shot in the TV series [*The Young Indiana Jones Chronicles*] for $1,500," Lucas noted, "that would have cost a studio $30,000 if they were doing the same shot for a feature film."[3] He began offering his digital editing studios to support other filmmakers attempting to take advantage of the new technologies. He and his team at Skywalker Ranch learned a lot from working on these projects. "The techniques that we pioneered in the TV series that we're now using in features are going to be one of the major differences about the way movies are made. . . . [I]t does change the whole process of making films."[4]

And yet there are still pockets of resistance. Theater owners are reluctant to pay $125,000 for a projector, five times the cost of traditional projectors. Jack Valenti, president of the Motion Picture Association of America, naturally places the responsibility on the individual theater owners: "If the technology is what everybody says it is, it's going to be a boon to watching movies. You make the movie experience more enticing, and that's beneficial to the theater owners. I think it has to be a joint effort [between the distributors and the theater owners]."[5]

Even the technology has had to compromise itself after a fashion: The latest digital cameras by Sony are now able to shoot in 24 frames per second, versus the traditional 30 frames per second of conventional digital video. "In the film world, 24-frame is the de facto standard, and it is much loved and considered integral to the 'film' look," says Larry Thorpe, a Sony vice president responsible for the camera's development.[6]

And of course, some filmmakers are clinging to their old film stock, arguing that digital video will never match the resolution and detail of traditional 35-millimeter film and that technical improvements in the old ways will postpone the switch indefinitely (the song remains the same).

To make matters worse, constructing a cooperative leap to the digital platform is made harder by antitrust laws that may prohibit negotiated agreements between distributors and exhibitors. Equally dangerous is the possibility of a few powerful firms dictating what everyone else has to do. Add in the uncertainty of investing in technologies before there is an accepted standard, and most individual inhabitants of the Hollywood cluster are reluctant to jump on the bandwagon.

The Ties That Blind

The dense connections that make up small worlds do more than just make change costly—they make it difficult to recognize the possibilities for such change in the first place. The many strong and frequent interactions within any single world ensure that inhabitants are surrounded by other people who are doing the same things, sharing the same ideas, and using the same objects. For the most part, the people who might disagree, the heretics, and their ideas, the subversive technologies, are kept out of the mainstream. We already know that a group's culture, or groupthink, can blind its members to potentially valuable alternatives, and that an organization's culture creates shared perspectives and emotions among its members. But Professor Jennifer Chatman of the University of California at Berkeley and Karen Jehn of Wharton have found that these common cultures are just as powerful in building shared perspectives within industries.[7] As Lee Roy Beach writes in *The Psychology of Decision Making,* "people who share cultures often arrive at similar frames for situations, frames that might be very different from those arrived at by outsiders."[8] So whether we draw the boundary of a small world around a group, an organization, or an industry, we must recognize that small worlds shape perceptions in ways that prevent inhabitants from seeing the value of people, ideas, and objects that reside outside of their traditional boundaries. The ties that bind are the ties that blind.

Karl Weick, a social psychologist and organizational scholar, once studied a team of smoke jumpers, firefighters who parachute into the backcountry to battle remote blazes while they are still small. Members of the group he studied died when a "10 o'clock fire" (meaning they thought they could have it out by 10:00 that morning) trapped them inside a steep canyon called the Mann Gulch. Norman Maclean wrote about this tragedy in *Young Men and Fire,* using the testimony of the three survivors and an extensive study of Mann Gulch. Karl Weick then applied his understanding of social psychology to make sense of what Maclean found. When the men realized the fire had turned toward them, they found themselves in a race with the advancing fire up the steep canyon walls. One of the amazing things Maclean found was that their tools— heavy poleaxes, saws, and shovels, as well as backpacks—were abandoned hundreds of yards from where they first turned from fighting the fire to escaping from it. They ran for almost as far as they could run, carrying the tools they had brought with them despite the fact those tools were now worse than useless. Their inability to drop their heavy tools and packs may ultimately have prevented them from outrunning the fire (which two of the survivors had managed to do, having dropped their packs early).

To the firefighters, those tools were more than simple objects: They represented who they were, why they were there, and what they were trained to do. Dropping their tools meant abandoning their existing knowledge and relationships. This may not seem such a hard choice to make, but because they had not been trained for such a moment, they had no alternative models of behavior. In moments of uncertainty and danger, clinging to the old way may seem a better alternative than no way at all.

It's easy to single out a few organizations that couldn't let go of their old knowledge, refusing to see and adapt to breakthrough technologies that pushed them aside. Often, however, these are the very same organizations that led the previous revolution. Somehow, these visionary firms went blind.

In 1886, only four years after Edison threw the switch at the Pearl Street Station in downtown New York, George Westinghouse opened an electric generating plant in Buffalo and began one of the most famous standards wars in technological history. Edison had introduced electricity to the general public using a system that produced a low-voltage direct current for transmission and use. In contrast, the new Westinghouse plant produced high-voltage alternating current. The arguments for and against each system are many and muddled, but simply put, the advantage of alternating current electricity lay in more efficient transmission over distances, whereas the disadvantage lay in the complexities and danger of an undeveloped system. The Battle of the Systems, as it became known, was played out mainly in the press between 1887 and 1892. In the end, Edison lost more than just the technical standard—he also lost his reputation as an inventive genius. The historian Harold Passer once wrote, "In 1879, Edison was a brave and courageous inventor; in 1889, he was a cautious and conservative defender of the status quo."[9]

What happened in between? If we believe that innovations are the product of the inventive genius, we're at a loss to explain it. But if we consider how Edison first relied on, and then explicitly abandoned, a strategy of bridging the many small worlds of his time, we can better understand the outcome. In 1882, he announced, "[T]he electric lighting system is now perfected. I will now bend all my time and energies to its introduction to the public."[10] Despite Edison's usual hyperbole, in this he was telling the truth. He moved from Menlo Park to Manhattan to be close to the business headquarters of Edison Electric Light Company, saying "I'm going to be a business man, I'm a regular contractor for electric lighting plants and I'm going to take a long vacation in the matter of invention."[11] Edison had turned his attention to building the necessary community around his emerging innovation. And despite losing the Battle of the Systems, Edison did build a successful and lasting company around the elements he originally pieced together in his Menlo Park lab: General Electric was the product of the Edison Electric Light Company and its acquisitions. But in doing so, he severed the very ties—burned the bridges to other worlds—that had made his Menlo Park laboratory so prolific.

The transformation of both Edison and Ford from courageous inventors to defenders of the status quo reveals the paradox inherent in technology brokering. The skills required to bridge distant worlds and generate novel combinations are ill suited to the focused process of building new worlds around such innovations, and those skills required to build new worlds are ill suited to ranging widely in search of alternatives. Firms in pursuit of innovation must learn to develop, and maintain, these distinct skills within a single organization. Technology brokers must continually bridge small worlds in ways that give them control over the knowledge they find in each, yet do so without letting that knowledge control them.

The Advantages of Bridging Old Worlds

Bridging old worlds offers a means for organizations to overcome the competency traps and perceptual blocks that typically hinder the innovation process. These activities work for two related reasons. First, bridging exposes an organization's members to the flow of the many different people, ideas, and objects that move within other worlds. Second, bridging changes the way people look at the new technologies they find in those other worlds, *and* it changes how they look at the people, ideas, and objects of their own world.

Fighting Fire with Fire

Overcoming the established competencies of an existing world, whether it's an organization's manufacturing system or an industry's network of suppliers, producers, and customers, is what makes innovation such a risky business. Many new ventures fail not for lack of a good idea, but because they can't hold on long enough to build their own economies of scale and develop their own networks of suppliers and customers. The bridging activities of technology brokering offer a way to avoid, or at least minimize, this risk.

By combining existing people, ideas, and objects, innovators can exploit the years, if not decades, of evolution that produced these resources elsewhere. At Ford Motor Company, for example, the pre-established expertise and objects of the machine tool industry were developed in the continuous-flow production lines of

the canning industry, cigarette industry, and breweries and granaries. As Ford himself said, he "assembled into a car the discoveries of other men behind whom were centuries of work." [12] By the
time Henry Ford adopted these manufacturing machines and techniques, there were engineers and mechanics already well versed in
their use and ready to adapt those machines to fit the needs of the
automobile industry. That's why the introduction of the first assembly line at Ford, in the magneto assembly room, increased productivity by almost 40 percent the very first day, and why productivity
had increased over 400 percent by the end of the year. Similarly, on
the final assembly line, workers originally took just under six man-
hours (350 minutes) to assemble a car. One year later, as Ford's engineers worked the bugs out of the new assembly line process, that
number was down to an hour and a half (93 minutes).

In a similar fashion, the ability of Design Continuum's product
development team to complete their development of the Reebok
Pump shoe was due in large part to their preestablished expertise
with IV bags and their properties, and with the pumps and valves of
other medical equipment. The fact that the IV bag manufacturer
became a supplier to Reebok in the large-scale production of the
sneaker made possible both the massive roll-out and the rapid rise
in production volumes that Reebok experienced in the first year. It
also testifies to the benefits of drawing upon technologies that have
already developed a set of experts (the IV bag designers and manufacturers), objects (the materials of IV bags and the ultrasonic weld-
ing machines that seal them), and ideas (about how to design IV
bags and how to design inflatable splints).

Bridging distant worlds in the innovation process becomes all
the more critical when incumbent technologies have the advantage
of economies of scale and entrenched market infrastructures (suppliers, retailers, third-party vendors, even regulators). The new
machine tools and methods worked at Ford from the very beginning—but they also cost Ford less because they rode the economies
of scale of a machine tool industry that in the previous fifty years
rose with (and fueled) the industrial expansion of the United States.

Reebok's inflatable insert cost $1.50 because it relied on an established infrastructure—the materials and equipment suppliers, the design and manufacturing expertise, and the capacity of the existing IV bag industry. Bridging provides organizations with access to the well-developed technologies of other worlds, as well as to the wealth of connections that support them in those worlds.

Bridging and Creative Insight

The more worlds you bridge, the more you have a foot in each of these world's different flows, and the more you're able to see and exploit the existing technologies as they emerge and evolve in their own settings. At the same time, having one foot in another world also means having one foot outside any one world. These two phrases sound the same, but mean something very different. Consider the girl in the Little Feat song "Rocket in My Pocket" who has one foot on the platform and the other on the train. Having one foot outside your world means you can be less beholden to the people, ideas, and objects that would otherwise bind, and blind, you. Bridging multiple worlds, in essence, makes you less susceptible to the pressures of conforming in any one because you have somewhere else to go.

Bridging activities do more, though, than just loosen the grip of local norms and values. At their heart, bridging activities provide the conditions for creativity, for the Eureka moment when new possibilities suddenly become apparent. The very notion that we can come up with new ideas has come under increasing attack by cognitive psychologists interested in understanding how people solve novel problems. A number of psychologists who have studied creativity, such as Dean Simonton and Howard Gardner, have argued that recombination is the fundamental mechanism behind creative insight. Einstein once said that such "combinatory play seems to be the essential feature in productive thought."[13] We can see Einstein's theory of relativity through the lens of recombination.

Einstein developed a theoretical framework that combined current understandings of what were previously unconnected ideas and phenomena. In a purely historical sense, he combined conceptions of space and time, matter and energy. Einstein built on the ideas of Boltzmann, Hertz, Poincaré, Mach, Planck, and others, but combined them in a way that enabled him to take what was best and leave behind the vestiges of older scientific practices and communities. As Howard Gardner writes in *Creating Minds,*

> Einstein's breakthrough was classic in that it sought to unify the elements of a physical analysis, and it placed the older examples and principles within a broader framework. But it was revolutionary in that, ever afterward, we have thought differently about space and time, matter and energy.[14]

Indeed, the art historian E. H. Gombrich once suggested there's no such thing as the immaculate perception: People don't suddenly come up with new ideas; they piece them together from what they already know. People often fail to come up with new understandings of what's happening, new ways of dealing with problems, when they lack the wide-ranging set of ideas from which to piece together alternatives. Those closest to Einstein's discovery, the very individuals whose work Einstein recombined—Mach, Planck, Lorentz, Poincaré—never wholly embraced his work. Chance did not favor these very prepared minds. Quite the opposite: Each was *too* familiar with, and too committed to, what had come before to see how Einstein's new combination could be something greater than the sum of its parts. Max Planck, for example, referred to Einstein's theories as merely a generalization of Lorentz's work. And Einstein once said of Mach, whose work he admitted to closely building on, "It is not improbable that Mach would have discovered the theory of relativity, if, at the time when his mind was still young and susceptible, the problem of constancy of the speed of light had been discussed among physicists." [15]

Simonton argues that these recombinant thought processes shape how people approach their environment. Those who are more engaged in exploring new combinations are often more attuned to the world around them:

> Those people who make their minds accessible to chaotic
> combinatory play will also make their sense more open to the
> influx of fortuitous events in the outside world. Both the
> retrieval of material from memory and the orientation of
> attention to environmental stimuli are unrestricted.[16]

Rather than believing they have seen it all, or at least seen all that is
worth seeing, those in the habit of finding unexpected connections
begin to recognize in each new person they meet, each new idea they
hear, and each new object they find the potential for new combinations with others.

The trick is to develop in-depth knowledge within a given field
but, *at the same time,* develop the willingness to take that knowledge
apart and combine it in new ways. This is difficult because, as the
fire at Mann Gulch shows us, people are reluctant to abandon their
old knowledge—their tools—even in the face of near-certain disaster. Bridging distant worlds provides a way to acquire knowledge
without acquiring the ties that typically bind such knowledge to
particular worlds.

Einstein himself admitted that his ability to revolutionize physics
came not from his intellect but rather from his position relative to
others more deeply embedded in the field. He did his most innovative work while on the periphery of the scientific community he
overturned. As he once said of this position:

> Such isolation is sometimes bitter but I do not regret being cut
> off from the understanding and sympathy of other men. . . . I am
> compensated for it by being rendered independent of the cus-
> toms, opinions and prejudices of others and am not tempted to
> rest my peace of mind upon such shifting foundations.[17]

One foot on the platform, the other on the train. In the same way,
Elvis Presley also cut himself off from the "understandings and
sympathies of other men" while growing up in Memphis, where he
was accepted by neither the black community nor the white for his
peripheral participation in each. We can give Einstein, Elvis, and

others credit for seeing farther than others. But if we are truly interested in building organizations where this can happen routinely, we need to think about how they bridged different worlds to get where they did and see what they saw.

How Organizations Bridge Small Worlds

Bridging the networked landscape involves moving among these worlds in ways that enable individuals and organizations to see how the people, ideas, and objects within any one can be used in new ways elsewhere. The resulting experiences with the resources of distant and different worlds become the raw materials for solving problems in other worlds.

There is a risk, however, to acquiring such knowledge, and this risk lies at the heart of the networked landscape: the small worlds phenomenon. In small worlds, as discussed earlier, the ties that bind easily become the ties that blind. Whether you are framing a house or designing a circuit, technical knowledge entails knowing how to combine the set of available resources in *particular* ways to achieve *particular* ends. But too often that knowledge begins to look like the *only* way, and the *only* end worth achieving. Worse, for those who have invested in a given technology, it can actually become the only economical way to achieve an end. So while knowledge is generally treated as a good thing in most conversations about organizations, when it comes to innovation it is a double-edged sword.

On the one hand, knowledge represents the raw materials for recognizing and creating radical innovations. Try designing a new integrated circuit today without advanced degrees in electrical engineering, materials science, and quantum mechanics. In this way, bridging involves learning—acquiring knowledge that can be used again in other ways and in other contexts. On the other hand, knowledge represents the old ways of thinking that prevent people from seeing new opportunities. The makers of vacuum-tube transistors could not pursue the benefits of the first silicon transistors in large part because of their expertise (and investments) in old technologies, not their ignorance of the new ones. The knowledge of designing circuits included the notion of elegance—of using as few tubes as possible—an elegance that first hundreds then thousands then millions of transistors on a single integrated circuit blew right past. And in this way, bridging enables you to see connections where others do not by enabling you to ignore the existing ties that others take for granted. In this way, bridging is not simply the sum of your contacts in different industries, but your ability to move, think, and see easily across small worlds.

How can organizations learn about a wide range of technologies without becoming bound by that knowledge? There is no single right way to do this. There are no prepackaged "Seven Industries in Seven Days" tours. Instead there are many ways, some small and some big, to gain access to the people, ideas, and objects of other worlds. With each option, the trick is to develop a deep knowledge and, at the same time, the ability to question what you know, take it apart, and combine it in new ways. Let's briefly consider a few of these options here.

Breadth over Depth

Moving among different worlds directly shapes people's ability to learn in different contexts and to see how what they've learned might work somewhere else. The advantage, in this case, is to know a little about a lot of things rather than a lot about a little. One of the managers at Design Continuum, the design firm discussed in chapter 1 that developed the Reebok Pump, put it this way: "We probably have a better perspective of the broad technology base than the client does. They know such a narrow slice right now, which is basically their expertise."

Anybody who acquires deep expertise does so at the expense of breadth. The challenge is to understand how much depth is enough, and how much is too much. The risk is not simply in what could have been learned elsewhere but also, as the later careers of Ford and

Edison have shown, in how committed individuals and organizations can become to their own expertise. As Abraham Maslow once said, "To a child with a hammer, everything looks like a nail."

Gian Zaccai, CEO of Design Continuum, believes that moving among many different industries "frees you from the dogma of any one industry and their firm belief in the links between problems and solutions." Building experiences in many small worlds makes it possible to approach each new problem with a more open mind. Another Design Continuum manager explained the firm's philosophy as follows:

> The main story is approaching each problem with a certain level of naïveté, of not being biased and conditioned by having been in the industry that you're trying to be innovative for. Not knowing all the reasons why something has failed. Not knowing all the reasons why you've invested all this equipment, all this money in this equipment.

The diversity of such work builds what technology brokers describe as a more flexible mind-set, a willingness to try new perspectives and to search for new combinations.

Take, for example, another project at Design Continuum involving a pulsed lavage, a medical product used in emergency rooms for cleansing wounds. The solution had to provide a pulsed flow of saline solution, had to meet medical product guidelines for cleanliness and safety, and had to be low cost and disposable. Working on the project, the design team recognized similarities between this problem and those of a previous product the organization had developed years earlier, a battery-powered squirt gun. On the surface, an emergency room tool and a child's toy seem unrelated. But by recognizing nonobvious similarities between the two products, the team was able to rapidly combine the low-cost electric pump and battery of the toy squirt gun with the materials and design guidelines of medical products to develop a successful new pulsed lavage.

The existence of super soaker squirt guns was not buried within an obscure or isolated industry—the product was on the shelves of almost every toy store in America. Nor was the technology behind the product inaccessibly complex or subtle. A screwdriver or hammer would have given anyone with ten dollars a wide-open view of the underlying mechanisms. What made Design Continuum able to recognize the potential that super soaker squirt guns held for an emergency room tool when nobody else did? For one thing, it was difficult for engineers who had spent twenty or more years of their life in the medical products world, with its set of technologies, language, culture, and complexity, to admit that the next step in their product's evolution might reside in a kid's toy worth three dollars in plastic parts, motors, and tubing. It was easier for the engineers at Design Continuum. They had, after all, designed such a toy before. Their identity as engineers wasn't bound by the dense web of connections that grounded the medical products client within its single industry. As a result, they could go places to look for new solutions, and could find ideas, objects, and people that others doing the same work might balk at. Put more simply, as William Klann did at Ford Motor Company, "If they can kill pigs and cows that way, we can build cars that way."

Get Your Hands Dirty

Reading *Wired* magazine or *Popular Mechanics* won't do it. Neither will walking the local mall. Such actions certainly help, but bridging distant worlds means learning enough about the people, the ideas, and the objects in each to see how they work and, sometimes, how they don't. This means working within worlds, gaining hands-on experience with the problems and solutions at hand and coming to understand what the people know, what the ideas mean, and what the objects can do. It is the difference between learning that a bicycle can be ridden and learning how to ride a bicycle.

Edison was once hired to develop an undersea telegraph cable. The main problem was in insulating the wires to keep water from leaking in and to keep the signals from crossing over to other lines. To do this, Edison and his engineers experimented with a carbon putty material derived from lamp-black, essentially the collected soot from the smoke of burning kerosene. The material worked well on the lab bench, but when the cable was submerged in water, there was cross talk between the wires. Edison's team had, in essence, stumbled across a material that changed its electrical resistance in response to changes in pressure. Though they abandoned the idea of using the soot as an insulator, they had learned a valuable lesson about that material.

Later, Edison was asked to improve on another recent innovation, the telephone, and, in particular, its microphone, which at that point was very weak. Edison's team remembered the carbon mixture that had failed them in the Atlantic cable experiments, and used it to create a microphone that converted sound waves into electrical signals. Changes in pressure as sound hit the material were converted into changes in the current moving through. That microphone was considered one of the key breakthroughs that made the telephone a successful product, and its design—a small black puck surrounded by perforated tin—did not change for another hundred years. The ability of Edison's team to see their old knowledge in new ways enabled them to see how a failed experiment in one setting could be used successfully in a very different one. Had they not gotten their hands dirty, they would never have been able to do this.

Bring the Outside In

Many bridging activities take time and resources. In addition, many organizations attempt to actively inject new perspectives by bringing the outside in: by hiring people from other industries or with varied backgrounds, by hiring consultants with potentially valuable experience in places the organization hasn't been, or by inviting people from academics or from different industries to give lectures.

Hiring people from outside the organization or industry can be highly rewarding. Robert Sutton, a professor at Stanford, writes in *Weird Ideas That Work* of Guidant Corporation, the makers of surgical stents that can be inserted into arteries to prevent their blockage or collapse. The materials and manufacturing methods of these stents present Guidant with probably its most serious technical challenge. They took advantage of the collapsing aerospace industry in Southern California to hire a group of engineers who had deep expertise in the high-tech materials and methods that were used in that world but were mainly unknown anywhere else. This strategy worked for Guidant. It is risky, however, because when you hire people for their expertise they may bring along their own fixed ideas about how things should be done.

Other smaller ways to bring the outside in involve bringing in outside speakers in an attempt to introduce the ideas of other worlds to your organization. Often, these are monthly or weekly scheduled presentations, designed not to advance people's expertise so much as poke at it, to provoke new ways of thinking by showing them different perspectives and different worlds. But the most effective of these momentary bridges into distant worlds turn into longer and very productive relationships. In the late 1980s and early 1990s, a professor at Stanford, Hau Lee, did some pioneering work on the design and optimization of manufacturing supply chains. Supply chains are the long set of links between material and component suppliers, shipping services, factories, warehouses, and retail outlets. The sheer number of different places, activities, and interactions involved is overwhelming, but for most firms the situation gets worse because as they add to or change their product lines, the original logic behind many decisions gets lost. Hau Lee and his academic colleagues were able to develop fairly comprehensive modeling techniques that could save organizations millions of dollars by clarifying and optimizing the design of their supply chains.

Hewlett-Packard's main campus is just down the street from Stanford University, and after a series of meetings that showed the practical value of applying Lee's academic work, Professor Lee ended up spending his sabbatical year working closely with Corey Billington, a former student of his who was now at Hewlett-Packard, to apply the ideas of supply chain management. One result of their work was the formal establishment of SPaM, the Strategic

Planning and Modeling group at HP, a small group devoted to analyzing and developing optimized supply chain solutions for the many different divisions at Hewlett-Packard. Within a few years, they were credited with saving the firm over $150 million in costs. We'll talk more about SPaM in a later chapter because it became a successful technology broker in its own right, linking the otherwise disconnected divisions within HP. The group had its origins from bringing the outside—in this case promising academic research—into the firm and building on its promise.

Take the Best, Leave the Rest

The danger of bringing existing technologies into a new organization or a new market is that you will bring with them much that is irrelevant to their new uses, if not downright obsolete. The introduction of the Bessemer process into the American steel manufacturing industry in the late 1860s provides a good example. The Bessemer process, credited to Englishman Henry Bessemer in 1855, made possible the mass production of steel by introducing a blast of air into molten iron to filter out unwanted impurities. The Bessemer process revolutionized the steel industry by enabling the low-cost production of high-quality steel; low-cost steel revolutionized the building industry by enabling the building of the first skyscrapers, and the military industry by enabling better guns and ships.

Historian Elting Morrison describes how, between 1864 and 1871, ten American steel companies adopted the Bessemer process. Nine did so by importing English workmen; the tenth was the Cambria Company. At the start, the other companies made better use of the process, but by the end of the 1870s, Cambria dominated the market. Morrison quotes the president of Cambria, who explained his choice of adopting the ideas and objects of the Bessemer process but leaving the experienced people behind: "We started the converter plant without a single man who had seen even the outside of a Bessemer plant. We thus had willing pupils with no prejudices and no reminiscences of what they had done in the old country." [18]

As the Bessemer process continued to evolve in use, the Cambria workmen were more than willing to explore new ways of making steel, while those who owed their jobs to their initial knowledge of the process resisted abandoning the original methods.

Similarly, historian David Hounshell suggests that Henry Ford benefited first by hiring Walter Flanders and Max Wollering, and then benefited again when, less than two years later, they left Ford for a more attractive offer with the Wayne Automobile Company. After Flanders and Wollering left, Ford's engineers continued to explore new ways to use the technologies they had introduced, dramatically improving on their performance in the new Ford system. Flanders and Wollering stayed long enough to show Ford the value of dedicated machine tools for the production of accurate parts at high volumes, but not so long as to set in place their old understanding of how to use them. Henry Ford's purchase of the Keim Sheet Metal Stamping Company serves as another example. The Keim Company produced sheet metal parts for the bicycle industry and had developed new techniques for stamping sheet metal into rounded forms. Ford thought this technology would be useful in redesigning several parts previously made from cast iron. When Ford's engineers tried to exploit these new technologies, they ran into problems. But as they learned more about the new technologies, they were able to find other, unexpected uses for the types of stamped sheet metal that Keim's people, expertise, and equipment could produce.

In both cases, Cambria and Ford exploited the new technologies that they had imported from outside their worlds, and once these technologies were adopted, continued exploring these existing technologies to find how they could be used in new ways.

• • •

Chapter 1 described how technology brokering allows people to think outside of the box by giving them other boxes to think in. Bridging provides those other boxes. At one level, it's that simple. Access to the people, ideas, and objects of other worlds gives people an advantage in seeing how those resources can be used in new ways. But at the same time, bridging small worlds is not that simple. Small worlds, like the boxes people think in, constrain innovation in two very different ways. Because small worlds are living, interconnected communities, attempting changes in any one part of the system meets resistance by the rest of the system. Small worlds also constrain inhabitants by limiting what they see as possible and appropriate, giving them the ties that bind them to other people, ideas, and objects inside their world and that, in the process, blind them to alternatives on the outside.

History is filled with examples of organizations and industries swept away by the winds of creative destruction. It's easy to place the blame on nearsighted individuals who, unlike their farsighted counterparts the inventors, could not see or embrace the future. But these explanations start to look shallow when we discover that the same people, like Edison and Ford, play both roles. Because of the constraints that small worlds place on innovation and change, technologies in one place may be valuable to but remain unseen or untapped by others. By bridging these worlds, technology brokers develop the ability to see how these resources can be combined with others and put to new use. To the extent that we remain blind to the dense and intricate interactions within webs of innovation, we cannot appreciate the abilities of those who can move among the worlds those webs create.

Bridging activities bring the people of organizations into contact with problems and resources of many different worlds. There are as many ways to bridge distant worlds as there are ways to skin the proverbial cat. But just as important, there is no one right way. We can look at many single innovations and uncover a critical link between two worlds—for example, the moment when the people, ideas, or objects of a world such as the machine tool industry entered into another, the nascent auto industry. But in the pursuit of innovation, bridging works because of the broad links to possible resources that become available to organizations, not because of the depth of any one connection. Technology brokering requires many simultaneous bridging activities because these activities both represent and create the open minds necessary to see new connections and new combinations.

The paradox inherent in the innovation process is that innovators need wide-ranging ties across distant worlds to generate the innovative ideas in the first place, yet they also need strong, focused ties to build communities around emerging innovations. Firms must commit resources to both. The answer is not to resolve the paradox, but rather to appreciate what each seemingly conflicting goal provides the organization. Bridging brings the people, ideas, and objects of distant worlds into the organization and into new combinations. The next step is to build new worlds around these new combinations. This is the subject of the next chapter.

5

Building New Worlds

Inventors and their inventions stand out from the noise and confusion of everyday history. Edison is as well known today as any modern entrepreneur, and the lightbulb itself has become the dominant icon of the inventive process. Most of our stories of innovation, in school textbooks and business journals, favor the idea of inventor heroes, following what historians of technology such as Abbot Payton Usher criticized in 1929 as "Great Man Theories of Innovation." Consider the following list:

Johannes Gutenberg	Printing press	1450
James Watt	Steam engine	1769
Eli Whitney	Cotton gin	1793
Thomas Fulton	Steamship	1807
Michael Faraday	Electric motor	1821
Cyrus McCormick	Reaper	1831
Samuel Colt	Revolver	1835
Elias Howe	Sewing machine	1845
Alexander Graham Bell	Telephone	1876
Thomas Edison	Phonograph	1877
Thomas Edison	Lightbulb	1879
Guglielmo Marchese Marconi	Radio	1895

Henry Ford	Automobile	1908
Pablo Picasso	Cubism	1910
Philo T. Farnsworth	Television	1925
William Shockley	Transistor	1948
Watson and Crick	DNA double-helix	1953
Elvis Presley	Rock and roll	1957
Steve Jobs	Personal computer	1977

Choosing a single person, place, and time for every innovation, however, means stripping away all the connections that linked these particular individuals to the other people, ideas, and existing objects of their worlds. We may end up with nice stories about heroic individuals, but we also end up with dangerous lessons about the pursuit of innovation.

Chapter 4 focused on the role of bridging distant worlds to tap into the revolutionary potential that lies in combining the existing and already well-developed resources that lie elsewhere. Technology brokering—as the strategic pursuit of innovation—requires bridging these distant worlds, but it also requires building new worlds to support and extend the innovations that come from those bridging activities. Sometimes building new worlds means creating new project teams or even divisions within organizations. Sometimes it means creating new organizations. And sometimes it means creating new markets or industries that bring together the people, ideas, and objects that, just a short while ago, would not have seemed to have a reason to work together.

The argument of this chapter is that building new worlds doesn't just help revolutionary innovations, it's what makes them revolutionary in the first place. From a network perspective, breakthrough innovations are those that trigger radical shifts in established networks, from one order to another, seemingly overnight. These shifts aren't random. They are the result of conscious actions on the part of entrepreneurs. Edison's lightbulb succeeded where his predecessors' did not because he built a new community around his original innovation—a community of suppliers, investors, engineers, even technicians. The activities that build a new world around an innovation provide two key advantages: In the beginning, these worlds create the collective efforts often necessary to turn visions into realities; over time, they create the communities in which the early, immature realities evolve into revolutions. Before we consider these two roles, let's look at why they are so difficult to see in past stories of innovation.

The Cult of the Inventor

Once, the story goes, Edison met with a cub reporter who had come to interview the Wizard of Menlo Park:

> While the reporter was being ushered in, the Old Man disguised himself to resemble the heroic image of "The Great Inventor, Thomas A. Edison." . . . Suddenly gone were his natural boyishness of manner, his happy hooliganism. His features were frozen into immobility, he became statuesque in the armchair, and his unblinking eyes assumed a faraway look.[1]

Francis Jehl, Edison's longtime assistant who joined him in Menlo Park and remained with him through most of his career, remembers when they first realized the power of Edison's name. At that point, he explained, they began the process of turning Edison the man into Edison the myth. To the public, Edison was an inventive genius. To Francis Jehl and many of the other engineers in the lab, "Edison [was] in reality a collective noun and [meant] the work of many men."[2]

The reason collectives often tolerate the anointing of a single "great" individual—whether it be Thomas Edison, Henry Ford, Steve Jobs, Bill Gates, or any others from the list—is that it pays. It pays to have a single name and date associated with any idea because that provides evidence, in the court of public opinion, of who "owns" the idea. And it pays by providing legitimacy and celebrity to a particular few individuals in the struggle for new investors and suppliers, or in the race to have their invention become the new standard.

The notion that a single name and date can identify the moment of invention reflects the myth of the lone genius, the cult of the inventor. The economic historian Nathan Rosenberg has argued that our persistent misconceptions about the innovation process are a product not only of our need for clean histories but also, at the moment, of the entrepreneur's need for ownership of ideas in the courts of law and of public opinion:

> The public image of technology has been decisively shaped by popular writers . . . mesmerized by the dramatic story of a small number of major inventions—steam engines, cotton gins, railroads, automobiles, penicillin, radios, computers, etc. . . . Indeed, not only our patent law but also our history textbooks and even our language all conspire in insuring that a single name and date is attached to each invention.[3]

Those who would be anointed as inventive geniuses are often complicit in such mythmaking; Edison was no exception.

Worse than simply being incomplete and inaccurate accounts of what happened, however, these simple stories distort our ideas of how to pursue innovation, how to manage it, and even how to make sense of it when it happens again. Every "modern-day Edison" who graces the cover of *Time* and *Newsweek* touting his or her invention, every business guru who insists we abandon the past to embrace the future, and every manager who insists upon demonstrating his or her individual genius takes us one step further away from understanding and emulating the successful innovations of the past.

The previous chapter described how the activities that bridge distant worlds create the necessary conditions for seeing new ways to combine extant resources. Bridging activities not only bring organizations into contact with a wide range of potentially valuable resources, but also change people's perspectives on what is sacred and what they take for granted in each of these worlds. But just seeing these new combinations is not enough. In fact, almost by definition, innovations aren't revolutionary *until* new networks form, seemingly overnight, to exploit them.

This chapter considers the second set of activities that technology brokering entails: building new worlds from the pieces of old ones.

In the same way, the process of building new networks of people, ideas, and objects is more than simply a matter of connecting resources. The networks that crystallize around an innovation change the way people think about what they are doing and, over time, make the original innovation revolutionary.

Rarely, if ever, are the networks that surround an innovation in its earliest stages given the credit they are due. Ralph Waldo Emerson's famous advice, "Build a better mousetrap, and the world will beat a path to your door," simply isn't true. The world will *not* beat a path to your door. As John H. Lienhard, professor of mechanical engineering and history at the University of Houston, notes, the patent office has issued some 4,400 patents for better mousetraps, and only 20 or so have made any money (the most successful, the spring trap, was patented in 1899).[4] Each year, 400 more people apply for patents on improved mousetraps, maybe set out a doormat, and wait for the world to beat its path to them.

But a better mousetrap, like anything else, will succeed only when those who envision the idea convince others to join in their new venture—as investors, suppliers, employees, retailers, customers, and even competitors. These others bring their own connections with them, like Walter Flanders brought some of the best ideas and machines of mass production to the Ford Motor Company. The impacts we see are often the result of the community that picked up and ran with the initial well-intentioned, but underdeveloped, ideas. Take Emerson's now-famous quote. In actuality, he never said it. The quote originated some seven years after Emerson's death. What Emerson actually said was, "[I]f a man has good corn, or wood, or boards, or pigs, to sell . . . you will find a broad, hard-beaten road to his house."[5] Emerson was not talking about innovation but simply about selling a good product. The quote became so much more because others picked it up and ran with it. This is the same story we see for many, if not most, innovations.

The role of networks in innovation begins at the earliest stages of the innovation process, where they provide the collective support necessary to risk going against the established ways of doing things.

Over time, these collectives turn into established communities of their own and their innovations become the established technologies that others seek to overthrow. The development of the transistor provides a useful example.

Building the World of the Transistor

The Intel Pentium IV microprocessor has 42 million transistors. A typical computer, with its microprocessor and assorted other chips, might use 200 million transistors. Both numbers are climbing fast. Intel recently announced it had developed a transistor that is 15 nanometers long, or 15 billionths of a meter—so small that you would have to place a thousand side by side to match the width of a human hair. The transistor is the primary building block of computing. Without it, the information revolution would not have happened—would not still be happening.

History has given William B. Shockley much of the credit for developing the transistor. Yet viewed from a network perspective, the web surrounding that innovation reveals the roles played by a wide range of other people, ideas, and objects. Some worked alongside Shockley at Bell Laboratories. Others came before, making Shockley's "invention" possible. And others came afterward, making those earlier experiments meaningful by turning the transistor into much more than its original form. Without this network, it is hard to imagine the transistor coming into existence, let alone evolving into what it has become.

The transistor so permeates today's products that, like the lightbulb, it is difficult to imagine life without it. But the technology came together in 1947, as most solutions do, to solve a problem that now seems small in comparison with what we use it for. Originally, Bell Labs, the research arm of AT&T, was interested in developing a solid-state transistor for two very real problems that AT&T faced in offering transcontinental phone service: amplifying and switching signals.

Since 1906, Bell had used the vacuum tube triode, developed by Lee De Forest, to amplify electric signals.[6] But the triode, despite forty years of continuous improvement, was unreliable; it used considerable power and, turning much of that power into heat, burned out regularly. AT&T was intensely interested in replacing tube amplifiers with something more durable. At the same time, the problems of using mechanical relays to route telephone calls from one end of the country to the other grew as telephone traffic grew. These relays were mechanical switches that opened and closed depending on where the call was going—creating temporary circuits from one phone to another anywhere in the country. To complete calls the telephone network needed hundreds of thousands of these devices, which meant enormous costs for both equipment and regular maintenance. So AT&T was also intensely interested in developing an electronic switch to replace their mechanical ones.

That set the stage for a concerted effort on the part of Bell Labs to develop a solid-state transistor. At the end of World War II, Bell Lab's director of research, Mervin Kelly, thought a solution lay in semiconductors, a type of material that physicists were experimenting with in the 1920s and 1930s. Scientists were exploring a class of materials that could be made to conduct electricity or not on command. Both vacuum tubes and mechanical relays acted in much the same way, and Kelly sensed the possibilities for replacing them both with semiconductors. Of course, how to design and manufacture semiconductor switches and triodes was the problem. Kelly recruited William Shockley, a Ph.D. from MIT and a brilliant theorist, to build a team to explore this problem. Shockley in turn recruited Walter Brattain, an experimental physicist at Bell Labs, and John Bardeen, another theoretical physicist from the University of Minnesota.

Surprisingly, Shockley's first contribution (beyond hiring Brattain and Bardeen) was to insist that they pursue an idea he had come up with years earlier. It was a bad idea, but in trying to make it work and then trying to figure out why it didn't, Brattain and Bardeen made key leaps in understanding semiconductors. While Shockley spent most of his time working at home, Bardeen and Brattain worked closely together in the laboratory. Bardeen, as a theorist, suggested experiments and interpreted their results, while Brattain built and ran the experiments. Following the trail of Shockley's failed idea, Bardeen had the historic insight that it was the surface state of the semiconductors that mattered to how electrons flowed through the material. Over the next month, Bardeen and Brattain worked on building devices that got them closer and closer to their goal.

On December 16, 1947, unbeknownst to Shockley, Bardeen and Brattain built the first point-contact transistor. It was about a half-inch tall and consisted of a strip of gold foil folded over the point of a plastic triangle, all held over a crystal of germanium (a precursor to silicon). The assembly was the world's first semiconductor amplifier: When a small current went through one of the gold contacts, a larger current came out the other. According to Walter Brattain's brother, Bob, "When John Bardeen went home that evening, all he said to Jane was, 'I think we discovered something today.' She was busy getting dinner and didn't pay much attention to it."[7]

Shockley, on the other hand, took the news hard. Both pleased that it worked and furious that he had been left out, Shockley focused his efforts on improving the transistor, excluding Bardeen and Brattain from most of this subsequent work. Walter Brattain said in 1947 that Shockley called them both in shortly after the demonstration and told them that "sometimes the people who do the work don't get the credit for it. He thought then that he could write a patent, starting with the field effect, on the whole damn thing."[8] Bell Labs introduced this "invention" in June of 1948, coining the name *transistor*. It took Shockley two more years to come up with an improved version that was more rugged and more easily manufactured and, for Shockley at least, something he could call his own.

History has since given disproportionate credit to Shockley. If we are looking for the web that surrounds the invention of the transistor, however, we can begin with the close collaboration between Brattain and Bardeen in the laboratory. And yet around these three individuals were many more. Before these momentous events, for example, we should acknowledge the central role played by Mervin Kelly in sponsoring the research into semiconductors at Bell Labs. If we look past Bell Labs, we can see the roles played by Erwin Schroedinger, Eugene Wigner, and Frederick Seitz—the scientists who began unraveling the mysterious properties of semiconductors in the 1920s and 1930s. Looking further, we can even see the connections that run from Bardeen and Brattain's early transistor back to De Forest's triode and Fleming's rectifying diode all the way to Edison's electric lightbulb.[9]

But to stop the story of the transistor here is just as misleading. When Bell Labs introduced the transistor in 1948, there was little fanfare in the press or in the engineering community. The transistor in 1948 was nothing more than a durable, reliable, smaller, albeit more expensive, replacement for the vacuum tube amplifiers and switches that engineers and manufacturers were used to dealing with in designing electric circuits. Most electrical equipment had around a dozen such components in them—amplifiers, diodes, capacitors, and resistors—and replacing tubes with transistors was only profitable if customers would pay (a lot more) for the advantages of slightly smaller size and increased durability. Even then, transistors made very bad resistors and capacitors. Worse, there was a limit to the miniaturization that transistors brought because, although transistors got smaller, the wires needed to connect them didn't, nor did the hands needed to assemble and solder them together.

It wasn't until the 1950s that the events of the late 1940s began to appear truly revolutionary. Much of the success of the transistor as we know it came about because, in the 1950s, a community of engineers, investors, and customers began to form and grow around the transistor. The truly revolutionary value of the technology itself didn't emerge until Robert Noyce and Gordon Moore, on the West Coast, and Jack Kilby, in Texas, came up with ways to take a design for a circuit made with solid-state transistors and build it into a single component: an integrated circuit. It was only once these engineers had hit upon the concept of building the entire circuit on a chip that the transistor started to look like what it does now.

But to give credit solely to Noyce, Moore, and Kilby is, again, to neglect the web of other individuals, organizations, and ideas that surrounded them and also enabled the integrated circuit to come into being. Noyce and Moore were brought together, like Bardeen and Brattain, by William Shockley, who had left AT&T to found Shockley Semiconductor. Once again, Shockley demonstrated first his knack for recognizing and pulling together great people, and then for driving them away. Rather quickly, Noyce and Moore recognized Shockley's management style and, along with six other engineers, left (Shockley would later call them the "traitorous eight"). They quickly found funding from Fairchild Camera and Instrument Corporation, which was looking for a way into the emerging transistor business. The new firm, Fairchild Semiconductor, sold its first 100 transistors to IBM for $150 each. Two years later, in 1959, the company hit upon the idea of making the entire electric circuit out of transistors.[10]

The generation of electrical engineers working in the 1950s had been raised to think about circuit design in terms of achieving the best signal quality with the fewest components (since signal quality mattered and components were expensive). Elegance lay in simplicity and could be achieved by finding specific, single-purpose components that were just right for the job. By this way of thinking, transistors were poor-quality, general-purpose components. The concept of an integrated circuit stood the existing ideas about circuit design upside down, since it meant thinking in terms of using many bad components instead of a few good ones. The key insight that Noyce and Moore had (and Kilby at Texas Instruments) was that if you used *enough* bad transistors you could build a good circuit. You just had to start thinking in terms of hundreds and thousands of transistors where once six to twelve were enough.

The community of engineers began to construct a set of ideas around this new notion of combining transistors that made the original "invention" of the transistor revolutionary. Noyce and Moore, working together, and Kilby, working alone, hit on this idea at the same time partly because the ideas were already floating around the community. But if we pull back another step, we can also see that even the idea of the integrated circuit relied on an ever-expanding community to make *it* valuable.

The deciding point in the patent battle between Noyce and Moore from Fairchild and Jack Kilby from Texas Instruments came down to the techniques that Noyce and Moore used to connect the transistors. In other words, it wasn't enough to integrate the transistors in a single chip. One had to integrate the connections between them—the lines that ran from one transistor to the next. For this, Kilby's patent drawing showed the traditional wires. By contrast, the patent of Noyce and Moore showed a revolutionary and ingenious way of layering conductors in planes above the transistors. This idea came about because Jean Hoerni, working with Noyce and Moore, one day recognized that you could put a layer of silicon oxide on top of the transistors, protecting them; this insight led to the possibility of layering, or printing, conductors right over the transistors. Known as the planar process, this technique was as critical to manufacturing integrated circuits as transistors were.

One of the early customers for Fairchild's integrated circuits was the military, for use in missiles and rockets, where cost was not an issue but size and durability were. Only through these early contracts were the integrated circuit pioneers able to bring prices down to the point at which commercial opportunities came knocking. Thus, the technological landscape in which the transistor emerged now included not only the designers and manufacturers of integrated circuits, but also the military—their first and best customers.

Finally, the true potential of integrated circuits lay not in replacing the old components used in analog electronics but rather in the new world of digital computing. This new world owed much to Von Neumann's development of a binary computer language that allowed computers to treat signals as 1s and 0s, and thus to use transistors as simple switches (on = 1, off = 0). It also owed a debt to a nineteenth-century cobbler's son, George Boole, who taught himself mathematics and philosophy and developed a new science of symbolic logic in which all reasoning is represented by a series of And, Not, and Or statements. The combination of Boolean logic and binary representation meant transistors could do what they were good for in the first place—switching current on and off. Having so many of them doing it so many times, however, caused them to become much more than the sum of their parts.

The world from which the transistor emerged was densely connected. The people, ideas, and objects in that world owed their success to the development of complementary technologies, skills, and ideas. To say that Shockley invented the transistor is to deny the connections that made it possible for Shockley to contribute in the first place and that made it possible for the transistor to move from Brattain's laboratory bench into so many of the products we use today.

The ultimate impact of this early community has been famously charted in the Fairchild Family Tree—the Fairchildren, as they have been called. Initially brought together by William Shockley, these eight original engineers continued to build on the idea. As the new technologies of the integrated circuit came together, this group was able to recognize the advances in manufacturing and in circuit design—and even venture capital—that would be needed in the coming years. Noyce and Moore went on to found Intel. Eugene Kleiner founded Kleiner, Perkins, Caufield & Byers, the venture capital firm. AMD, LSI Logic, National Semiconductor, Signetics, and Four Phase all emerged directly from the community that came together at Fairchild. In turn, Linear Technology, Cirrus Logic, VLSI Technology, Sierra Semiconductor, Chips and Technology, and Cypress all came from these companies.

Other Connections

Was it a coincidence that so many players in the semiconductor industry came from the group that formed at Fairchild? Perhaps, but the same types of connections can be seen in the Whiz Kids who came together in World War II under Robert Lovett and Tex Thornton: Arjay Miller, Robert McNamara, and J. Edward Lundy. This group of statisticians brought quantitative analysis to management. At the War Department, their methods often flew in the face of tradition and instinct. But their shared belief in themselves gave them the confidence as young lieutenants to push generals around. They were such a tight-knit group that they stuck together after the war. Henry Ford saw their value and hired them. Miller would go on to run Ford Motor Company. So did Robert McNamara, who also served as Secretary of Defense from 1961 to 1968. Tex Thornton left Ford soon after the Whiz Kids arrived, going on, ultimately, to found Litton Industries.[11]

The same story can be told in the biotechnology industry. Cetus Corporation, where Kary Mullis developed the techniques for PCR in the early 1980s, spawned from its ranks a range of biotech laboratories that inhabited the middle ground between university research labs and the big pharmaceutical companies. And in the video game industry, the group of MIT students in the Tech Model Railroad Club who developed the first arcade video game, Spacewar, in the early 1960s soon after spread out across the country to shape the future of that industry.[12]

Many stories of innovation, when you get past the smoke and mirrors, thus reveal a backstage filled with other people, ideas, and objects that were as critical—if not more so—than the one presented onstage. Ultimately, the amount of credit we insist on giving to individuals in the innovation process is absurd. Communities like those that formed in the early days around the transistor, around recombinant DNA and PCR, and around operations research were every bit as responsible for making those ideas stick, grow, and ultimately become revolutions.

Building New Worlds

The webs of innovation that form around emerging technologies are not the signs of a better mousetrap. In fact, the construction of these webs is a central part of the innovation process. Consider the life cycle: An innovation emerges when one or a few people recognize the potential in an idea or an object for uses beyond what's already been done. They share this vision with a few others—a colleague down the hall or a buddy over in software. Those others collectively contribute their own ideas and their own skills, and by doing so push the idea along and encourage each other to push even further. They pitch the idea—maybe to a manager or potential investors, who add yet more resources, and to other interested colleagues, potential suppliers, or retailers. Over time, a community begins to take shape which is connected around the emerging technology. The efforts of this growing community accelerate the evolution of the new idea, and their diverse perspectives push it in new directions.

This process of building a new world around an innovation reflects two very real and different ways in which the webs that surround emerging technologies enable the innovation process. In the beginning, these webs create collectives—usually small groups of people working closely together (sometimes in collaboration, sometimes in competition). Over time, these same webs turn into larger communities whose tight-knit interactions propel the new technology forward.

Collective Deviance: Thinking Different, Together

If you think about it, there's no real difference in the early stages of innovation between entrepreneurs and deviants. Successful innovations are just those deviations that survived adolescence. In their youth, each was just a brash new way of doing things differently, one deviant idea among many. Neither Einstein nor Elvis was embraced by the establishment before, or immediately after, he presented the world with his new ideas. The same and worse receptions await new ideas in organizations.

The collective, a small group of individuals committed to a common goal, offers a powerful way to overcome this initial challenge. This role can be seen in the early days of the impressionist movement in the 1860s. While history gives prominence to individual artists—Renoir, Monet, and Cézanne—art historians have noted how these individuals began as part of a single small group.

Social psychologist Michael Farrell recognized that this collective enabled the individual artists to commit to, and create, a movement that directly challenged the established art world. In splitting from the dominant styles of the art world, the artists' circle of early impressionists worked closely to develop their emerging style and to jointly construct an environment of support and motivation for their creative efforts.[13] They worked so closely together that their paintings were often indistinguishable: When two paintings were on display in a gallery much later, Monet could not say which was his and which was Renoir's without looking at the signature. Only later, when the impressionist movement was established, did each artist make efforts to distinguish himself as an individual. Many works of art, Farrell argues, particularly those from the early stages of new movements, should be viewed as the product of collectives and not of any individual artist.

Collectives like the impressionists provide two critical resources for an early innovation: a broad pool of ideas and a strong network of support. The first resource, a broad pool of ideas, comes about because the collective brings individuals together in ways that allow them to build on each other's ideas, to turn a wacky comment or hesitant suggestion into a brilliant insight. The collective works when it becomes difficult, if not impossible, to identify whose idea it was in the first place. Farrell, in describing the early days of the impressionists, noted: "A chance idea that might have been discarded if the painter had been alone was supported by the group. Risky decisions were validated and the group began to develop its own subculture."[14] The project team that developed the Reebok Pump at Design Continuum was another such collective. When someone suggested putting an inflatable splint into a shoe, the others could have laughed it off as one more wacky idea in a brainstorming session filled with many wacky ideas. Instead, someone else built on the idea. The idea of using an IV bag to act as the inflatable bladder made the idea of an inflatable splint not only realistic, but good. Fundamentally, the difference between a good idea and a bad one, in a collective, depends entirely on what the others decide to do with it.

The second critical advantage that these early collectives provide is a common belief in the collective's cause and its chances for success just when these are needed most, when the ideas (and people) are attempting to go against the established ways of doing things. In 1951, the psychologist Solomon Asch asked how effective individual judgment really was in the face of social pressure to conform. He brought groups of students together in a single room, purportedly to test their visual judgment. The students were all shown a card with a line drawn on it, and then a card with three different lines, and asked which line was the same length as the one on the first card. The trick, and with social psychologists there is always a trick, was that seven of the eight students were in cahoots with the experimenter and gave a uniform false answer. Of those who completed the experiments alone (the control group), almost nobody made errors. And yet about a third of the subjects who were placed in groups went along with their group's (wrong) answer. In later studies, Asch found no real differences in the effects of the group size. Whether the group consisted of three or sixteen people, the pressure to conform remained the same. When subjects were asked their reasons for conforming, some doubted their perceptions in the face of so many other, conflicting answers; some never doubted their perceptions, but chose to go along with the group anyway; and some insisted that they (and the group) were right.

This experiment involved just a line: nothing personal, no friendships involved, no departmental budgets on the line, no installed base to cut into, no established traditions or sacred cows. Just a line. And yet people, regardless of their background, found it painful to go against the majority. Asch found that the pressure to conform is more powerful than almost anyone expected at the time.

For our purposes, however, Solomon Asch found out something even more important. He found that the easiest way to get an individual to go against the larger group is to give that individual a group of his or her own. Adding one more independent subject to the group—from one to two—makes the effect of the group pressure disappear. When subjects had one other person who agreed with them, they were able to stand against the larger group. Asch also found that this collective deviance was a fragile thing. If he took one of the partners away in the middle of an experiment, the other often began conforming again.

In this way, collectives encourage individuals to think different, together. When you work with others who are visibly engaged in and passionate about the work, you feel better about it yourself. Emile Zola captures this power of collective deviance in his novel *The Masterpiece,* which fictionalized his time spent working alongside the impressionists. When the central character, based on Monet, was in despair, he went walking with his friends:

> They . . . sauntered along, with an air of taking over the entire width of the Boulevard des Invalides. When they spread out like this, they were like a free-and-easy band of soldiers off to the wars. . . . In this company and under this influence, Claude began to cheer up; in the warmth of shared hopes, his belief in himself revived.[15]

In this group, each artist's motivation (and identity) was shaped by his connections with the collective.

We tend to think that organizations play the role of collectives, providing all the necessary support for those within them. Yet the role of the collective is even more critical *inside* organizations, where standard operating procedures and "the way we do things around here" make just about any change seem deviant, and where hierarchies can turn even casual comments by superiors into powerful pressures to conform. The role of the collective, joining forces to fight the status quo, often spells the difference between good ideas stopping at the first conservative layer of management or pushing their way, painfully if necessary, all the way to the top.

Communities as Evolving Worlds

The collectives that initially produce an innovation turn into a community over time. What's the difference? As an innovation such as the transistor or the lightbulb develops, it moves from being a vision of what could be into a shared reality. The collective helps by pulling together previously disparate people, ideas, and objects and providing them with the necessary support to overcome their initial illegitimacy. Once the new venture crystallizes and acquires legitimacy, the need for the collective gives way to the advantages that only an established community can bring. Individuals doing the same work and playing the same roles in a collective give way to individuals playing competing or complementary roles: "I can manufacture chips better then they can; if not, then I'll focus on designing them."

The communities that evolve around new technologies are a complex and fascinating social phenomenon, but, for our purposes here, their value is simple. Revolutionary ideas may trigger the emergence of communities, but it is the evolution of technologies *within* these communities that makes those ideas revolutionary. When Bob Noyce and Gordon Moore (and Jean Hoerni) found a way to put multiple transistors into a circuit and onto a chip, they made the original development of the transistor that much more of a revolution. When Tim Berners-Lee and Robert Cailliau wrote the protocols (URLs, http, and HTML) for displaying content on the World Wide Web and convinced their superiors at CERN to not only support the protocols but also to give them away, and when Marc Andreessen and Eric Bina at the University of Illinois at Urbana-Champaign wrote Mosaic (which became Netscape), they made the Internet that much more of a revolution. And despite Edison's resistance, electric light became that much more revolutionary when Westinghouse introduced alternating current.

In fact, we can expect most of the actual improvements in the productivity and performance of a new technology to take place *in use*—and long after "individual inventors" have lost control of their ideas to the communities that are forming around them.[16] As communities grow around new technologies, they create the necessary feedback loops that sustain them. As one group gets better at manufacturing integrated circuits, another exploits those gains to design more advanced chips, and another uses those to develop better computers, which spur the demand for more and better manufacturing.

On a global scale, these kinds of feedback loops spurred the Industrial Revolution. Improvements in the steam engine increased the productivity of coal mining. More coal (and its by-product, coke) meant more and ultimately better iron. More iron meant more and better steam engines. More steam engines meant more coal, and so forth. At more local levels, the same interactions enable stable communities to form around emerging products or processes within organizations. The small group established at Intel to work on microprocessors grew into a sustainable community in time to displace Intel's core business, memory chips. As the opportunities to profit from these stable interactions become more certain, more individuals and organizations join the communities with the express purpose of pursuing those profits.

Whether pulling individuals together across organizations or within a single one, these communities take shape around emerging innovations. As more and more people join a community, the web itself becomes easily recognizable from the outside. In organizations, it soon becomes officially sanctioned, maybe as a new development project, as a research center, or even as a new division. Outside of organizations, it begins to look like an emerging market (one of the most defining characteristics of the evolving community being a readily identifiable set of customers), an industry, or a "cluster" of firms located in a particular region.[17]

Building Activities

Building new worlds from the pieces of old ones means creating meaningful and valuable links between previously unconnected people, ideas, and objects. Technology brokering relies on building these new networks to both generate and build on innovations, first in creating collective ventures and then in establishing self-sustaining communities. These links must be meaningful and valuable to the others who might enlist in the cause.

The risk in building these new networks lies in losing ownership of the very innovations at their core. Some of this risk is simply a vestige of the cult of the inventor. It's hard for individuals to seek out and build collectives when they think the path to greatness requires going it alone. Philo T. Farnsworth, for example, is often credited with inventing the television but losing it to David Sarnoff and RCA. Evan Schwartz describes in *The Last Lone Inventor: A Tale of Genius, Deceit and the Birth of Television* how the inventor had dedicated his life to being like Thomas Edison, Alexander Graham Bell, and Samuel Morse, the "lone inventor who could transform the world." [18] But the fact is, building the technology that became television as we know it required building a community that could do more than simply send and receive images. The community needed to also build and sell televisions, to create content, to establish transmission networks, and so forth. Farnsworth, with his dreams of being the lone genius, was ill suited from the start for building such a complex community.

But some of this risk is very real. Bringing other individuals and organizations in to share in the development of an emerging technology can often mean losing control over its key elements. IBM, of course, discovered this in the development of the personal computer. The company was, in many ways, a victim of the necessities of the innovation process.

The story is well known. When IBM began work on the personal computer, it was in a rush to enter a market that it had blown off as inconsequential to its core business. Needing to compete with the market success of the Apple II and Commodore 64, IBM pieced together a system that used an off-the-shelf microprocessor, the 8088 from Intel, and outsourced the development of its operating system to a small software firm in Seattle named Microsoft. The result was not necessarily pretty. The PC, as IBM called it, made no great technological leaps over what Apple already offered. In fact, once Apple saw the PC, it welcomed the competition—IBM's presence gave the personal computer market legitimacy among business customers. Apple even took out a full-page ad in the *Wall Street Journal* saying "Welcome IBM. Seriously." But IBM had done one thing right: Whereas Apple had built a wonderful but proprietary system, IBM had created an open system

that attracted a wide number of parts suppliers, software program-
mers, and computer manufacturers. It had created a community that,
as it evolved, ensured that the PC would revolutionize the business
world. In the process, of course, IBM might have given away the keys to
the kingdom. Microsoft and Intel soon dominated the PC-compatible
market. But by bringing these firms on board early, IBM built the necessary community that ensured its innovations would endure.

Organizations in pursuit of innovations must learn to build
new networks around their emerging ideas without losing control
of them. Like the activities of bridging, there are no certain recipes
for success. There are no clear rules for how much is enough and
how much is too much. Every situation is different, but a clear ap-
preciation for the role of collectives and communities is the right
place to start. Let's briefly consider some of the activities that organizations engage in to build networks, first by building collectives
and then communities.

Mix and Match

Michael Riordan, coauthor of *Crystal Fire*, once said that Brattain and Bardeen "were two very complementary human beings. It
was like Bardeen was the brains of this joint organism and Brattain
was the hands."[19] As mentioned in chapter 1, a look behind many
revolutionary innovations or discoveries will reveal "inventors"
working closely with at least one other person, such as Edison and
Charles Batchelor, Steve Jobs and Steve Wozniak, and Bill Gates
and Paul Allen. In many ways, these partnerships were the first and
critical link around which larger collectives could form. Like Riordan implies of Brattain and Bardeen, these partnerships were successful because they brought together complementary personalities,
skills, and ideas. Jobs's charisma and Wozniak's technical prowess
was a great combination. So was Edison's vision and salesmanship
and Batchelor's mechanical skills.

Organizations are often terrible places for partnerships because
they rarely reward, promote, or keep such pairs together. Organizations

like to think in terms of positions or roles, but not of individuals and their unique personalities, much less the particular combination of two or more individuals. But often this is where the greatest ideas can emerge and develop. When was the last time your organization hired a pair? How about a whole team? The idea is not so outlandish. In the video game industry, firms often hire entire design teams rather than try to piece one together. The same phenomenon is happening in the networking industry, and Cisco's successful growth strategy depends on acquiring small firms (over seventy since 1993) for their established expertise.[20]

Similarly, team building has somewhat of a bad reputation—as an activity, it implies a treatment for dysfunctional teams. In the context of innovation, however, *team building* means the process of putting together the team in the first place: of finding the right mix of individuals, skills, and experiences to turn a vision into reality. Many different factors go into mixing and matching a team. At Design Continuum, for example, each new project requires a particular set of engineering, human factors, and other design skills and experiences that dictates who should be on the team. These different backgrounds represent the knowledge (and network contacts) that each engineer and designer can bring to the project from his or her experience working in different worlds. But the team also needs the right mix of personalities that will allow them to work well together as a collective and to build ties outside the team to clients, suppliers, and potential users. For example, Deborah Ancona and David Caldwell, researchers at MIT, studied forty-five new-product development teams in five high-tech companies, with a focus on those activities that spanned the boundaries between the team and the outside world.[21] They identified three different roles that teams need to fill: *ambassadors,* who represent the team to outsiders and protect it from external threats; *coordinators,* who link the team's activities with external groups, including handling scheduling, negotiation, and design issues; and finally, *scouts,* who scan the external environment for valuable technologies or market information. Mixing and matching teams requires piecing together the right people who can both bridge distant worlds and build new ones.

Multiple Networks

It's difficult to know in advance which backgrounds, which experiences, and which skills are needed in a new project. In fact, finding out which people, ideas, and objects to recombine *is* the innovation process. So chances are, new project teams have a mix of obvious skill sets, but lack the nonobvious ones. Problems arise in teams like this because they simply don't know what they don't know. Good teams maintain the awareness that their best solutions will draw from and build on wide-ranging but already existing ideas, and will make efforts to exploit the experiences of others in the organization and elsewhere.

Building and maintaining connections to others takes time and energy. Indeed, that may be the first law of social networks: There's no such thing as a free network. But there are differences in the costs of these network ties. Interactions within teams, for example, can be intense and, because they occur often, can take a lot of time and attention. But we exist in many different networks at the same time— a working group or team at work, our families (local and extended), our friendship circles, maybe a church or community group—some of which are quite intense, but many more of which are not. Most of the time, these networks remain dormant while we attend to other activities. While we are at home, we are not thinking of work (one hopes), and vice versa while we are focused at work. This is the momentary nature of social networks. They can be turned on and off depending on the situation. In organizations, these momentary networks can be of tremendous value because, for relatively little time and energy, they can bring together distant people.

Brainstorming meetings offer a good example of a momentary network, although this is one of the technique's more overlooked aspects (and values). Brainstorming has been around since Alec

Osborn first wrote about it in *Applied Imagination* as a tool for generating creative ideas. The original idea was to gather a group of people who, for the duration of the meeting, would suspend all judgment and try to come up with as many possible solutions as they could to a particular problem, such as how to put ten pounds of components into a five-pound laptop, how to navigate a 500-channel television set, or how to link a 1980s-vintage database to a Web browser interface. What's not mentioned, but is one of the essential secrets to successful brainstorming, is that these meetings bring together people who would not ordinarily come together on a particular problem.[22] The meetings activate dormant networks around a particular problem for the duration of the session.

As an engineer, I sat in on my share of brainstorming sessions. Some have been extremely successful, and I left energized and enlightened. Others were such a disappointment that I left wondering what other projects I might find work on. The difference often hinged on who was invited. Bringing an existing team together for a brainstorming session when it has already been working on the same set of problems for weeks, if not months, is expecting to find new ideas from the people most likely to share the same old ideas. Returning to Granovetter, the strength of brainstorming lies in the strength of the weak ties it taps into. Brainstorming creates momentary networks that link people from across the organization and across project teams, building bridges between their diverse and otherwise disconnected experiences and the needs of the current project.

Communities of practice are, like brainstorming, a means for bringing together people who would otherwise not interact in organizations. The term *communities of practice* originated with research by Jean Lave and Etienne Wenger on how people learn and how that learning is inextricably bound up with how they work and how they communicate with others.[23] Wenger's study of the people responsible for processing claims in an insurance firm, for example, showed just how important the community was for creating and sharing often very complex and tacit knowledge. John

Seely Brown and Paul Duguid, in *The Social Life of Information,* have since described how communities of practice are both more pervasive—appearing in research and development laboratories and in field service organizations—and more powerful than previously considered. Communities of practice are groups that form across organizational boundaries because of shared interests—networks that are not the result of organizational edicts but rather that emerge naturally as individuals run across and build relationships with similar individuals. The phenomenon itself is an old one but is becoming more prevalent in organizations as technology makes it easier for people to interact across the company and across the globe. The effects of these communities, like the effects of brainstorming, are to build and maintain multiple networks in the organization that add opportunities to bridge distant worlds.

Equal but Separate

Often, the best way to bring people together is to divide them up. The promise of many management trends, from flattening the organization to communities of practice to computer-supported collaboration, is to bring all of the disparate elements of the organization into one big, happy, and well-connected family. But these efforts often make such demands on everybody's time—attending meetings, answering e-mails, checking the corporate intranet—that they soon fade away. One alternative is to create equal, but separate, groups within the larger organization, fragmenting the larger network in order to force smaller collectives into action.

Harvey Earl ran GM's automotive styling group from 1927 until he retired in 1958. Alfred Sloan, GM's president at the time, recognized that the basic engineering of the automobile had stabilized and that styling would soon become a key strategic advantage in the market. As an independent designer, Earl had designed the first LaSalle, and based on that work Sloan gave him the task of building GM's Art & Colour department. Within the first year, Earl had built

a department of fifty designers to oversee the design of GM's growing range of cars and trucks. In the beginning, all fifty designers oc-
cupied a single room. Earl separated them into five groups using the
large, movable blackboards on which they sketched out their ideas.
The idea was not to cut them off completely from the rest of the
group, but to focus them on their own groups and their own work:
They could overhear the other groups, but not see their designs.

In essence, Harvey Earl created equal but separate groups so that
each group could create and build on its own ideas without outside
influence. He reconnected these separate groups by walking between them himself or by holding design competitions—asking the
groups to each design "a future small fastback sedan" or "an owner-
driven luxury car."[24] IDEO, a design firm discussed in more detail in
chapter 7, broke into similar groups when it found that its size had
made the costs of dense ties greater than the value of the community
they produced. Breaking into smaller, tightly knit studios that were
loosely connected to one another kept the value of small groups
while maintaining the larger network of weak ties.

A Short, Happy Life

The danger with collectives and communities is that they often
outlive their usefulness. Collectives build a common belief around a
new venture that is necessary to overcome the resistance of tradition. But that common belief becomes a closed mind over time.
Ralph Katz and Thomas J. Allen first recognized this problem as the
not invented here (NIH) *syndrome.*[25] They looked at over fifty R&D
project teams and studied the relationship between each team's productivity and the amount of time individuals had spent in the team.
Their research revealed that teams first become more productive as
they find out about each other's skills and the right ways to put those
skills together, and then become less productive as they become
fixed in their ways and confident that they know all there is to know
about their field (a confidence made only greater by the support of
their teammates).

The term *skunkworks* is well known now, and the tactic of creating a skunkworks is often considered the ideal way to build a collective that will tackle the established traditions of the organization. The notion of skunkworks came from the Lockheed group of that name, a group of engineers and aviators who isolated themselves from the rest of the organization and produced such revolutionary aircraft as the U-2 and the SR-71. Michael Schrage, writing in *Fortune*, succinctly captures the dangers that this innovation tactic brings (and signals).[26] Skunkworks are a means to circumvent the bureaucracy, the politics, and the short-term goals of the larger organization in order to build a collective that works closely together. But in so doing, skunkworks also sever the team's connections to the rest of the organization. Ultimately, those isolated groups rely on the rest of the organization to embrace their innovations, yet with few links between the development group and the rest of the organization they face a difficult challenge getting their ideas heard at all. Schrage quotes a friend who built one such skunkworks: Others in the larger organization "try to kill every good idea we have." The experience at Apple was worse, where Jobs developed the Macintosh as a skunkworks project (right down to restricting access to the building and flying the Jolly Roger flag). Sure, the Macintosh was a revolutionary leap past the Apple II, but the sight of engineers from both camps fighting in a local bar showed that building a collective by burning bridges to the rest of the organization and dismantling the multiple networks that also play key roles in the innovation process can do as much damage as good.

Thus, part and parcel of building collectives and communities is knowing their limits: when they can become too insulated and when they should be dismantled.

•   •   •

On the night of August 8, 2001, a party was thrown for the IBM PC, which turned twenty years old. It received considerable attention in the press as "The Birthday of the Personal Computer." *USA Today* carried a full-page story in the business section, complete with graphical explanations of the computer and its growth.[27] Whose pictures graced the articles? Microsoft's Bill Gates and Intel's Andy Grove. James Cannavino, who was project manager of the IBM PC, went all but unnoticed. Steve Jobs declined to attend, and who can blame him? He had introduced the Apple II personal computer four years earlier than the IBM PC. Totally forgotten was Ed Roberts, who insiders acknowledge for his role as the founder of Micro Instrumentation Telemetry Systems (MITS), which introduced the Altair in 1975, providing the market with its first recognizable personal computer (and providing Bill Gates with his first recognizable employment in the personal computer industry).

Who threw this bash? Bill Gates and Andy Grove. Microsoft and Intel have played a large role in the evolution of the PC since 1981, but what role did they play in its conception and birth? Both were suppliers to IBM, one of an operating system it hadn't originally written and the other of an off-the-shelf microprocessor. There was little uproar, however, concerning the bias in this recognition. Gates and Grove might not have been the parents of the PC, but they were certainly the winners. In the twenty years since the events took place, Gates and Grove have become the fathers of the personal computer. And if we needed to rewrite a little history to make the myth come out right, so be it.

A similar birthday bash took place on October 21, 1929, on the fiftieth anniversary of Edison's introduction of the lightbulb. Henry Ford hosted the party, moving Edison's Menlo Park laboratory (and seven carloads of Menlo Park dirt) to Dearborn to become part of his Greenfield Village Museum. Edison was feted for his development of the electric lightbulb, and, in the process, electricity's powers were celebrated. The role played by General Electric was subtle but pervasive, and Edison's wife Mina wrote in her diary the day before: "I feel that dearie [Thomas] is so much more than the electric light and that the light jubilee is one grand advertisement for General Electric and the light companies, that [he] has just been made the excuse."[28]

When innovation is seen as the work of heroic individuals throwing off the oppressive chains of established society, we're in for trouble. Too many times entrepreneurs have attempted to walk in the footsteps of Edison, Ford, or whoever—determined to be as boldly individualistic as history tells us these lone geniuses were. But they weren't. What set them apart, and what sets apart technology brokers, is the recognition that innovation requires not just a new idea (built from combinations of old ones) but also the collective effort necessary to make that new idea work against the doubt and uncertainty of the process. The world will not beat a path to your door. Instead, innovation requires building a community of like-minded and wholly committed individuals who see their shared future in the success of the emerging technologies and industries.

So to succeed, technology brokers actually must walk a delicate line between establishing the broad-ranging networks required to see and recombine valuable new ideas across a range of industries and, once new innovations are constructed, building the necessary collective action and community around those innovations. Technology brokers must pursue strategies that put them on the periphery of existing worlds, yet retain their ability to become the core of new ones. Some are better at bridging multiple domains, others at building communities around their ideas. But whether one is a manager in a large organization or an entrepreneur building one's own organization, the lessons of technology brokers offer insights into balancing these two competing strategies.

PART THREE

How Firms Pursue Innovation Through Technology Brokering

6

Technology Brokering in Practice

There are many different ways that firms can pursue a strategy of technology brokering—as many ways as there are small worlds and boundaries between them. The opportunities for recombinant innovation exist in bridging the differences among the people, ideas, and objects of previously disparate industries, whether between the meatpacking and automobile industries of 1900 or the toy and medical industries today. The same opportunities for innovation lie in bridging the differences between markets, between organizations, or between groups within organizations.

Similarly, there are differences in the level of commitment to bridging old worlds and building new ones. Some technology brokering strategies require committing most of the organization's resources to moving among these worlds, while devoting less resources to building new communities around the resulting innovations. Other strategies balance resources between bridging and building—often by creating explicit roles for such groups within the organization. Still other strategies focus on building and maintaining a firm's strong ties within a single industry or market, and retain only the capability to respond effectively should brokering opportunities arise in the firm's midst. Let's briefly consider some examples.

Edison's Menlo Park laboratory and Design Continuum dedicated themselves to bridging distant and otherwise disconnected worlds. Such firms move among worlds, often as consultants but also as entrepreneurs (Edison managed to do both). For example, Elmer Sperry was a contemporary of Edison who, over the course of his career, attained 350 patents—an impressive number when compared with anyone but Edison. The list of Sperry's innovations is as broad ranging as Edison's, and covers everything from arc lighting to auto-piloting aircraft, from electric generators to gyroscopic stabilization of ships, and from mining machinery to golf caddies. His peers elected him to the National Academy of Sciences— at the time a remarkable feat for a practicing engineer—long before Edison, whom they regarded as more entrepreneur than engineer.

Elmer Sperry's work offers a good example of the successful dedicated pursuit of technology brokering. Sperry was best known for his pioneering application of feedback control mechanisms to a range of industries that had little or no previous knowledge of such solutions. Technologies such as the electric motor emerged in one industry and rapidly diffused to others. Those individuals and firms that gained early experience with them were at an advantage when it came to adapting those technologies to the needs of other industries. Sperry's work, while broad ranging, had its greatest effect in the application of electronic feedback control mechanisms, first in arc lights and electric generators, and then in mining, shipping, and airplanes, to name just a few. To the historian Thomas Hughes, who has written at length about Sperry's career and the technical details of his inventions, Sperry was "a solution looking for feedback problems," an inventor who focused his efforts on the "fast moving front of advancing technology."[1] Perhaps most important, however, was Elmer Sperry's awareness of his strategy of technology brokering. He once said:

> If I spend a lifetime on a dynamo I can probably make my little contribution toward increasing the efficiency of that machine six or seven percent. Now then, there are a whole lot of

[industries] that need electricity, about four- or five-hundred
percent. Let me tackle one of those.[2]

Sperry knew the value of moving among small worlds, and the
possibilities for bridging the valuable divides between those objects, ideas, and people that were emerging in the worlds of the
telegraph and electric light and the many other industries that had
little or no knowledge of them. Sperry's choice of strategies was not
one of desperation. He had early on proved himself a brilliant and
resourceful engineer and, at the time, had rejected an offer from a
large corporation to advance the technologies he had initially developed. Instead, he chose the freedom of a technology brokering
strategy because it allowed him to maintain control over the problems and places where he chose to work.

The Many Faces of Technology Brokering

The strategy of technology brokering is not limited to engineering
firms. Many people have tried to understand what fueled the success
of Silicon Valley. And while much of the attention has gone to the
engineers and entrepreneurs who pieced together revolutionary
new technologies, we need to acknowledge the role of the law firms
and venture capital firms that were also intimately involved in these
new ventures. The venture capitalists and lawyers who worked with
each new venture had worked with many others before them. Each
new venture, particularly in the 1960s, 1970s, and 1980s, formed a
small world populated by engineers, computer scientists, or molecular biologists who were deeply focused on their technologies. Yet
the success of these new ventures depended as much on strategic
focus, on leadership, on marketing, and on financial controls as it
did on technology. The venture capitalists and lawyers could, and
did, tap into their networks to bring together promising new ventures and seasoned CEOs, bring together the complementary technologies of different companies, or even pool the financial support

of different investors in ways that exploited their position spanning the many small worlds of the Valley and in ways that ensured the success of these new ventures.[3]

Mark Suchman, a sociologist at Stanford, has described the role of law firms such as Wilson, Sonsini, Goodrich and Rosati in providing the necessary dealmaking and counseling capabilities needed by the relatively naïve and unconnected start-ups.[4] Similarly, Martin Kenney and Richard Florida describe the same role played by venture capitalists such as Art Rock (who provided much of the seed money for Fairchild Semiconductor and, later, many of its spin-offs) and Kleiner, Perkins, Caufield & Byers.[5] Atari, Apple Computer, Sun, Cisco, and almost every other firm in Silicon Valley that was born in the 1960s and beyond were in some way supported by venture capital funding and then, as they grew, by the connections these investors provided with other firms in their portfolios. While the primary role of these professionals is as lawyers or investors, they depend on the success of their clients and in many cases help make that success real by using their own experience in the same industry to solve (or successfully avoid) the problems their clients face. Their job requires an in-depth knowledge of how things are done in a particular field, a knowledge that even competing firms are willing to share for the benefits of establishing or hewing to a common set of standards.

Another set of firms that exploit their position spanning multiple worlds are the suppliers of common components that another industry uses, such as the circuit boards, power supplies, or connectors that all computer manufacturers put in their machines. These firms, by working on development projects with a number of competing firms, often learn who is working on what, and where the valuable ideas are.[6] Their livelihood rests on not sharing this information with competing customers, but they are often able to move the people, ideas, and objects that develop in one industry into others. The rapid diffusion of machine tools in the 1800s occurred because the people and firms that built machines for use in industries such as firearms production or textiles went in search of other industries where those same machines might be valuable.

Firms such as Browne and Sharpe, which emerged from the world of sewing machines, and Providence Tool Company, from armory production, formed a machine tool industry dedicated to building general-purpose machines.[7] With each new application, their products improved, and those improvements fed back to older customers and opened doors to newer ones.

Some customers also act as brokers, but for them it is less a strategy for innovation than a by-product of the unique position in which they find themselves. Customers move often among firms in the same industry—among competitors, retailers, repair shops, and after-market manufacturers—and serious customers often push the boundaries of the market's products. The engine mechanics of auto racing, for example, are constantly experimenting with ways to eke out one more horsepower and are constantly bumping into the limits of the technologies they use. Likewise, the engineers and artists at Pixar, creators of *Toy Story,* are pursuing more lifelike computer animations and constantly experimenting with new graphics and new algorithms, pushing the limits of both hardware and software. Firms can often find valuable new information from such customers working at the margins of their own market. At these far extremes, customers are rebuilding, reprogramming, and recombining bits and pieces from competing products or adding their own designs. Eric von Hippel of MIT and Stefan Thompke of Harvard have found such lead users to be significant sources of innovation when the organization recognizes them as such. Lead users often sit on the boundaries between peripheral and mass markets, and from there can see (and often build) valuable new combinations of existing technologies from both.[8]

Some central research laboratories also act as technology brokers. Although their charter often is to conduct basic research, many labs actually serve as gatekeepers that, from their scientific backgrounds and their experiences within their industry, can often spot emerging technologies that would be useful for the firm. Economist Willard Mueller studied the chemicals firm DuPont, looking for the origins of the basic inventions underlying their innovation process.

He investigated the twenty-five major product and process innovations that took place between 1920 and 1950, which together accounted for 45 percent of DuPont's total sales in 1948. Of the twenty-five total innovations, DuPont developed only ten internally and acquired the rest; of the eighteen product innovations, DuPont developed only five.[9] DuPont's R&D labs, while charged with basic research, were acting as gatekeepers between the needs of the firm and market and the technologies that were emerging elsewhere. When they saw valuable new ideas, they would bring them in and adapt them to fit their needs.

Some firms have recognized and institutionalized the valuable role of such central services. BMW's Designworks/USA serves as the automobile manufacturer's U.S. design headquarters. BMW acquired Designworks in 1995, after working with the firm on a number of projects. However, bringing the twenty-five-year-old design firm in-house threatened to cut its designers off from the rich variety of projects they had worked on before, and hence cripple their ability to bring new ideas into the organization. Instead, Designworks continues to do outside design work. As a result, Designworks designers keep their design skills sharp by learning about and working in a number of outside worlds and bringing those experiences back into the automotive industry.

Technology Brokering Strategies

In each of the examples discussed previously, the individuals and organizations share a fundamental quality: They bridge otherwise disconnected worlds. The differences between them have more to do with how they (and we) slice the network than with how it is experienced by those who live it every day. A dedicated strategy of technology brokering isn't for everyone, but many firms can exploit the lessons that such firms provide. Many firms can benefit from recognizing that although they might not make good technology brokers, the chances are good that brokers could thrive within their boundaries. There are many places within firms—between project teams, between divisions, between plants—where competition, politics, geography, and lack of communication have created small worlds by creating gaps in the flow of ideas and people across the organization. Here are opportunities for technology brokers to operate within the fragmented landscape of the modern organization, bridging those worlds and building innovative combinations of people, objects, and ideas.

By working across many different worlds and building network connections to the people, objects, and ideas of these different worlds, firms that organize around the pursuit of innovation increase the chances that they will see solutions in one world that solve the needs of another. By remaining on the periphery of these different worlds, rather than committing to any one, they avoid the need to limit themselves to working with only one or a few problems or technologies. And by avoiding these limits, they retain the flexibility to mix and match the many problems and solutions they come across.

Such strategies ultimately boil down to a few key decisions that managers must make about their firm and their markets: whether to (1) commit themselves to a full-time strategy of technology brokering, (2) remain focused on the markets and customers they serve but create groups within their bounds that are focused on bridging worlds and building recombinant innovations, or (3) develop the ability to recognize and seize one-time opportunities for brokering.

In the first strategy, the entire firm can dedicate itself to the pursuit of innovation through technology brokering, and seek a position in the larger network that allows it to move among worlds. Examples are Edison's Menlo Park laboratory and Design Continuum. This strategy is uncommon for the simple reason that it is difficult. A chicken-and-egg dilemma exists, in that technology brokering becomes easier the more worlds one moves through, the more experiences one gains, and the more skilled one becomes at bridging and building new combinations of resources. But moving through different worlds requires having something to contribute in each, and this requires the ability to broker technologies that, at the start, often aren't there. Many technology brokering firms got their start by bringing one set of technologies into new worlds. Over time, learning from these new worlds added to their knowledge stocks about different people, ideas, and objects. By pursuing dedicated strategies of technology brokering, these firms have been able to build organizations, hone work practices, and establish cultures that directly support their innovation process. Whether or not such a strategy is appropriate to all firms, the lessons these firms offer about technology brokering are invaluable. Chapter 7 describes in detail the interactions between the innovation strategies of dedicated technology brokers and their structure, culture, and work practices.

The second way that firms can pursue technology brokering strategies is by constructing smaller groups *internally* that are dedicated to bridging different worlds and building recombinant innovations. This is often a very effective strategy because large organizations tend to already span multiple small worlds in their environment, but do so by divisions that rarely interact. The potential exists in many of these firms to recombine the people, ideas, and objects of the different worlds they move through, but it requires cooperation and communication among divisions. Most organizations recognize this untapped potential and attempt to reduce the barriers between divisions either at higher levels or by enabling more interactions between the people of different divisions doing the work. The former strategy often fails, however, because the higher levels of management rarely have the kind of deep understanding of emerging market opportunities and technologies needed to recognize new opportunities across other worlds. The latter strategy, of mixing those who do have that deep knowledge, often fails because such people are simply too busy acquiring and using that deep knowledge to do their existing jobs. A third alternative is to build dedicated groups within these larger organizations that can move among the different divisions and their different worlds. These groups act as consultants to the different divisions, often even budgeted through their internal clients. They are freed from the operating responsibilities within any one market, but not from the need to provide value to their different clients. Chapter 8 describes these internal technology brokering groups and how they can be most effective.

Finally, technology brokering can be, and most often is, conducted by organizations as single opportunities to move the technologies of one world into another, opportunities that emerge unexpectedly and disappear rapidly. Sometimes this happens when an organization sees technologies in another world and realizes the potential they hold for its own world—Ford's recognition, for example, that Walter Flanders and Max Wollering, and their ideas and experiences with machine tools, would be valuable in building cars. Other opportunities arise when an organization realizes that one or more of its technologies could become valuable in another market. This describes the development of Viagra, whose initially disappointing performance in clinical trials as a relief for angina (by dilating the coronary arteries) led Pfizer scientists to consider another valuable market. In pure numbers, this is likely the most common form of technology brokering. But it is also the most serendipitous—relying on the coincidence of open minds, fertile imaginations, and receptive managers. For every recombinant innovation that established firms introduce in other worlds, countless more go unrecognized or unrealized. However, a number of firms have succeeded in exploiting emergent opportunities for technology brokering, and chapter 9 looks at how they were able to turn accidental recombinations into successful innovations.

Technology Brokering as a Firm

This chapter focuses on those firms that organize solely around the process of technology brokering. For these firms, the pursuit of innovation is not a process of deviating from the established routine—it is the established routine. The success of any project, in the eyes of the engineers, designers, project managers, and executives involved, is measured by how new and improved the proposed solution is from what came before.

But it's not change for the sake of change. Rather, change is focused on immediate benefits because technology brokering relies on traditional expertise. Traditions established in the canning industry are what made Ford's use of mass production so effective so quickly. Expertise in IV bag manufacturing made Reebok's Pump shoe possible. For technology brokers, change works not because they are constantly shifting and unfocused, but because they move quickly to recognize and build new networks of people, ideas, and objects around each new project on which they work.

These firms face the constant pressure to innovate, but they are free to seek out the most effective strategies for gaining access to the technologies of different worlds. They are also free to build their organizations—their structures, practices, and cultures—around the recombination of these existing ideas. Looking backstage at their innovation processes, firms such as Edison's and Elmer Sperry's yesterday and Design Continuum today share many features that have enabled them to bridge many small worlds and to rapidly build communities around the opportunities they discover.

Not all firms can dedicate themselves to the continuous pursuit of innovation. For the rest of us, it's more important to recognize when and where we can create groups within large organizations that can pursue technology brokering strategies full time, or to recognize when to create communities around recombinant innovations when the opportunities emerge. We consider these challenges in the next two chapters. Yet although dedicated technology brokers are relatively rare, their organizations hold valuable lessons for those who want to pursue similar strategies.

When we look inside these firms, we see that a strategy of moving among different worlds is not enough. The network position is critical, but it only creates the conditions for technology brokering. People inside the firm must still recognize how the resources of one world can solve the problems of another. To actually make the connections, to bridge the different worlds and build new communities around these new ventures, requires an organizational structure, practices, and culture that support their network position. Whereas the firm may move among worlds, it's the *individuals* of the firm who gain experiences in those worlds and who must make the connections when they or someone else faces a problem in another context. Understanding how the organization is built to make these connections possible—at the level of the people doing the work—is necessary for understanding how these firms are able to continuously innovate.

In particular, the links between a firm's network position and its organizational structure, work practices, and culture emerge as interdependent features of a technology brokering strategy. Together with a firm's organizational structures and work practices, this strategy creates an internal marketplace of ideas and a culture of wisdom where new ideas and objects can move around freely and each person's contributions can quickly take on new value for each new problem the organization faces. Technology brokering without these structures, practices, and culture won't work any more than these structures, practices, and culture will work without moving among multiple worlds.

This chapter describes some of the more successful firms pursuing technology brokering innovation strategies. While a traditional focus on invention and inventors has put these firms in the spotlight and made them look like beehives swarming with creative geniuses, the perspective of technology brokering pulls back the curtain to reveal much more important work going on backstage.

Take the product design and innovation services firm IDEO, for example. The business press has called its founder, David Kelley, a modern-day Edison. Tom Peters wrote about the creative buzz that filled IDEO's hallways, and Ted Koppel praised the firm for its creative genius when it redesigned the traditional grocery cart on an episode of *Nightline*. Much has been written about the innovative nature of the company's product designs. By way of explanation, people have described IDEO's organizational structure (flat and project-based), the people (smart and irreverent), their process (frequent brainstorming and rapid prototyping), and the culture (always open and sharing).

Countless firms have tried to replicate IDEO's magic inside their own four walls. And yet most will fail. That's because although IDEO's magic includes its particular way of organizing, it depends just as much on the firm's dedicated strategy as a technology broker. Let's talk first about IDEO, and then about how firms like IDEO integrate their strategies for technology brokering with their organizational structure, work practices, and culture.

IDEO: A Technology Broker in Action

IDEO is a modern technology broker. Since its founding in 1978 as Hovey-Kelley Design, the firm has been poised to ride the diffusing wave of computer technologies from Silicon Valley outward by providing innovation and design services to clients in a range of industries. Founder and chairman David Kelley once stated the firm's strategy even more simply than Sperry, saying, "We want to be the high-tech company to low-tech companies."[1] The company has done a remarkable job of it. IDEO's headquarters occupy six buildings spread along a quarter-mile stretch of High Street in downtown Palo Alto. Branch offices are located in San Francisco, Boulder, Chicago, Boston, London, Munich, and Tokyo.

One of IDEO's early projects was the design of the first Apple mouse, where the firm cut its teeth on the emerging technologies and possibilities of the personal computer industry. Since that early job, IDEO has designed over 4,000 new products for almost 1,000 different clients. It has worked in over fifty different industries, on products that range from portable computers to toy guitars, from medical products the size of small automobiles to toothbrushes for kids, and from the mechanical whale in *Free Willy* to water bottles for bicycles. IDEO designed interiors for Amtrak's Acela high-speed train, the Leap chair for Steelcase, insulin pens for Eli Lilly, the Palm V, Polaroid's i-Zone instant camera, Nike sunglasses, Smith ski goggles, Logitech joysticks, Crest's Neat Squeeze stand-up toothpaste tube, electronic books, computers, medical equipment, and surgical devices. It recently merged its expertise in information technology with its design of environments, using what the firm knows about high technology to produce a unique experience for shoppers in fashion house Prada's flagship New York store.

IDEO is almost as well known for its creative process as for its innovative products. Although Alex Osborn introduced brainstorming as a creativity tool in advertising in the early 1960s, it was IDEO that made the process famous. Tom Peters first wrote about IDEO in 1992 and devoted several pages to how the company had raised the art of brainstorming to a new level, thrown traditional management hierarchies out the window, and made the engineering process fun.[2] Every time new reporters come through IDEO's offices, they are bowled over by the open loft-like work spaces and the many products, parts, prototypes, sketches, foam models, and toys that are scattered everywhere. It looks like a cross between a high-tech engineering office and a kindergarten before clean-up.

Companies can remodel their office spaces, adding open lofts and shared work areas. They can change everyone's title to make everyone equal. They can put toys in the lobby. Clients have even moved their engineers to work side by side with IDEO engineers on their projects in order to absorb the culture, learn the new networks, and return home with them. Will any of this make them as innovative as IDEO? No.

IDEO's people and work practices are unique, but they are as much a result of IDEO's innovation strategies as they are a cornerstone of it. Underlying this creative cacophony is a singular advantage IDEO enjoys over its clients and many others. By virtue of having worked in so many different industries, the company is far more likely to see (or simply remember) new ways of solving long-standing problems in one industry by importing ideas from others. As Steve Jobs once said, "When we have some wacko problem, chances are that someone at [IDEO] has the skills to take care of it."[3] Or as Kelley himself has said,

> Working with companies in such dissimilar industries as medical instruments, furniture, toys, and computers has given us a broad view of the latest technologies available and has taught us how to do quality product development and how to do it quickly and efficiently.[4]

IDEO will seek out projects in industries it finds "interesting" and "full of potential" and even risk taking a loss on the project just to gain access to new worlds.

By most measures, IDEO is continuously innovative. In 2002, IDEO engineers and designers won nine of the prestigious awards in *Business Week*'s annual design competition. The company has won more *Business Week* Industrial Design Excellence Awards than any other firm: forty-eight in the last five years alone. The second-place finisher among design firms took twenty-two, while Apple led all corporations during that same time with sixteen. IDEO is frequently mentioned in the popular press and in numerous appearances on CNN, PBS, ABC, CBS, and CNBC for its innovative designs. Recent books have described IDEO's design culture and process, from Tom Kelley's (brother of founder David Kelley) *The Art of Innovation* to Jeremy Myerson's delightfully illustrated exploration of the firm, *IDEO: Masters of Innovation*.

IDEO's clients range from start-ups seeking the technical skills they lack in-house to *Fortune* 50 firms seeking the innovative ideas, flexible thinking, and broader perspectives they lack in-house. Some clients have their own manufacturing expertise, others have marketing know-how, and others have exciting new technologies. At IDEO, the core activity is neither manufacturing products nor pure research and development, sales, or marketing. Instead, IDEO's engineers and designers are engaged, every day, in designing new products, new environments, even new innovation strategies for their clients— and the firm's success depends on routinely surprising its clients with innovative solutions.

For each new project, IDEO uses the experiences its engineers and designers have gained while working for so many different clients in so many different industries. The resulting innovations are recombinations of objects, ideas, and even people they learned about while working elsewhere. For example, the bicycle manufacturer Specialized asked IDEO to design a new and different water bottle, and the project team came up with a spill-proof nozzle that didn't require opening and closing: Just squeeze the bottle and the nozzle pops open. The team first developed that idea when, five years earlier, they were working on a shampoo bottle that could hang upside down in the shower. They first heard about the idea when working with a medical products company and seeing valve designs for artificial hearts.

IDEO has recently recognized the full potential of its network position. By moving among so many small worlds, it has acquired more than just a lot of good objects and ideas. IDEO has also acquired links to a range of vendors, suppliers, and manufacturers that are particularly innovative or easy to work with, to research scientists with deep knowledge of emerging materials, to product companies that are central to particular markets. IDEO has realized it is not just in the business of combining existing objects and ideas in novel ways, but also in the business of building communities around those recombinant innovations.

Building on its ability to create new applications that combine emerging technologies with other objects and ideas, IDEO then uses its vast network of people and firms to build a community around those innovative new products and processes. One such project came through working with ElekSen, a switching and sensing company that develops new technologies around the combination of conductive fabric and microchip technologies. ElekTex is the first technology released by ElekSen: a lightweight, durable, and flexible "smart fabric" that is potentially valuable in a range of different industries and markets. But although ElekSen has the capabilities to develop this technology, it lacks the access, customer knowledge, and manufacturing resources that would allow the company to successfully launch its innovation in any one market. IDEO helped ElekSen identify a range of potential new products for ElekTex, developed these ideas to a prototype stage, and then helped ElekSen find manufacturers with which to partner.

The first application to hit the market came from a partnership with Logitech, which builds keyboards, mice, and trackballs for computers (and with which IDEO has designed a number of products). Logitech introduced a fabric case for PDAs that unfolds into a keyboard, the KeyCase. The KeyCase makes use of Logitech's central position, resources, and connection within the computer market, while exploiting ElekSen's deep technical expertise. IDEO, by virtue of its position spanning multiple worlds, was able to bridge the gap between ElekSen and Logitech and, through its design capabilities, build common ties between them.

Linking Innovation to Structure, Practice, and Culture

Technology brokers such as IDEO benefit from having worked in a wide range of different industries. They not only see radically different sets of technologies, but also see radically different uses for the same underlying technology. For example, Whirlpool recently hired IDEO to help them design a revolutionary new home appliance for taking odors and wrinkles out of clothes—the Personal Valet. The Personal Valet essentially reduces the need for dry cleaning (except for removing visible stains) by using a special wetting agent, which is misted onto clothes. The major challenge IDEO faced was engineering a system that would consistently mix and spray this solution, getting sufficient particularization to evenly penetrate clothes without spotting. Such particularization requires the solution to reach the speed of sound, Mach 1, as it exits the nozzle of the mister. IDEO's engineers both understood this problem and had seen previous solutions in the world of pharmaceuticals, where they had helped Inhale Therapeutic Systems (now Nektar Therapeutics) develop a product for diabetics that delivered an inhalable dose of insulin. This insulin device required turning a pellet of insulin powder into a fine particular mist. Through this project, IDEO's engineers learned a great deal from the fine particle scientists also involved. This experience provided central elements of the design of the Personal Valet misting system.

The experiences IDEO gains from clients in so many different industries are the experiences of the designers as they work on projects in these different worlds. There's no guarantee that just because IDEO worked elsewhere before, the ideas the firm learned from that project can be applied to another project where they might produce a dramatic innovation. The network position simply gives IDEO access to many different technologies and the objects, ideas, and people that they represent.

It does a large corporation little good to work in different industries if it cannot move and recombine the ideas, objects, and people it finds in one that might be valuable in another. Sure, top-level executives can back different divisions like so many racehorses, but the synergies available from such a diverse set of experiences are often lost in the process. By the same token, a firm's employees can share everything they know with one another, but if all they know are the same customers, the same products, and the same manufacturing practices, then those interactions lose much of their value. In these cases, a strong organizational memory can be a detriment because it traps firms in the past. But if a firm can move easily among worlds, and in doing so can recognize how the problems it faces today resemble problems it has seen solved somewhere else before and can bring those solutions forward, then innovation can happen.

IDEO makes its network position work because its organizational structure, work practices, and culture all support the brokering process. IDEO, Edison, Design Continuum, Elmer Sperry, and others that have pursued dedicated strategies as technology brokers all share a set of underlying organizing principles that enable them to exploit their brokerage position. These principles are inextricably bound to a strategy of technology brokering and are explored in the following sections.

A Fluid Structure

The structure of work in technology brokering firms plays a critical role in such firms' overall innovation strategy. For starters, the traditional bureaucratic hierarchy is practically nonexistent. At places like IDEO, there might be a handful of "managers" who work together to assign individuals to projects. But even these managers spend time on projects, often taking on engineering or design work to "keep their hands dirty."

For technology brokers, the focus is on the work—on solving the problems of current projects and clients and on getting new projects lined up. Spending time and energy building—and then complaining about—a hierarchy doesn't do these firms much good because they don't know what kind of work, in which kind of world, they will be facing on the next project. That doesn't mean there is no hierarchy at IDEO, for example, or at Edison's Menlo Park lab. Even without a formal hierarchy, everyone still knows who the best designers are, who the best project leads are, where to turn for help, and who the ultimate boss is. What it does mean is that none of these is set in stone.

As in Hollywood, everybody is only as good as his or her last project. Nobody has a fixed position to strive for or defend; nobody has control over critical organizational resources. But that doesn't mean there is no authority or advancement. Just getting rid of job titles and corner offices isn't enough, because people find other ways to measure success. It's human nature to compete, even in the most collaborative of environments (people just end up competing on how collaborative they are). Being first among equals is a powerful goal. The flat structure of IDEO or Design Continuum or even Edison's lab is a natural fallout of the structure of the work these entities do and how they organize to do it, not a cause of their success.

Rather than flat, think fluid. Technology brokers have a flat structure because that's the way it averages out over time, not because that's the way it always is. For each project at IDEO, for example, there is a clear project manager, a clear boss (the client), and clear roles for everyone on the team. But on the next project, the old manager might now be working for someone she managed the last time. And depending on the nature of the problem, the client, and the industry, different engineers or designers become the experts. For a project on haircutting, an engineer's agricultural background of growing up around harvesting machines is an interesting but peripheral perspective to bring into the team. But for the next project, redesigning a tractor cockpit, he takes a more central role in the work.

Technology brokers constantly face new challenges in new worlds, and they tailor each project team to face those challenges. When that project is over, they reshuffle teams and offices. These firms can do this because the nature of the work, as a continual flow of new problems and solutions, differs dramatically from what more traditional firms see. Reshuffle the job assignments once too often at more traditional firms and it will feel like everyone is starting from scratch. That's because most organizations must structure around stable processes of designing, manufacturing, selling, and supporting a relatively unchanging (albeit ever-improving) set of technologies to solve for a limited set of existing problems. Sure, some interesting insights might come from a reshuffling exercise, but the costs to the company's short-term efficiency and focus can be devastating.

Within technology brokers, individuals work on a range of problems in a range of different industries, often moving to another industry after only a single project. Teams form and disband around individual projects, often pulling in additional members for brainstorming sessions or short bursts of effort. The teams are often small, averaging from two to seven people and changing in size over time depending on the demands of the project. This movement of people on and off teams benefits projects because it allows teams to draw on the unique experiences and knowledge of members of the firm as they are needed, without drawing them away from other projects.

Sean Corcorran, a studio manager at IDEO, has deliberately pushed the boundaries of this fluid structure with an initiative called "the 15-minute move." When his studio was moving into a new office space, a converted auto repair shop in downtown Palo Alto, he challenged the engineers and designers to come up with office furniture and a layout that could be broken down and completely reassembled in fifteen minutes. The offices had to remain the personal territories of the individuals working in them, but had to be relocatable about the space to keep up with the changing structures of each new project team. Their solution: Embed more power, network, and phone connections in the floor than necessary so that the studio staff can reconfigure the space at will; put all furniture on wheels so that everyone's stuff moves without having to box (or unbox) everything; and design and build desk-mounted privacy screens and storage systems that don't get in the way of moving quickly. To completely change traditional office spaces takes days, if not weeks, of downtime. Although Sean Corcorran's group hasn't broken fifteen minutes yet, they've trimmed the process to under ninety minutes—that's simply a long lunch break.

This kind of fluid structure—organizing around projects as they come up, and reorganizing quickly around the next—is more than a nice tool for managers. By frequently and easily migrating between projects, people develop varied experiences that reflect the varied projects that technology brokers engage in. "As a designer, you love variety," one project manager at IDEO explained. "Not having to do the same thing for years on end keeps you fresh and it makes you more confident that you can use something you learned in this area and move from there." At IDEO, it's rare for individuals to remain working within any one industry for more than one or two projects. As teams often disband completely after one project, it is easy for individuals to move from one industry to another. People often can work on more than one project, if the demands of each are not enough to occupy them full time or if their particular skills are needed in more than one project. This movement, while reflecting a fluid structure, provides individuals with a wide range of experiences.

The constant flow of people and new projects also builds dense networks among people across the company and helps them to learn about each other's distinct knowledge and skills. These contacts become part of each employee's personal network that others can turn to when they face a problem in the future. Sometimes teams are often deliberately drawn from across multiple offices to ensure that they will have the widest possible range of personal networks to draw on, because each team member's personal network typically covers much of his or her office.

The fluid structure of work in technology brokering firms supports innovation because it exposes the firm's members to a continual flow of new problems requiring novel solutions. When they find a potential opportunity, technology brokers quickly build a group or organization around it that can focus on pursuing particular ideas in single markets. Some, like Edison, spin off these new organizations, like electric light, the use of magnets in iron mining, the phonograph, and electric railroads. Others, like IDEO, build more loosely connected relationships between themselves and their broad network of suppliers and manufacturers. When Palm hired IDEO to design the Palm V, both firms recognized the valuable role that useful accessories—protective cases and stylus pens—would play in making the product a success. They designed these accessories to complement the Palm V and, using vendors they had worked with before, contracted to have them built and supplied right alongside the Palm. Like the networked environment outside, technology brokers are constantly bridging potential barriers between projects and between individuals within the firm, building new groups around each new project they face.

Work Practices

Technology brokers have discovered how to bridge the disparate worlds they move among outside their boundaries, and how to build new ventures from the technologies and people they come across. In the process, they have developed four intertwined work practices that help them do this: capturing good ideas, keeping ideas alive, imagining new uses for old ideas, and putting promising concepts to the test. Although the markets and settings of different brokers are diverse, their approaches are not. Indeed, the four intertwined processes are remarkably alike across companies and industries.

Capturing Good Ideas   The first step is to bring in promising ideas. Because technology brokers span multiple markets, industries, and geographic locations, they keep seeing proven technologies, products, business practices, and business models. Brokers recognize that these old ideas are their main source of raw material for new ideas, even when they are not sure how an old idea might help in the future. When brokers come across a promising idea, they don't just file it away. They play with it in their minds—and when possible with their hands—to figure out how and why it works, to learn what is good and bad about it, and to start spinning fantasies about new ways to use it.

Designers at IDEO, for example, seem obsessed with learning about materials and products they have no immediate use for. At lunch one day, Professor Robert Sutton and I watched two engineers take apart the napkin container to look at the springs inside. Another time, we brought a new digital camera to a brainstorming session, and the meeting was delayed for ten minutes while engineers took apart our new toy to see how it was designed and manufactured. IDEO designers visit the local Palo Alto hardware store to see new products and remind themselves of old ideas, and they take field trips to places such as the Barbie Hall of Fame, an airplane junkyard, and a competition where custom-built robots fight to the death.

Technology brokers capture even more ideas from doing focused work on specific problems, especially when studying new industries or visiting new locations. Each new project offers lessons. Recall Thomas Edison's instructions about how to start a new project: "1st. Study the present construction. 2nd. Ask for all past experiences . . . study and read everything you can on the subject."[5] Today, firms like IDEO and Design Continuum do pretty much the same thing when they're trying to come up with new designs. They collect related products and writings on those products, and—perhaps most important—they observe users. When Design Continuum was hired to improve the tools and techniques used in knee surgery, its engineers went to a convention for surgeons, where they had the doctors re-create the surgical process in a way that allowed the engineers to watch and talk with users. One of the engineers described the scene:

> We wanted to observe the procedures, so we had a cadaver
> lab, which was actually in a swank hotel. One room was the
> lecture room and the other held twelve cadavers. They had
> the room chilled down to 50 degrees, had the cadavers in
> there and had a guard twenty-four hours a day making sure
> nobody accidentally walked in. We just wanted to see how
> doctors used the tools, the little blocks and stuff they use for
> doing the procedures.

The result? Designers noticed that surgeons had developed elaborate habits to make up for what one engineer described as the "missing third arm"; this inspired them to develop a new surgical tool that allowed doctors to hold, rotate, and operate on the kneecap.

Similarly, when Design Continuum was asked to develop an innovative kitchen faucet for a client that had been producing products in the industry for decades, it undertook a massive benchmarking exercise in order to learn not just about kitchen faucet valves, but also about valves used in automobiles, medical products, and toys. The final design, drawing on many of those ideas, was for a pullout faucet that housed an integrated filter and circuitry to track filter life. The faucet delighted the client, whose engineers had assumed, after many years in the business, that they knew everything there was to know about valves.

All of this curiosity means that technology brokers create massive collections of ideas. Some will lead to innovations; some will not. The important thing is that they're there. Edison once said, "To invent, you need a good imagination and a pile of junk."[6]

Keeping Ideas Alive The second step, keeping ideas alive, is crucial because ideas can't be used if they are forgotten. Cognitive psychologists have shown that the biggest hurdle to solving problems often isn't ignorance, it's that people can't put their fingers on the necessary information at the right time even if they've already learned it. Organizational memories are even tougher to maintain. Companies lose what they learn when people leave. Geographic distance, political squabbles, internal competition, and bad incentive systems may hinder the spread of ideas.

The product design firms we studied were particularly good at keeping ideas alive, in part because much of each company's stockpile of ideas is embedded in objects that designers can look at, touch, and play with (it's easier to search through an actual junk pile than a virtual one). IDEO has made a science of accumulating junk. Many designers put plastic parts, toys, prototypes, drawings, and sketches on display in their offices. One engineer, Dennis Boyle, has an amazingly eclectic assortment of items that he constantly talks about and brings to brainstorming meetings to inspire new designs. It includes twenty-three battery-powered toy cars and robots, thirteen plastic hotel keys collected during trips, a flashlight that goes on when the handle is squeezed, an industrial pump, eleven prototypes of a portable computer, fourteen prototypes of a computer docking station, six computers in various stages of disassembly, fifteen binders from past projects, a pile of disk drives, a collection of toothpaste tubes, a toy football with wings, a pair of ski goggles he designed, a Frisbee that flies under water, and dozens of other products and parts. He portrays this collection as "a congealed process—three-dimensional snapshots of the ideas from previous projects."

Building on such collections, IDEO designers have amassed a shared collection of over 400 materials and products in what they call the Tech Box, a set of filing cabinets in each of IDEO's locales that houses many of the cool mechanical and electrical gizmos, ideas, artifacts, and materials that designers run across in their projects: tiny batteries, switches, glow-in-the dark fabric, flexible circuit boards, electric motors, piezoelectric speakers and lights, holographic candy, flexible and resilient hinges, a metal-plated walnut, vacuum-sealed copper pipes with freon inside, a widget from the bottom of a Guinness can that gives the beer a foamy head when you open it, plywood tubes, and flip-flops from Hawaii. It began as part of Dennis Boyle's collection of interesting things, but it became a status game as people in his studio competed to contribute cool new stuff. Every time someone sees something that looks like it might be a valuable solution later on, he or she drops it off at the Tech Box and it gets logged, put on a Web site, and sent to similar Tech Boxes at all the different offices. When a problem comes up in a new project, designers can grab what looks related from the Tech Box and try to find a useful connection.

Just as Dennis Boyle's "knowledge management system" would be useless if he didn't constantly talk about the items and discuss how they might be used, the memories in the Tech Boxes would eventually die if designers didn't constantly look at the stuff, play with it, and use it in their work. Each Tech Box is now maintained by a local curator, and each piece is documented on IDEO's intranet. Designers can find out what each product or material is and who knows most about it inside and outside IDEO. Engineer Christine Kurjan, head curator of IDEO's Tech Boxes, hosts a regular conference call with the local curators in which they talk about new additions and the uses to which items are being put in new projects.

It's harder to keep ideas alive when they're not embedded in tangible objects. The people who design knowledge management systems for large consulting firms like Accenture and McKinsey originally thought that lists of best practices, reports, and PowerPoint presentations would be sufficient. They assumed that consultants would be able to solve problems just by reading through databases. But even at these firms, consultants quickly found that the systems are most useful as annotated Yellow Pages, helping them find out who to talk to about how the knowledge was really used and might be used again. Perceiving a need to link consultants together rather than refer them to stored information, McKinsey created its Rapid Response Team, which promises to link—within twenty-four hours—any consultant facing a problem to others who might have useful knowledge. The team accomplishes this feat largely by knowing who knows what at McKinsey.

Spreading information about who knows what is a powerful way to keep ideas alive. Edison was renowned for his ability to remember how old ideas were used and by whom. The most respected people at IDEO are part pack rat (because they have great private collections of stuff), part librarian (because they know who knows what), and part Good Samaritan (because they go out of their way to share what they know and to help others).

Imagining New Uses for Old Ideas The third set of work practices occurs when people recognize new uses for the ideas they've captured and kept alive. Often those applications are blindingly simple. When Edison's inventors were developing the lightbulb, bulbs kept falling out of their fixtures. One day, a technician wondered whether the threaded cap that could be screwed down so tightly on a kerosene bottle would hold lightbulbs in their sockets. They tried it, it worked, and the design hasn't changed since. Old ideas can become powerful solutions to new problems if brokers are skilled at seeing such analogies.

Design Continuum engineers used analogical thinking to develop the pulsed lavage, the medical product for cleansing wounds with a flow of saline solution described in chapter 4. In thinking about pulsed lavage, the engineers saw connections to battery-powered squirt guns. Once they'd seen these similarities—similarities that would not have occurred to most observers—the engineers could incorporate the squirt gun's inexpensive electric pump and battery into a successful design for a new medical product.

An effective technology broker develops creative answers to hard problems because people within the organization talk a lot about their work and about who might help them do it better. Company-wide gatherings, formal brainstorming sessions, and informal hall-way conversations are just some of the venues where people share their problems and solutions. Gian Zaccai, the CEO of Design Continuum, recognized the power of bringing people together face to face:

> You pick two people, with different experiences and maybe
> even different training and put them together and you've got
> that kind of a synergy, an exchange of ideas. Because what-
> ever this person says will provoke a hundred different ideas in
> this other one and a hundred different memories.[7]

Many brokers also use a physical layout that enables (perhaps *forces* is a better word) such interaction. At the Menlo Park labora-tory in New Jersey, Edison's muckers worked in a single large room: As one put it, "we were all interested in what we were doing and what the others were doing."[8] Bill Gross put his Internet start-up factory, Idealab!, in a 50,000-square-foot, one-story building in Pasadena, California. Although the demise of the Internet boom has led people to question the mania behind so many start-ups, there's no denying Idealab!'s effectiveness in quickly creating new firms around new ideas. Idealab! has few walls, so that everyone is forced to run into everyone else. Bill Gross's office is in the center, with concentric circles around it. The innermost desks are for start-ups in the earliest phases, when new ideas and support from others are most crucial. As businesses grow, they move farther from the center. When they reach a critical mass of around seventy employees, as eToys and CarsDirect.com have done, they leave the incubator for their own buildings.

IDEO's studios are also laid out so that everyone sees and hears everyone else's design problems. Hang out for a while and you will see hundreds of unplanned interactions in which designers overhear nearby conversations, realize they could help, and stop whatever they are doing to make suggestions. One day engineers Larry Shubert and Roby Stancel were designing a device for an electric razor that would vacuum up cut hair. They were meeting at a table in front of Rickson Sun's workstation. He soon shut his sliding door to muffle the noise from the meeting, but he could still hear them. He emerged a few minutes later to say he'd once worked on a similar design problem: a vacuum system for carrying away fumes from a hot scalpel that cauterized skin during surgery. Sun brought out samples of tubing that might be used in the new design and a report he had written about the kinds of plastic tubing available from vendors. The encounter shows how having the right attitude drives people to help each other solve problems. Larry Shubert commented, "Once Rickson realized he could help us, he had to do it, or he wouldn't be a good IDEO designer."

Putting Promising Concepts to the Test A good idea for a new product or business practice isn't worth much by itself. It needs to be turned into something that can be tested and, if successful, integrated into the rest of what a company does, makes, or sells. Quickly turning an imaginative idea into a real service, product, process, or business model is the final step in the brokering cycle. *Real* means concrete enough to be tested; *quickly* means early enough in the process that mistakes can be caught and improvements made. "The real measure of success," Edison said, "is the number of experiments that can be crowded into 24 hours."[9]

Technology brokers are not the only businesses that use prototypes, experiments, simulations, models, and pilot programs to test and refine ideas. The difference is that collecting and generating ideas, and testing them quickly, are more than just some of the things brokers do: They are the main things brokers do.

Brokers must be good at testing ideas, at judging them on merit without letting politics or precedent get in the way. A broker's attitude toward ideas is usually "Easy come, easy go." Brokers treat ideas as inexpensive and easily replaceable playthings that they are supposed to enjoy, understand, push to the limit, break, and change in ways the ideas' inventors never imagined. If an idea seems to solve a current problem, they build on it. If an idea doesn't work out, they look for another. Brokers rarely keep trying to make something work in the face of evidence that it won't. They focus on finding the best ideas for solving problems, not on solutions for which they can claim glory. We could call it the *nothing-is-invented-here attitude*. It means they reach out—early and often—to anyone who might help them solve problems and test ideas. Brokers view the more familiar "not invented here" syndrome—in which people, believing they know more than others in their field, reject all new ideas that come from outside their group—as inefficient, arrogant, and ultimately fatal to innovation.

Almost immediately after thinking of a promising concept, a development team at a place such as IDEO or Design Continuum builds a prototype, shows it to users, tests it, and improves it. The team then repeats the sequence over and over. Prototypes can be anything from crude gadgets to elaborate mock-ups. IDEO designers in the Boston office built a full-size foam model of an Amtrak train to test ideas about seating, layout, and signage. To make more refined prototypes, IDEO's machine shop uses computerized milling machines and other sophisticated tools. IDEO's machinists can take a rough sketch and quickly turn it into a working model.

Putting a concept to the test not only helps determine if it has commercial value, but also teaches brokers lessons they might be able to use later, even when an idea is a complete flop. Brokers benefit from failures, because in learning about why an idea failed, they get hints about other problems the idea might solve someday. Recall Edison's efforts to design a new telegraph cable that would span the

Atlantic Ocean. His engineers' experience with carbon putty as a failed electrical insulation proved invaluable a few years later in another application, the inexpensive, effective, and reliable microphone that helped make the telephone commercially feasible.

Culture

Culture represents the shared rules, both implicit and explicit, that shape the behaviors and experiences of individuals within a firm. Culture has a profound effect on innovation via the value it places on tradition versus change, the stigma that is associated with ignorance and failure, the role of competition versus collaboration, and the value placed on invention versus using old ideas.

The culture of technology brokers supports the structure and work practices within these organizations by creating a shared sense of purpose and process. Individuals are motivated to learn as much as they can about each new industry they enter because they share the value placed on learning about things that others might not have seen before. They are willing to help people working on different projects—for an hour, a day, or a month—because they recognize that's how it's done in their community. And they ask for help from the rest of the organization, even when it means admitting ignorance and failure, because they are more interested in finding the best existing ideas than in demonstrating their ability to invent new ones.

In many firms, these kinds of behaviors can derail an individual's project and even career. To admit that a major problem exists often means giving ammunition to rival teams and managers for why they should have your budget, headcount, or promotion. One engineer at IDEO described how, when he arrived at IDEO, he learned to draw upon the ideas of others in the organization:

> Where I worked before, you just didn't ask for help. It was a
> sign of weakness. . . . [At IDEO] we don't have time to screw
> around. At the first hint I don't know something, I'll ask

> "Does anyone know about this?" The whole thing here is
> you've got to leverage as much as possible. You ask for help—
> you are expected to ask for help here.

Similarly, an engineer at Design Continuum compared her experiences there to her previous experiences in a large corporation:

> It's freely joked about here that you'll never get it right the first
> time, freely joked about all the time: "Oh so what went wrong?"
> or, "How long were you here this weekend fixing it?"—that sort
> of thing. In the corporate world they're working on the same
> product all the time and they just don't realize that things can go
> wrong [when you try something new]. I think that's what you
> learn as an engineer here: *you have to fail your way to success.*

In technology brokering firms, sharing problems and admitting failures isn't just accepted, it's expected. You can even get into trouble if you don't. At IDEO, for example, as long as you've gotten the best minds of the company to look at your problem, failing isn't a problem. Fail alone, however, and you get little sympathy.

This culture reflects the willingness of members to seek help from others and to share their own ideas, and can best be summarized as an "attitude of wisdom."[10] People who have an attitude of wisdom are cooperative because they are neither too arrogant nor too insecure to ask others for help. At IDEO the attitude of wisdom encourages designers to communicate the problems they face or offer past solutions with potential value to these new problems, providing a comfortable environment for individual designers to act as technology brokers. A senior designer described this attitude:

> We are all very smart people, but given the complexity and con-
> stant trade-offs associated with the design process, brilliance
> comes from the minds of lots of smart people rather than the
> actions of one brilliant designer. A true genius wouldn't be
> happy here. But I don't know if they exist. I have never met
> one smart enough to consider all of those variables at once.

By actively seeking ideas, both outside the firm and within, people demonstrate they are humble enough to accept other people's ideas and at the same time confident enough to seek them out, especially when this requires a tacit admission of their own ignorance. When engineers call a brainstorming meeting at IDEO, they are admitting they have a problem and believe others can help them. And yet they are gaining the respect of their peers, who in the process become familiar with the difficulty of their project.

A strategy of technology brokering encourages the attitude of wisdom because of the flow of new objects, ideas, and people that technology brokers are continually exposed to. A Design Continuum project manager described the values that come from their movement among so many small worlds:

> The variety teaches you the perspective of looking around and not staying focused on your industry and the cards that you're dealt in this game. And you have that different perspective partially through the experience of just being exposed to all different kinds of programs directly but also just getting in the habit of doing that. You can see that you need to apply other manufacturing processes to places that have never heard of them.

That freedom comes because technology brokering changes more than just *what* people know—the process also changes the way people think about what they know. Deep expertise is both a blessing and a curse.

W. B. Cannon, writing in "The Role of Chance in Discovery," reminds us that there is a deeper level to Pasteur's dictum that chance favors the prepared mind:

> There is another implication in Pasteur's dictum . . . that is the importance of avoiding rigid adherence to fixed ideas. It is quite natural for the uninstructed intelligence to find a comfortable security and serenity in a set of conventional opinions which have been satisfactorily prearranged. The

> unusual is promptly dismissed because it is not wanted; it does not conform to the preconceived plan. The possibility of adventures in ideas is unknown to such benighted persons.[11]

Wisdom is not about what you know, but how you know it. If knowledge is a measure of the grasp an individual has of a given subject, wisdom is a measure of his grip. Does he hold his ideas tightly or loosely? Will he let go when they show signs of wear or inappropriateness? There is, in legend at least, a famous Balinese monkey trap made of rope and a coconut with a small hole and a shiny spoon inside. The hole is large enough to fit a monkey's hand, but too small for its fist around the spoon. The trap works because the monkey, after reaching in to grab the spoon, refuses to release his grip on what is finally in his grasp.

Much of what holds back incumbent firms and individuals is their inability to give up the knowledge they have spent so much time acquiring in their worlds, or to consider the vast reservoir of ideas that reside in other worlds. To people who have spent twenty years of their life designing surgical instruments, the idea that a super soaker squirt gun has just as much to contribute to their work runs up against the firm grasp with which people come to hold their own expertise.

Technology brokers slowly acquire the attitude of wisdom because they are forever discovering new ideas in other worlds. For someone like Jim Yurchenco, one of the original engineers at IDEO, moving among worlds creates a toolbox filled with tools, but with all the labels taken off about how they *should* be used.

Managing Technology Brokers

The chicken-and-egg dilemma for firms pursuing strategies of technology brokering thus returns. To be effective, technology brokering requires a structure, set of practices, and culture that bring together people with a wide variety of experiences and encourage them to figure out how what they know might help others. But for these organizational features to work as an effective innovation strategy requires a network position across different worlds. The movement among many small worlds is what gives technology brokers, and in reality the people who work within these firms, the wide-ranging experiences that make them willing and able to search for distant connections.

As I've said before, you can have all the beer-busts, staff meetings, communities-of-practice leaders, intranets, knowledge databases, and free sodas you can afford, but if the variety of experiences isn't there, all these management techniques won't make people creative. And if the problem at hand is the same one the group, division, or organization faced in the last project, what makes you think the group will come up with anything different this time?

In short, the structure, work practices, and culture of technology brokers combine to create an internal marketplace where individuals get ahead by thinking like technology brokers themselves. Individual designers and engineers at IDEO, for example, recognize the value of their own differences—what they know that others in the organization do not. As one once remarked, "If somebody else walks into the meeting with a coffee mug like yours, it's time to find another one." Within technology brokers, everyone feels pressure to conform, but it's a conformity to *dis*conformity. Everyone is valuable to the firm to the extent that he or she brings in new ideas from the outside. And everyone is valuable to the extent that he or she can draw on these diverse ideas to build new combinations of objects, ideas, and people into successful ventures.

Technology brokers create these internal markets through their structure, by continually injecting new market needs (and new technologies) into the organization through projects with multiple clients and by continually shifting people across project teams. They do this through their work practices, by bringing people together from across the organization to work on each new problem. And they do this through their culture, by creating a world in which borrowing good ideas is more valued than inventing them, in which harvesting ideas from across the organization is even better than coming up with them alone, and in which sharing ideas gets people more credit than withholding them.

. . .

This chapter described the strategies used by firms that organize solely around the process of technology brokering. For these firms, the pursuit of innovation is not a deviation from their everyday routines but rather the singular purpose and organizing principle behind their survival. Although such technology brokers are rare, there is much they can teach us about how they have linked their innovation strategies to their structure, work practices, and culture.

A dedicated technology brokering strategy bridges small worlds, exploiting a position between worlds to combine existing objects, ideas, and people in new ways that promise new ventures, and building the necessary communities around these new ventures that will ensure their success. Such a strategy works because these firms are continuously moving into new worlds. This innovation strategy, together with their organizational structures and work practices, creates an internal marketplace of ideas and a culture of wisdom where new ideas and artifacts can move around freely and each person's contributions can quickly take on new value for each new problem the organization faces.

Technology brokering without these structures, practices, and culture won't work any more than these structures, practices, and culture will work without moving among multiple worlds. However, not all firms can dedicate themselves to the continuous pursuit of innovation. For the rest of us, it's more important to recognize when and where we can create groups within large organizations that can pursue technology brokering strategies full time, or to recognize when to create communities around new recombinant innovations when opportunities emerge. The next two chapters consider these challenges.

8

Technology Brokering Within the Firm

Read most of the writing on strategy and you will come away with the idea that firms are single, cohesive, and coherent players in the competitive landscape. It's an appealing image. After all, the combined resources of an entire firm can be quite powerful. Such large firms as IBM, Hewlett-Packard, Motorola, and Boeing work in many different industries. They see the ideas, objects, and people in each one, and they see the problems—and market opportunities—as well. Imagine what these firms could do if all their people could share these experiences, and if they could find and exploit the many potential synergies among their different technologies and different market segments.

And yet the saying "If HP only knew what HP knew" is so accurate that I've heard it used in countless firms. I doubt anyone would deny it applies to their firm as well. Talk to anyone in large companies, from the CEO down to the project manager, and they will admit that their firm is anything but cohesive. Organizations are their own fragmented landscapes, broken into the many small worlds of their divisions, groups, and teams.

To everyone but the top dog, firms *are* the competitive land-scape—that's where competitors are easily identifiable as they fight for promotions, for headcount, for budgets. You'll never hear that in the official party line, though. In fact, most strategies are built on the assumption that once a clear vision is put forth, everyone will pull together, selflessly pooling their resources for the common good of the company. That rarely happens. People don't get promoted for losing focus on their own markets or for pulling resources away from their own projects in support of the overarching vision. Not in today's world, where profit and loss are accounted for at the divisional level and where every project has to promise a return on investment in just a few years.

One executive, a midlevel project manager in a high-technology firm, captured the contradiction better than I ever could. After a seminar on managing product development projects, he wrote to me about the gap between his organization's innovation strategy and its culture:

> Our organization's main strategy promotes and encourages interaction among divisional groups to facilitate communications and to learn from and help each other.... However, in reality our culture over the years has instilled the beliefs of independence, taking the initiative, and being self-deterministic. ...At the functional manager level, helping is seen as "collaborating with the competition" and considered a contemptible act. The manager's and group's focus is on making themselves look good, not such a bad thing, but at the same time hoping the other groups and divisions looked bad.

Does this sound familiar? It does to me. When I was designing products at Apple, there was the competition out there—the Dells, Compaqs, HPs—and there was the competition down the hall: the other engineers vying for project management responsibilities, the other managers vying for budget and headcount, the other project teams vying for competing technical choices, and the division heads fighting desperately for their share of the revenue while resisting, equally desperately, their share of the overhead. Who can blame them? That's how everyone gets measured. But more important, who is to say that it is the wrong approach? In fact, it's the right one.

Given the speed with which new technologies emerge and old ones fade away, and with which new competitors appear and established firms crumple, firms need managers who can focus on developing the particular markets and technologies needed for success. It's unrealistic to expect that the same people who can compete so ruthlessly in the market will turn around and blithely give it all away to others inside the firm. You can't turn a large organization into one happy family any more than you can turn a large family into one. In modern organizations, no amount of memos, moving speeches, and off-site seminars on the virtues of knowledge sharing is likely to overcome the values of individuality and independence that pit one person against the other and one department against the other. So what should one do?

Embrace the differences. The focus that each manager, each division, each group brings to its unique situation is what powers the short-term growth of the company. Mess with that and you're messing with the pistons of a car already moving at sixty miles per hour. Even more, their focus creates the kinds of small worlds in which valuable new technologies emerge and develop. In the paradox that is innovation, the fragmented groups within large companies become the sources of new ideas in other groups. While the problem remains getting potentially valuable ideas out of their different small worlds and across the organization, it's important not to lose sight of the sources of those ideas.

From a perspective of recombinant innovation, large firms often have vast amounts of untapped potential. Once new combinations are identified, it can be easier for managers to shift resources around inside the firm to build the new ties in the organizational network that pull together the necessary resources—easier, at least, then trying to align the interests and actions of investors, suppliers, and others in the marketplace.

But the trick remains recognizing these opportunities for recombination. Think of each division within a large firm in the same way as we thought about industries earlier, as bundles of resources and market opportunities. Each division is, one hopes, doing a good job applying its existing combinations of ideas, objects, and people to solving the needs of a particular market. But that leaves the outer areas untapped. These are the regions where resources in one small world could potentially solve the problems of another. And it's not just the resources that these divisions are using now—it's also the ones they have seen in their markets, the ones they have experimented with but put aside, and the ones that, to them at least, are failed experiments.

For example, take the story of Duco, DuPont's revolutionary paint that brought color to the automotive world. Many people have heard the famous phrase uttered by Henry Ford, "They can have any color they want, so long as it's black." Most of the time, it's used to explain Ford's dogged pursuit of economies of scale with the Model T: one car, one color. But Ford was simply stating the obvious. Back then, there was no easy way to paint automobiles; to get the same durable finish in any color other than black took weeks of hand-painting. Then, in 1923, along came Duco, a sprayable lacquer that offered a range of colors. The story of how DuPont scientists developed Duco is a story of how ideas—indeed, wrong ones—in one corner of the organization became revolutions in another.

DuPont began when Eleuthère Irénée du Pont de Nemours (E. I. DuPont) left France in 1802 for Delaware, establishing the Eleutherian Mills to manufacture and sell gunpowder. By 1811, DuPont was the largest maker of gunpowder in America. For DuPont, the nineteenth century was a story of its dominance in the explosives industries. In 1902, though, control of the family business went to three of Eleuthère's grandsons, who decided to take the company in new directions. The company's extensive knowledge of cellulose chemistry, fundamental to explosives, was beginning to show signs of value in other uses and other industries. Nitrocellulose, the combination of nitric acid and cotton or wood pulp, made smokeless powder. But when mixed with ether and alcohol, it also created a nonexplosive solution that hardened into film. Over the next several decades, DuPont scientists worked to develop applications for this material across a range of industries.

In 1920, in DuPont's Redpath Laboratory in Parlin, New Jersey, scientists were working to develop a new photographic film using nitrocellulose.[1] They came back on a Monday to discover that the solution they had been working with on Friday had hardened. It was relatively useless as photographic film, but they experimented with it further nonetheless. Finding that the solution could take color easily, they realized they had stumbled onto a potentially valuable solution to the problem of developing a color lacquer for cars. They worked closely with engineers from General Motors to refine this product into a useful automotive lacquer, and the results appeared on GM's Oakland models, released in 1923. The time required to paint cars in color dropped from two weeks to two days. Had the scientists assigned to improving photographic film tossed out their failed experiment—after all, it was useless in that industry—DuPont might never have developed Duco.

Business history is rife with such serendipitous recombinations. Recall the story of 3M's Post-it Notes, in which a poorly performing adhesive became valuable by finding other uses for it. Or of Pfizer's Viagra, which failed in clinical trials as a cardiovascular medicine; when patients resisted returning their samples, however, researchers realized the unexpected use for the drug. Even Edison's phonograph had similar origins. In an attempt to develop a telegraph recorder, Edison recognized in the scratchy drag of a needle across a spinning cylinder the possibilities of the phonograph.

But these recombinations can happen regularly as well—they can become part of the overall innovation strategy of the firm. Hewlett-Packard dominates the personal computer printer business in part because it spent much of the 1980s and 1990s building expertise in laser printers, inkjet devices, and pen plotters. It moved the resources it developed in each of these markets—the ideas, objects, and even people—into the others: sometimes willingly, sometimes competitively. But in the process, the company continues to improve its expertise in each. Right now, it is poised to take on the much larger professional printing markets, bringing what it has learned with it.

Although the company's success in printing continues, Hewlett-Packard may have killed a golden goose in 1999 when Lew Platt, then CEO, split the company in two. Hewlett-Packard would focus on computers and imaging, while Agilent would focus on test and measurement devices.

"We are taking this action to sharpen the strategic focus of our businesses, improve their agility and increase their responsiveness to customers and partners," Lew Platt explained. "This will offer exciting opportunities for our employees and will enhance the two new companies' growth and earnings potential."[2]

But there were hidden costs. Hewlett-Packard was a company that had grown from two young engineers making oscilloscopes into a multidivisional powerhouse through what came to be known as "next-bench" engineering. Engineers would develop products based on the needs of the engineers working at the next bench. If you can't measure something, design a new measuring device. If you can't design it, develop a new CAD system. As digital technologies diffused into other industries, Hewlett-Packard moved there too. Soon it had profitable businesses in medical monitoring systems, computing, test and measurement, and communications.

In 1994, Lew Platt recognized the advantages this diversity of experiences gave HP. In his annual report to shareholders that year, he noted:

> We have a terrific advantage when we combine our areas of
> expertise. A lot of innovative solutions are coming from HP
> in telecommunications and in the medical business because
> of the combined strengths of HP's computing, communica-
> tions, and measurement business.

Splitting Hewlett-Packard and Agilent in 1999 was a good way for the stock market to put dollar values on what were becoming very different businesses: the overinflated computer industry and the more mundane (but potentially more cutting-edge) work in testing and measurement. The process, however, took a company well positioned to recombine its resources across divisions in new ways for new markets and severed the ties between these divisions.

One Big Happy Family

The holy grail of knowledge management efforts seems to be a system in which everyone's knowledge is available all the time to everyone else in the organization. The idea is of a big happy family where everyone is involved in, and supportive of, everyone else's work. People are willing to drop what they are doing to see if they can lend a hand. It's not a bad idea. The reasoning behind it is sound—it's frustrating knowing that you are working on a problem that someone, somewhere in the company, has already solved. It will take you days, but might take him or her five minutes. One manager in an engineering group made this plain:

> There are cases where the person who has the knowledge is sitting right next to you and it goes unnoticed and you plow a lot of ground you didn't necessarily have to. There's still a lot duplication of effort. There just isn't any way that I know of to make all knowledge that has ever been done on something available to the person at the time in which they need it. It's all a matter of getting the right knowledge into the right hands at the right time.

It *is* all a matter of getting the right knowledge into the right hands at the right time. But the danger behind most traditional knowledge management efforts is that they might succeed. Imagine a company where everyone helps everyone else. Who's doing the work?

Frederick Brooks, writing about the realities of software development, introduced into organizations the now famous equation about networks, namely, that for every person you add to the network, the number of interactions everyone must attend to increases as $n(n-1)/2$. Three people have three times as many relationships to attend to as two; four people have six times as many. Brooks used this reality of networks to question the mythical man-month as a way of measuring labor in product development. Brooks's law is that "Adding manpower to a late software project makes it later."[3] The same could be said for trying to connect everyone in the organization into one big brain: Adding more people to the knowledge management effort only makes the firm dumber. The more time and attention people devote to sharing what they already know, the less they focus on performing their own jobs and the less time they spend developing the ideas, objects, and people that help them in those jobs.

You might counter with the notion that information technology is the answer. Information technology captures everyone's knowledge in a central database, where people can access it without bothering anyone else. But these systems are only as good as the information that gets entered. It takes time and energy to record all the learning that happened on a single project, let alone a decade of experiences within a particular market or with a particular technology. Worse, there's no guarantee that what you find valuable will ever see the light of day. It's like prerecording your half of a conversation. Further, databases are good at storing answers when the questions are known in advance, but creativity has been defined as what you do when you don't know what to do. In these cases, people often don't even know the right questions to ask. This is why Picasso once said, "Computers are useless; they only give you answers."

In short, trying to bring everyone together, in person or in databases, is not the answer. People need to focus on their work, and for most of the firm, that work entails building and maintaining strong ties within its market—staying close to a few key suppliers, customers, regulators, and competitors. These are the differences in focus that develop deep expertise in existing technologies and deep understandings of the needs of a particular market. This expertise and understanding is the raw material of new innovations, and needs to be supported. Effective innovation strategies that attempt to recombine the organization's existing technologies in new ways need to exploit those differences without undermining them.

Internal Technology Brokers

For the most part, organizations discover the innovative potential that comes from recombinations of their existing resources through size and serendipity. Serendipity is the gift of making useful discoveries by accident. Size simply brings more ideas, objects, and people into the organizational mix, increasing the odds that accidental combinations will happen. But serendipity and size are not advantages on which you want to rely.

Some firms have built strategies around the pursuit of recombinant innovation. These firms do so in the same ways that Edison built his Menlo Park lab, or IDEO built its consulting firm—by bridging the many small worlds of their landscape, and building new combinations of the ideas, objects, and people they found there. In essence, they built internal technology brokers: groups that moved relatively freely between the different divisions within large organizations, recognizing how ideas in one group could be used in others.

These internal technology brokers are not central research labs, where Ph.D.'s wander the halls inventing the future. Stories such as the origin of DuPont's Duco suggest that this is where the action is, but the picture is not true. Duco was serendipity illustrated. Most R&D labs have a five- to ten-year horizon: They look at where the firm could be, not where it is. Technology brokers, on the other hand, don't invent. Internal technology brokers, like their counterparts in the wild, are more interested in redistributing the future that is already here. For them, the action is on the factory floor, in the engineering war rooms, and with the marketing groups of the different divisions, because that's where the new ideas, the new products and processes, and the new understandings about the market are being honed.

How can one tell the difference between research labs and internal technology brokers? The most important difference involves where the learning takes place. Does it come from basic science or from the field? Are the answers commercially valuable today or five years from now, assuming another round of research funding? Both kinds of research are necessary, but it's important not to confuse the two. One is a process of invention, of science feeding technology. The other is a process of recombination, of the best (and sometimes worst) practices of one division feeding others.

The trick is recognizing when a technology brokering group can be built, and knowing what resources the group needs. Often it starts when a small group in one corner of the organization develops a technology that seems promising beyond its limited market. Those closest to the technology will know this better than anyone else, because they are intimately aware of the untapped potential, the limitations, and the possibilities of the emerging technology. But the critical step is separating these people and their work from the demands of their existing market, changing their focus from the relentless push to dominate a single industry to a relentless push to get into many different ones.

Consider a tale of two centers: Xerox's Palo Alto Research Center (PARC) and 3M's Optical Technology Center (OTC). Their histories are similar, but their differences are revealing.

Xerox PARC

Xerox started out in 1906 as the Haloid Company, a maker of photography paper. In 1947, it bought xerography technology, a means of making dry copies (replacing the mimeograph machine first developed by Thomas Edison), eventually changing its name to Xerox to reflect the success of this technology. Today, it has around $17 billion in revenues and is still one of the leading document processing companies in the world.

In the late 1960s, the digital future was dawning. Xerox, wanting to take advantage of the emerging digital technologies, formed the Palo Alto Research Center, which was given the charter of creating the "architecture of information."

PARC's research output was astonishing. It is credited with developing the first personal computer, the Alto; the concept of personal distributed computing; the graphical user interface (adopted by Apple for the Macintosh in 1984 and by Microsoft as Windows a decade later); the first commercial mouse; Ethernet; client/server architecture; object-oriented programming; laser printing; and many of the basic protocols of the Internet. And yet Xerox has become famous for "fumbling the future" by failing to adopt and market any of PARC's ideas.[4] The ideas, objects, and people of Xerox PARC contributed to the commercial success of many flagship companies of the computer age: Apple, Microsoft, 3Com, Hewlett-Packard, Digital Equipment Corporation, Adobe. Xerox's failure to capitalize on the impressive output of the PARC researchers may stem from PARC's charter: Creating the architecture of information is a lofty goal. Such a charter carries with it responsibility for inventing a distant future.

PARC's work was truly visionary, but visions take a long time to develop. And as discussed in chapter 5, they take a committed group of people dedicated to building the necessary networks around the emerging idea. PARC succeeded in generating ideas, but failed to build the needed community and commitment for them inside Xerox. That's why many of PARC's ideas succeeded outside Xerox, where small groups of individuals could put the right pieces together and slowly build new markets around them. Could this have happened with PARC inside Xerox? Maybe. To see how, let's turn to another internal group within a large firm, a group that took a different approach to the innovation process.

3M's Optical Technology Center

Minnesota Mining and Manufacturing, 3M, was founded in 1902 (four years before the Haloid Company), by five businessmen in Twin Harbors, Minnesota, to mine what they thought was corundum, a low-cost abrasive ideal for making sandpaper. They were wrong about the mineral, which turned out to be something else, so the company moved to Duluth, making sandpaper but buying abrasives from another source. The company moved from sandpaper to adhesive tape and continued to diversify into a wide range of industrial and commercial products. Today, it is a $16 billion company with more than forty business units in industries and markets all over the world, from industrial products to consumer goods and from health care to electronics.

3M is known for its innovative capabilities. It is famous for its commitment to individual innovation—expecting scientists and engineers to spend 15 percent of their time on discretionary projects, exploration, and experimentation. The intent is to tap into its collection of talented individuals, giving them the support to invent the next great thing for 3M. The success of Post-it Notes celebrates and perpetuates the belief that this management style, focused on the individual as inventor, is what fuels 3M's growth. But there are other ways in which 3M has managed to innovate, and perhaps more effectively establish a practice of continuous innovation, than by hoping for more great individuals and their inventions.

In 1960, Roger Appeldorn began work at 3M as a lab assistant in the Thermo-Fax Department, working on thermographic imaging technologies. There he discovered a way to disrupt the surface of a transparent film by heating it locally. The disrupted areas displayed a unique property, appearing white but, when projected, providing a black image. His process had restructured the surface of the film and, as Appeldorn said, "You can change the other physical properties dramatically when you change the surface of something."[5]

The first 3M application of this new process was in the development of a low-cost overhead lens projector. In this case it was the layer of transparent film on the platen of the overhead lens projector, now ubiquitous in classrooms and corporate meetings alike. This film was designed to change the direction of the light coming from the bulb beneath the platen (and image), bending it up toward the overhead lens that projects the image on the screen. This first use for engineering the surface structure of a plastic film was based on ideas used in the Fresnel lens, a lens design built in 1819 that revolutionized the efficiency (and effective range) of lighthouses. The Fresnel lens (pronounced Fruh-nell) took the scattered light coming from a single lamp and refracted it out to sea in a concentrated horizontal beam. The traditional lamp design projected roughly 40 percent of its light out to sea. Using a set of concentric lenses, Fresnel was able to capture and redirect more of the lamplight, doubling efficiency to 80 percent.[6]

3M's engineers wanted to capture the light coming from a single projector lamp and redirect it toward the overhead lens, an identical problem. But rather than the large glass prisms of the original Fresnel lenses, the engineers at 3M figured out a way to make this design on a thin film of plastic, creating a thousand tiny geometric prisms on the surface of the plastic and laminating it onto the glass platen. This technology was called *microreplication*. Over time, the engineers came to realize it could have broader applications. "That was a profound realization," Appeldorn explained. "Because all 3M products have surfaces, microreplication had the potential to add something to all of them."[7]

The next use of microreplication involved optics again. Putting the Fresnel lens on traffic signals created a narrower beam, making it easier for motorists to recognize which lane the light was intended to control. In one lane, the light was sharp; in the other, it was now diffuse. Another application was in the development of reflective material for traffic signs. This technology, laminated onto a plastic sheeting, made possible lane lines that reflected more light back to the driver and traffic signs that were visible from a far greater distance. Here the surface features were cube corners, which were substantially better at reflecting the beam coming from a low angle, such as from a car's headlights or a road sign.

What makes the story of microreplication and of how 3M decided to capitalize on it so important is the company's recognition that, in microreplication, the future of 3M was already there—it was just unevenly distributed. By 1981, Roger Appeldorn was running a small business unit at 3M, responsible for its own P&L, involving the uses of microreplicated lenses in lighting systems. He knew there were other applications across 3M that could use microreplication, but with his unit's aging equipment and small markets, he couldn't justify investing in this untapped potential everywhere else (and for everyone else's markets).[8] As is the case for innovative ideas in many large companies, this could have been the end of the story. There is little incentive for people in one corner of the organization to invest time, energy, and considerable capital in order to make their ideas work for someone else's markets and for someone else's P&L statement. And in large firms, where the managers of individual business units are often competing with each other for performance evaluations and advancements, there are often *dis*incentives for such unselfish development work.

Not in this case. Together with his boss, Ron Mitsch, Appeldorn decided to make innovating with microreplication the focus of his group's strategy. 3M created the Optical Technology Center in 1983—a quasi-central laboratory dedicated to finding and developing new uses for microreplication rather than to dominating any single market. This was a strategy of brokering their existing technologies across 3M. There was much development work yet to be done, but this work was specific to applications and markets. For example, while manufacturing overhead lenses was a discrete process, applying microreplicated surfaces to tape products meant learning how to continuously laminate miles of tape in an hour. Once the OTC lab identified a potentially valuable new way of using microreplication, the lab could focus its development efforts on making it work.

But at the same time, this was not the traditional idea that most people have of an R&D lab in a major corporation. Many think that research and development should be focused on the future—on what technologies are five, ten, or more years away. This was the charter of Xerox PARC: to create the architecture of information. Unfortunately, PARC is as famous for failing to get Xerox to capitalize on these innovations as it is for producing them in the first place. In PARC's defense, that is the problem with inventing the future. At best, the ideas work in prototypes. But if the market is ready (and that's no guarantee), there's little chance that you can take a prototype on a lab bench and make a million of them tomorrow.

The Optical Technology Center, on the other hand, did what Edison did. It took ideas that had been developed already, and were being used in other markets, and found new ways to use them in new markets. Sure, there was some development effort in adapting them to new uses, but the engineers already had the basics down. They knew many of the limitations already, and could spot immediately if the new applications would work. Further, as the engineers found ways to make microreplication work in new markets, they continually learned about the particular technologies and demands of each of the different divisions. And they brought these new experiences with them to the next project. After a few years, the lessons they learned applying their original ideas in new places rivaled their original expertise in microreplication.

3M was in the right place for this kind of thinking. There was expertise in the company about both the market needs and the existing technologies of many different industries. But because 3M was organized around this expertise (and the markets to which they were dedicated), its organizational strategy and structure did not support having one division design products for another.

In this way, the Optical Technology Center was set up to play the role of technology broker within 3M, spanning multiple markets and bringing ideas from where they were known to where they were not. The OTC began with its own experiences with microreplication, but rapidly learned about existing technologies and ideas within the other areas of 3M from its attempts to combine microreplication with other technologies—for example, its continuous application to tape products. And because the OTC's strategy was not based on its performance in any single market, its incentives—indeed, its survival —hinged on its ability to continuously innovate across all of 3M's markets.

One of the more recent and revolutionary impacts of microreplication has come in the computing industry. 3M's Brightness Enhancement Film focuses the diffused light coming from a portable computer's LCD screen—capturing what would have gone to the sides and sending it all to the front. Also marketed as a privacy screen, this technology makes it difficult for the person sitting next to you on an airplane to see what is on your screen. Because much of the drain on a portable computer's batteries comes from lighting the display, the film's ability to focus light leads to energy savings of 20 percent to 30 percent. Computers with a standard battery life of three hours are able to run for an extra hour before recharging.

Another recent product came from 3M's Structured Adhesives group, in which the engineers working with microreplication created a surface of microscopic pyramids made from oxide grains on top of a flexible fabric substrate. This structured adhesive is ideal for high-precision sanding jobs on stainless steel, chromium, nickel, and titanium. Right now, these products are used for producing surgical instruments, artificial joints, jet blades, and golf clubs. One version of this abrasive, Apex, is capable of performing both rough sanding and fine-polishing work, and so replaces a manufacturing process that previously involved up to six steps in moving from coarse to fine sandpaper.

The technology of microreplication enables 3M to create tiny pyramids, spheres, cube corners, or edges in sizes from millimeters to micrometers to nanometers (a millionth of a millimeter). In addition to the uses noted previously, this technology has turned up on CD-ROMs, fluid transport systems, adhesives, light guidance tubes, speed tape (reducing drag on boat hulls and plane wings), and abrasives. Within fifteen years, microreplication accounted for over $1 billion in revenue. Where the company finds the next uses for microreplication is up to it.

Thus, the managers at 3M made a critical and, it turns out, highly effective decision. They created an internal organization, the Optical Technology Center, as a laboratory dedicated to brokering the ideas of microreplication into all of the other divisions at 3M. This way, the divisions could stay focused on what they knew and did best, and so could the engineers working with microreplication. But the difference was that because the divisions were ongoing manufacturing concerns, only part of their performance criteria depended on innovation. The bulk of their performance derived from efficient operations and effective sales of existing products. The OTC's performance, on the other hand, depended on its ability to continuously develop innovative new uses for microreplication. It was an invention factory, and would live by that strategy or fade away.

Creating the Structure and Culture of
Internal Technology Brokers

Internal technology brokers will thrive under the same conditions as external ones: where there are many small worlds in which ideas, objects, and people emerge and develop and across which there is little interaction. As a result, the same internal structure, work practices, and culture that were discussed as keys to success in chapter 7 hold true. Internal technology brokers must have focused innovation strategies, in which their success on each project and their long-term survival depends on their ability to provide innovative solutions to their clients—in this case the different groups, factories, or divisions of their larger organizations. Their budgets should come from the divisions they help, not from a corporate research account. Performance metrics need to be tied to the amount of revenue (or cost savings) they provide to their clients, not to the number of patents they generate or to the pioneering work they do that other firms commercialize.

This structure ensures that technology brokering groups will put the necessary emphasis on recombining the organization's existing ideas, objects, and people rather than on inventing new technologies. This structure also emphasizes building the necessary support for new ventures within each division, not throwing good but immature ideas over the wall. A good example of how these structures support internal technology brokers comes from such a group at Hewlett-Packard.

At Hewlett-Packard, pre- and post-Agilent, Corey Billington ran a group that called itself SPaM, for Strategic Planning and Modeling. The group began in 1989 when Billington, an engineer responsible for the capital budgeting process, began to study issues surrounding Hewlett-Packard's widespread manufacturing and distribution networks. Working with Hau Lee, a local professor of industrial engineering, Billington combined advances in computer spreadsheet capabilities and optimization modeling techniques being developed in academic research with the goal of creating computer models that would help HP to understand and improve upon its current manufacturing system. Billington and Lee's initial work resulted in the relocation of manufacturing facilities and the reallocation of work across the different facilities.

For internal technology brokers especially, it's not just about creating new combinations of resources for the different markets in which an organization moves. It's also about sharing best practices within the organization. Divisions often evolve different ways to organize factories, optimize supply chains, or manage people. When one division, or even one factory, develops a novel way to accomplish a business process, chances are good that other divisions are facing the same problems, and chances are good those other divisions will never know about the novel solution.

The supply chain environment represents a system of interactions that is too complex to allow for managerial intuition or linear thinking to shape major decisions. SPaM's computer models are used to predict how changes in the design of products or the location of distribution sites may bring about changes in the overall production costs. In a sense, these models describe the problems that each division faces in its environment within a computer simulation that allows managers to attempt solutions and observe possible outcomes.

From its beginning with a staff of interns, SPaM has since grown to more than eight full-time engineers and expanded its modeling approach to consider issues surrounding the entire supply chain involved in HP's manufacturing processes, from those suppliers that provide HP's factories with materials through the factory to distribution and warehousing and ultimately to retail stores and customers. The group now consults to division managers, developing models that allow those managers to make informed decisions regarding the supply chain design, including, for instance, the design of products for manufacturability, the location and allocation of work among factories, and the ordering process across the links of the chain. These consulting efforts, in the form of projects, require the SPaM team to capture in a single computer model the dynamic relationships that characterize each particular division's manufacturing and supply chain environment.

The differences between each of the division's environments ensure that the computer models developed for each project are never the same. And yet SPaM's consultants are constantly using parts of old models to create new models. Each new project develops unique modules that describe *particular* aspects of that division's environment. One such module might capture (in the cost analysis spreadsheet) customs fees that are incurred for a division that moves material between countries; another might capture the costs and benefits of using common parts across a range of products. Over time these modules accumulate and, as they're used again, evolve. Each new project becomes a unique combination of these old modules and new ones. In the process, SPaM consultants bring to each division new ways to account for its supply chain systems and new ways to cut costs, ways they learned from the other divisions with which they have worked. And with each new project, the SPaM group learns more. SPaM has consulted with over 80 of HP's roughly 150 divisions. When the group has gotten through the rest of the divisions, by its own reckoning, it can start again with what it has learned in the process.

Corey Billington early on recognized the different role that SPaM played within Hewlett-Packard. Division managers at HP compete with one another. Do well on your numbers, and your slice of the discretionary budget gets bigger. It's a good system that rewards good managers. But it discourages them from sharing their best practices with others. SPaM was not in competition with the divisions it helped, and that was a critical distinction that made it easy for any division manager to invite it in. The group was politically neutral. "We absolutely must be neutral." Billington explains, "If we're ever a political weapon, it would destroy the process of it."[9]

But just because it's a different role doesn't mean it's not a valued one. SPaM had only been around for eighteen months when Hewlett-Packard was forced to reconcile the ponderous nature of its central labs, where SPaM was located. Each division was asked to put a value on the different groups within the central labs. The study showed that most labs were breaking even, if not operating in the red, whereas the SPaM group was credited with approximately $150 million in realized cost savings. At the time, this savings reflected over two-thirds of the value that HP's operating divisions credited to the 600-employee corporate manufacturing services. How did the group do it? As one SPaM consultant explained, "They're relying on us to connect one division's experiences to another. Either that or, a lot of times, they don't know who else has done it."

Focus, Focus, Focus

One of the central tensions in managing innovation is balancing between short- and long-run performance. Short-run performance means being good at what you're already doing; long-run performance means being good at adapting to changes in the environment. It's never clear, though, how much of your time and resources to devote to exploiting your existing competencies and how much to focus on developing new ones. To make matters worse, it's practically impossible to ask people to do both at the same time—to be good at what they do and to continually experiment with changing what they do.

The oil companies used to be pretty explicit about dealing with this paradox. They would have two divisions: exploration and exploitation. Exploitation would be filled with engineers worrying about how to get the most oil out of each well and each field, and how to get it to market for the least cost and best price. But these were not the people you wanted out looking for oil, which took intuition, guts, and a willingness to make a lot of mistakes. Instead, the search for new wells was given to a different group altogether. Exploration was composed of the people who were willing to take risks and make big bets, and there was tolerance for the many failures that ultimately were necessary to succeed.

Internal technology brokers are similar to these exploration divisions in many ways. Their job is to explore for technologies in the organization that might be useful elsewhere. Failure, in the form of mistakes, comes with the job. And like their counterparts in the oil business, it's a sign of activity. For most of the firm, mistakes are something to be rooted out in pursuit of six-sigma efficiencies in their operations. But for internal brokering groups, mistakes are part of the learning process. As Edison said, "I have not failed. I've just found 10,000 ways that won't work." [10]

Most important, however, the value of creating internal technology brokers comes from separating out the tasks of bridging the organization's internal boundaries and of building new networks to support potentially innovative new ventures. There's little place for these tasks within divisions because success hinges on crossing (even tearing down) the barriers between divisions. Internal technology brokers can focus on bridging and building innovation networks; the rest of the organization can focus on improving what they already do well.

Increase Diversity

For many organizations, there is not enough diversity within the firm—not enough small worlds—to give internal groups the variety of work they need to successfully pursue technology brokering strategies. When this happens, these groups can also work with clients outside the organization and in other fields. Designworks/USA, the in-house design group for BMW mentioned earlier, is one such group. For twenty-five years, Designworks was a successful Southern California design firm before being acquired in 1995 by BMW.[11] But both Designworks and BMW recognized the benefits of working in, and moving among, a wide variety of markets and were loath to lose that advantage. So they formalized it: Half of Designworks/USA's revenue must come from outside

BMW. It comes in the form of projects with clients as diverse as Adidas and Peterbilt. Designworks/USA designed the Nokia 9110 Communicator, one of the first Internet-enabled phones. It designed a cataract surgery device, Smith ski goggles, Thermador cooktops, and bicycle components. It even redesigned the interior of a Boeing 747. As Henrik Fisker, president of Designworks/USA, puts it, "We have to compete with the rest of the world. It keeps us efficient." [12] By working with external clients, Designworks/USA brings in valuable experiences it wouldn't get simply by attending consumer product shows or reading design magazines. And Designworks/USA's designers get to play in more sandboxes, which, for a designer, is more fun than managing more people.

• • •

Not everybody can adopt the innovation strategies of technology brokers such as Edison, Sperry, IDEO, or Design Continuum. Most firms will find they're best at pursuing success in just one or a few markets, where they can build strong relationships with key customers and suppliers. Large firms, however, often move among the many small worlds of their different divisions. Within their walls, these firms already have the potential for innovating by moving existing ideas, objects, and people from one market to others in new combinations. Also within their walls, however, these firms have the barriers between divisions (or departments or groups) that make bridging worlds, recognizing opportunities, and building new ventures difficult.

For these firms, the answer often lies in constructing internal technology brokering groups chartered to move among the many small worlds of the firm rather than establish themselves in any one. Hewlett-Packard's SPaM and 3M's Optical Technology Center provide vivid examples that successful innovations can come from groups whose main responsibility is neither performing in the present nor inventing the future, but rather redistributing the future that's already here.

The benefits of internal technology brokers come from more than simply the dynamics of recombinant innovation. They also come from the multitiered markets that large firms create. Existing technologies can have potentially revolutionary impacts in the different markets in which the firm plays, but they can also have an impact on the organizational processes shared by the different divisions. Whereas 3M's Optical Technology Center directed its innovation strategies involving microreplication toward 3M's many different markets, HP's SPaM was able to innovate by focusing on the internal management of each division's supply chain.

The key to success is the realization that technology brokering happens on the ground, where people are most familiar with the capabilities of existing technologies and the problems of their markets and their work. Although senior executives are often in a position to link these otherwise disconnected divisions, they are often too distant from the technologies and the problems to recognize anything but the most obvious of matches. Even then, they are often in competition with those whose resources they could use.

Creating internal technology brokers requires creating the same conditions that firms such as Design Continuum and IDEO experience. This means posting these groups outside of individual divisions, where they might be subject to the distractions and resource constraints that follow profit and loss within a single market. It means creating the conditions in which they're rewarded for introducing existing technologies into the different small worlds of the organization—and not focusing their efforts within any single one. It also means building a structure and culture within these groups that rewards the group for bridging different worlds; recognizing valuable new ways to combine the organization's existing ideas, objects, and people; and building new networks around those recombinations.

Finally, not all firms are large enough, diversified enough externally, or fragmented enough internally to benefit from developing internal technology brokers around particular problems or technologies. Most companies fall in this middle ground; for them, the benefits of technology brokering arrive unpredictably. For such companies, committing the entire firm, or even a single group, diverts too many resources from the tasks at hand and brings too little payoff. The value of technology brokering for these firms lies in recognizing when opportunities for recombinant innovation do come along, and developing the know-how to seize those opportunities. Chapter 9 describes several such firms that have taken advantage of one-time opportunities for technology brokering, and describes how others can prepare to do so as well.

9

Exploiting Emergent Opportunities for Technology Brokering

So far, we have looked at firms, and groups within firms, that pursue strategies of continuous innovation by bridging multiple worlds and building new networks from the combinations of ideas, objects, and people they find. For most firms, these dedicated innovation strategies are difficult to duplicate, if not simply inappropriate. Some firms are large enough to build dedicated technology brokering groups spanning the fragmented organizational structure within their own borders. But many firms lack the resources to devote to the full-time pursuit of innovation.

For many, opportunities for technology brokering result from accidental connections between people moving on the periphery of the organization and the technologies they might run across in their travels in other markets or organizations. This was the case, for example, with Henry Ford and his engineers, who during a seven-year period brought together the set of technologies that would become mass production. Neither the Ford Motor Company nor Ford's team of engineers was organized for the purpose of bridging disparate worlds. They did, however, have the insight to recognize these opportunities and make the most of them. The lessons of technology brokering apply here in understanding what managers can do to make sure their organizations are prepared to recognize and respond quickly to such opportunities.

An organization's ability to exploit one-time opportunities for technology brokering lies in adopting and adapting *existing* ideas, objects, and people. Most opportunities for innovation don't involve unproven ideas, immature technologies, nonexistent suppliers, or long and costly learning curves. Most, like Henry Ford's mass production, make use of established ideas, objects, and people, and as a result, usually demonstrate real benefits quickly.

One-time opportunities for technology brokering are often hard to exploit, however, because the culture and structure that support technology brokering are largely absent in most organizations. For most organizations, as discussed in the previous chapters, the pursuit of efficiency overshadows the pursuit of innovation. Under these conditions, the bias tends towards the familiar. External information is filtered by existing expertise and practice: Those ideas, objects, and people that support the established competencies are noticed and incorporated; those that threaten to overturn these competencies with the promise of new and better ones are largely ignored or, if noticed, actively resisted.

Yet opportunities for recombination are what fuel entrepreneurial ventures. A recent example, still unfolding, is the case of Nexia Biotechnologies, a small firm in rural Quebec whose founding idea was the production of spider silk by goats.[1] In 1993, two Canadian venture capitalists who knew the field of biotechnology approached Jeffrey Turner, now Nexia's president but then a research scientist in the animal sciences department at McGill University. He had been working on transgenic animals, in his case goats, with the intention of introducing foreign genes into mammary glands. The thinking back then was to have goats produce what would ordinarily be exorbitantly expensive drugs. But Nexia wanted to produce something else: spider silk. It is by weight many times stronger than steel, but is also incredibly difficult to harvest. Introducing the gene of the golden orb weaver spider into goat eggs (in combination with a "genetic switch" to ensure that the gene only becomes active in the mammary glands) means that Nexia can now harvest spider silk in goats' milk to create a product it calls BioSteel. The company still faces the challenge of separating and strengthening the silk produced, but it took advantage of the 400 million years of evolution that designed the long-chain amino acids capable of such strength, and took advantage of a few hundred goats to construct those complex proteins. Nexia entered the market for high-strength, low-weight materials with a set of ideas, objects, and people (and goats) pulled mainly from biotechnology. It is now in negotiations with the Pentagon and others regarding how spider silk can be used to replace Kevlar, steel, and other materials.

These opportunities can also happen in established organizations, often by accident, as people moving on the periphery of an organization recognize how technologies in previously unrelated worlds fit the organization's existing needs. For an example, we can return to the development of PCR by Kary Mullis at Cetus Corporation. His background in molecular chemistry gave him a different set of technologies with which to consider the problem of replicating DNA strands. Because the origins of biotechnology were in molecular biology and biochemistry, the problem of replicating DNA was largely considered one of creating the biological conditions that built particular target genes from scratch. Mullis's background allowed him to invert this process: He saw the target genes as long-chain molecules, and approached the process as one of simply replicating, over and over, the existing strands of DNA. What was revolutionary was not the techniques, but rather their combination and the idea of mass production that lay behind them.

Opportunities also arise when synergies within the organization are noticed and pursued—sometimes through chance meetings between engineers or managers, where discussions turn to problems one or the other is facing. Such conversations often bring out the recognition that technologies in one corner of the organization could be useful in another, or that breakthrough products might come from combining the existing technologies of different divisions. Hewlett-Packard was known for this type of innovation: Improvements in paper handling in the company's inkjet printer divisions, for example, helped it design new laser printers, and improvements in its computer division often could be applied to its imaging and diagnostics products.

Opportunities also happen when the potential joining of worlds seems inevitable—known as *convergence*—and organizations want to get a jump on it. There's no avoiding the idea that our cellular phones, personal digital assistants, digital cameras, and music players should all, one day, be a single integrated device. Nor is there any question that, one day, our home computer, television, VCR, stereo, and probably telephone will all be integrated into a single digital hub. But many questions remain about just how that will happen and who will come out ahead in the process. Microsoft might control the personal computer market, but Sony's PlayStation 2 dominates the game console market and looks more and more like a potential rival for control of the digital hub. That has motivated Microsoft to develop the Xbox in a multibillion dollar gamble that the hub for integrating home computing, television, video recording, and games just might be the game console and not the PC. The Xbox is a combination of existing Microsoft software components, an Intel Pentium III microprocessor, and new Nvidia graphics chips. It took the Xbox team fourteen months to put the pieces together—impressive considering the Xbox was hardware and the company had been focused on building software. Whether Microsoft made its move in time is, as of this writing, still unclear. Either way, the race to exploit converging industries relies on exactly this ability to quickly bring together new combinations of existing technologies and, just as quickly, build new communities around them.

This is no easy task. The difficulties stem from how people in organizations typically respond to such innovative opportunities. These opportunities usually arrive looking like threats to the traditional ways of doing things, and thus threats to people's authority and identities, which are built on those traditional ways. Yet chance favors the prepared firm: Those that are prepared to recognize and respond to one-time opportunities for technology brokering will be able to exploit them when they do appear.

A Lost Opportunity at Xerox PARC

Xerox PARC offers a particular example of how inappropriate support can drive innovations away. It was at PARC that Bob Metcalfe and others developed Ethernet, the high-speed network protocol that allows computers to communicate with one another. Metcalfe arrived at Xerox PARC in 1973 with a Harvard Ph.D. and a Hawaiian tan, signs of the worlds he was about to connect to the ongoing work at PARC. He had learned about packet switching as a Harvard student working in the computer lab at nearby MIT. And he had learned about randomized retransmission (basically a way of making computers wait their turn to talk on a network) by working on Hawaii's Alohanet packet radio network. When he got to PARC, Metcalfe saw the work the center was doing with the Alto personal computers and recognized how his communication protocols could make it possible to link these computers, first into a local area network (LAN) and then onto the ARPAnet. As he said, "I used the ideas that I had collected from the ARPAnet and the Aloha network to, on May 22, 1973, invent Ethernet."

PARC was in effect one big sandbox in which many talented researchers invented modern computing. But their support from above was more like that from an indulgent parent than from an interested investor. Metcalfe worked hard to turn Ethernet into a standard, particularly by building an alliance between Xerox, Digital, and Intel. But when Xerox neglected to pursue commercializing the technology, Metcalfe left to found 3Com.[2] It was at 3Com, not Xerox, that Metcalfe made Ethernet work. The big break came in 1982 when 3Com worked with a semiconductor company to put Ethernet onto a chip that could be placed on a card and installed in the IBM PC. At 3Com, Metcalfe and others built the new networks of people, ideas, and objects that ensured Ethernet's success. Xerox's inability to capitalize on the resources in its midst is more the rule than the exception within large organizations, so to understand how firms can exploit emerging opportunities for technology brokering it's helpful to first consider why they can't.

Gunfire at Sea

There are few better organizations in which to study this inability than military bureaucracies. Built as they are upon the management of distant men and machines, often in times of chaos, these organizations face enormous pressures to perform in the short run. From the command structure to the supply lines to the field weaponry, consistency and reliability trump novelty much of the time. And yet weapons and tactics are continually changing, and the military, however painfully, perpetually faces the challenge of adapting to these changes. From the brutalities of trench warfare in World War I to the logistical nightmares of the Gulf War, the military is always in danger of "fighting the last war," of applying the strategies and tactics developed and honed in the last engagement despite their obsolescence in the current one. This section considers a historic example of this tendency.

At the end of the nineteenth century, America was emerging on the world stage both politically and industrially. World power, at that time, still rested on the global reach of navies, and the American navy had just achieved international stature in the Spanish-American War of 1898. Its decisive victories over the Spanish fleet during the war, along with new bases in Cuba, Puerto Rico, and the Philippines, made the U.S. Navy a world power overnight. It was following those successes that William S. Sims, a junior officer stationed in the friendly waters of the China Seas, introduced into the U.S. Navy one of the more revolutionary changes in naval artillery: continuous aim firing.

The story of this innovation is told with tremendous insight by Elting Morison in *Men, Machines, and Modern Times*.[3] I will try to do it justice here. To understand the innovation that was continuous aim firing, it's necessary to understand the previous technology of naval artillery. Naval artillery had, up until then, been a relatively inconsistent but obviously important resource. Its inconsistency was a result of the cumbersome process of loading, setting the range, and timing the firing of the gun all to the roll of a ship at sea. This inconsistency had two major consequences. The first had to do with performance. It was necessary, in battle, to fire enormous quantities to achieve relatively few direct hits. Although the U.S. Navy had demonstrated its superiority in the Spanish-American War, it had done so by firing 9,500 shots, of which 121 hit their target. This was not seen as a problem, particularly since the navy won the war; instead, it was simply the cost of doing business, the status quo. The second consequence in the 1890s was that naval strategy, culture, and politics evolved around gunnery's long history of inconsistency. Because it was difficult to rely on trading distant shots, ship commanders demonstrated their skill and courage by closing on the enemy, where the skills of close-quarter sailing and combat obviated the need for accurate cannon fire. The political position of the gunnery officers reflected this inconsistency as well; the path to promotion spent little time in gunnery. All of this would change, but only with great pain.

As Elting Morison describes, the ideas of continuous aim firing were already in existence in naval artillery in various forms before they came together in a way that improved performance, by some accounts as much as 3,000 percent. Sims did not invent continuous aim firing, nor was he the first to combine these elements into the technology we can identify as continuous aim firing. That honor belongs to Percy Scott, a British officer. Sims simply learned of this technology from Scott, introduced it on his ship, and then attempted to convince the U.S. Navy to adopt the practice. For this reason, it provides a wonderful example of the difficulties of introducing innovations into organizations.

But first, a brief description of the technical origins of continuous aim firing is in order. Continuous aim firing took advantage of three existing elements used by naval artillery in the 1890s. Gunnery, at the time, essentially consisted of finding the range of a target, setting the angle of the cannon for that range, and then firing just as the ship rolled back across the horizon. The elements involved in this process included a telescoping sight, which assisted gunners in finding the range but, because of the cannon's recoil, was impossible to use in firing; the gearing that set the angle of the gun; and the skills of the gunner in timing the firing to the ship's roll. Percy Scott developed continuous aim firing by enabling the gunner to maintain a continuous bead on the target regardless of the roll. This was done by, first, changing the gear ratio that adjusted the angle of the cannon, making it easier for gunners to raise and lower the gun in time with the ship. With a continuous view of the target, the telescoping sight became useful again, and could be mounted on a sliding sleeve that did not recoil with firing. Finally, Scott mounted a small target in front of his revised cannon that could be moved up and down to simulate the rolling ship, and a small-caliber rifle *in* the barrel of the gun, to allow gunners to easily and cheaply practice the movements necessary for continuous aim firing.

Like Henry Ford, Scott's new combination of existing elements had immediate and revolutionary effects. In 1899, five ships of the North Atlantic squadron of the British navy had fired for five minutes each at a target ship at a distance of 1,600 yards. In total, two hits were made on the sails. Six years later, one naval gunner in one minute scored fifteen hits on a seventy-five-foot by twenty-five-foot target at the same range, half within a bull's-eye fifty inches square.[4]

In 1900, William S. Sims was a junior officer on the battleship *Kentucky*, posted to the China Station. It was there, through coincidence, that he met Percy Scott, then commanding officer of the British ship H.M.S. *Terrible*, and, by chance and a prepared mind, learned of Scott's innovation. Sims adopted Scott's ideas and objects, and trained his own gunners in their use. Like Scott, he experienced dramatic improvements in accuracy. Sims had the benefit of adopting a technology that not only exploited existing components but was itself already in use in the British navy. He was not advocating a

lengthy period of research and development, a long process of edu-
cating the market or developing suppliers, or the prospect of a long
and costly learning curve. Continuous aim firing already worked
and worked well. But that didn't guarantee that the rest of the navy
would embrace the new technology.

Over the course of the next two years, he sent no fewer than thirteen official reports documenting his own experiences and those of
the British gunners. At first, Sims's reports were ignored by the Bu-
reaus of Ordnance and Navigation—filed and forgotten to such an
extent that they were later found half-eaten by cockroaches. So Sims
copied his reports to the other officers of the fleet. This action
prompted a response by the Bureau of Ordnance that flatly denied
the possibility of such an innovation: first, because British equipment was not any better than that of the United States; second, because the cause of inaccurate firing must lay in the gunnery officers
and training; and, finally, because tests revealed it to be impossible to
raise and lower a six-inch gun as fast as a ship's roll required. The bureau was right as far as it went: The average British equipment was no
better, except for the improvement made on Percy Scott's ships; the
training of gunnery officers was critical, but could not be improved
until the gunnery equipment was modified; and tests on land would
prove impossible because they required moving a cannon up and
down without the help of a rolling ship. This type of reaction is not
much different from the responses that Edison generated from the
established scientific communities of the United States and Britain
when he announced his system of electric lighting.

The responses of the established hierarchy shouldn't surprise us.
Such reactions are natural in most organizations where innovations
threaten to overturn established procedures and structures. Consider organizations as networks of relationships built up over time
to link together particular ideas, objects, and people. The close ties
among these three elements mean that organizational structures,
career paths, and even individual identities are built upon the particular relationships among the different elements. Changing these
relationships—in the case just described, changing the links among

the cannon, gearing, sights, and ideas about aiming—threatens to ripple out through the network. Changes that dramatically improved the accuracy of gunfire at sea threatened to change the rules of naval warfare, strategies for engagement, the importance of gunnery officers on ships, and the culture of closing on the enemy. And it is typical to find in organizations that the very people threatened by such changes are in charge of accepting or rejecting them. It's little wonder that the officers in Washington who Sims addressed, officers whose authority rested on their positions within the established system, responded defensively.

Faced with this denial, however, Sims increased the inflammatory nature of his reports. This new tactic swiftly triggered direct attacks by the established naval hierarchy on Sims's integrity and sanity. This caused Sims to far overstep his authority, skirt the chain of command, and write directly to the president of the United States, Theodore Roosevelt, describing the innovation and its effectiveness on Scott's ships and his own and describing the intransigence of the U.S. Navy. Roosevelt listened, having always had a strong interest in, and understanding of, the state of the navy.[5] At Roosevelt's command, Sims was returned to Washington and promoted to Inspector of Target Practice. Here, for six years under Roosevelt's protection, he was finally able to introduce the innovations of continuous aim firing throughout the fleet, ultimately becoming known as "the man who taught us how to shoot."

What lessons can we draw from this historical account? Besides the value of having the president's ear, this case highlights (1) the profound impact that existing technologies can have when they are brought together in new combinations, (2) the difficulty that organizations have in adopting innovation despite the existence, *within the firm*, of all of the necessary pieces and evidence of their usefulness, and (3) the sometimes bold interventions necessary to alter the established network structure of the organization and build a new community around the emerging idea.

This last point highlights the central paradox of the innovation process. Discovering the breakthrough value of new combinations of existing ideas requires bridging distant boundaries, as Sims did in meeting Percy Scott in the China Station, which usually happens on the periphery of organizations. However, innovation also requires building new network ties around these emerging combinations in order to ensure their success. And building new networks in organizations requires power, which comes from central positions. The problem is that people on the periphery have little power to wield within the organization, whereas people with power have little incentive to risk it by introducing innovations. Technology brokering, by taking advantage of one-time opportunities, requires unique collaborations between the periphery and the core, between those with potentially valuable ideas and those with power.

Building the Xbox

For a closer look at how the technology brokering process unfolds within organizations, let's consider the development of the Xbox at Microsoft. Unlike continuous aim firing or the assembly line, which demonstrated immediate improvements, the outcome of this innovation is far from certain. But its development took place over a similar period of time, involved similar clashes between established and emerging ideas, and weighed, ultimately, on decisions at the very top.

On January 6, 2001, Bill Gates introduced the Xbox, Microsoft's game console, at the Consumer Electronics Show in Las Vegas to a crowd that was equal parts fanatical and skeptical. Fanatical because, according to the technical specifications, the Xbox would revolutionize gaming. Skeptical because Microsoft was a PC software company first and foremost—it wasn't clear it could pull together a console, let alone the developers and games that would make it real. For now, the outcome of this venture remains uncertain. In the words of one hardcore gamer (and university professor), "The Xbox rocks." But Sony's PlayStation 2 remains the market favorite, and while Microsoft has pledged over $2 billion in resources toward the success of the Xbox, the company's $40+ billion war chest means that it's not betting the farm. The story of Xbox's development at Microsoft is a fascinating story of imminent convergence and of the individual and organizational efforts that had to happen to take advantage of that convergence before it was too late.

To understand the accomplishments of the Xbox team, it's first necessary to recognize that the personal computer and the game console are truly worlds apart. Although the PC allows users to play games, and although PC games have been a strong force in the development of advanced graphics, it wasn't until 1993 that the PC offered graphics on a par with game consoles. The early Windows operating system simply wasn't built for multimedia. Meanwhile, since the early days of Atari in the 1970s, game consoles had focused on graphics. In 2000, the PC gaming industry was just over $1.6 billion; the console market was twice that size. Consoles cost $200 to $300, computers much more. And developers found it hard designing games for the PC, where the technology was constantly changing. Video games even had their own community of gamers, developers, magazines, conventions, language, and values. In this world, Sony and its PlayStation dominated. Although everyone could see that the technologies underlying the PC and game consoles were similar and could imagine that one day the two would converge, it wasn't clear when or how. And it wasn't clear who.

If the game console became the hub of the home computing environment, Sony had a lock on it with its PlayStation systems, which it could easily upgrade to take on more tasks. The PlayStation already played DVDs; future generations could add such things as online gaming, digital video recording, Internet access, and e-mail. Microsoft's monopoly position, sitting between the computer and the consumer, was in danger of being outflanked, if it hadn't been already.

All this was becoming clear in 1999, when Seamus Blackley left the video game industry and reported for work at Microsoft's Redmond, Washington, campus. As a new Microsoft employee, he attended the Game Developers Conference in San Jose the following month. There Sony announced the details of its new PlayStation 2, whose graphics capabilities rivaled the PC. Blackley saw the people, ideas, and objects of an even better game console already within Microsoft. There was DirectX, a new software platform that allowed PC game developers to design games for the personal computer without having to know what components or system the games were running on. There were also the microprocessors, graphics chips, and hard drives of the personal computer, which, combined in the right way, could take gaming in whole new directions. Blackley and others within Microsoft who also bridged the two worlds of the PC and video games sensed the breakthroughs that could come from combining the best of these worlds. And so they set about introducing the innovation within Microsoft.

Dean Takahashi, in *Opening the Xbox,* describes how the Xbox wouldn't have happened had it not been for the group that quickly formed around Seamus Blackley and fought for support of the new project. It began, Blackley describes, as "three friends and a slide presentation." Or as Bill Gates describes it, "We had some guys at Microsoft who came and said, we should do a console."[6]

The group included Ted Hase, a manager who promoted PC game developers; Kevin Bachus, a marketing manager for programming software; and Otto Berkes, a graphics programmer extraordinaire. Together they began to build support within Microsoft for the new venture one engineer at a time. To say any one of them had the original idea would be crazy. As Takahashi describes, "It was never clear if [Blackley] started the project or joined an existing one."[7] This is the value of the collective effort—nobody is really sure who is inventing because, in fact, the inventions emerge in the interactions of the group. Making the Xbox a reality meant not simply putting the pieces of various products together in new ways, it also meant combining elements of the organization in new ways, and ultimately building a network that extended beyond the Xbox team and Microsoft and deep into the gaming community. Introducing the Xbox at the Game Developers Conference on March 10, 2000, Gates knew the future of this venture rested in their hands: "It's very exciting to be here today and have the opportunity to announce a whole new platform, a platform that all of you are going to take in directions that we can't even imagine."[8]

It's appealing to imagine new and revolutionary ventures as the product of skunkworks projects, like Steve Jobs's Macintosh team, hidden in a different building, flying the Jolly Roger flag, and thumbing their noses at the established organization. But this approach to introducing change easily backfires. That's because innovation requires both bridging distant worlds—bringing in ideas from outside the organization—and building new networks that connect those innovations to the rest of the organization and to the larger market. Jobs's Macintosh project succeeded because Jobs remained the CEO of the company through it all. But the Macintosh perhaps might have done even better had Jobs devoted less time to overthrowing the world and more to building new ties to the growing community of software and hardware vendors who were creating the larger PC market. Seizing opportunities for technology brokering requires effectively both bridging old worlds *and* building new ones.

The Xbox succeeded in part because Seamus Blackley and others came from the gaming world, where they had established their expertise and their credibility with critical game developers. But it also succeeded because Rick Thompson, Jay Allard, and others came from the Microsoft world, where they had built their own expertise and credibility. At times, each side needed the other; at other times, each side fought the other. But the cooperation and friction were necessary to ensure that Microsoft built the necessary combination of ideas, objects, and people within the firm and across the video game market.

Building New Ventures from Old Ideas

Managing one-time opportunities for technology brokering is similar to managing traditional internal innovation efforts, such as wholly new products and processes, and yet it is also similar to managing the adoption of external technologies, such as packaged information technology solutions. On the one hand, intrapreneurs who are trying to get their innovative ideas adopted must focus on adapting those ideas to fit the particular needs of the larger organization and intended market. On the other hand, they can exploit the established resources and track record of the existing technologies they are importing into the organization. Henry Ford and his engineers were able to walk the assembly lines of Chicago's meatpacking plants and see the ideas at work. Some of Ford's team had worked in the granaries and foundries, where they picked up the ideas (and objects) of continuous workflow. Exploiting opportunities for technology brokering requires balancing between the old and the new, bridging the distant worlds from which valuable ideas, objects, and people come, yet building those elements into a cohesive technology around which networks in the organization and in the market can crystallize.

Creating new combinations of existing technologies relies on many of the same structures and work practices of traditional development and adoption efforts. The necessities of managing new product development projects (such as heavyweight project managers, frequent prototyping, and concurrent engineering) have been well documented. So too have the organizational processes of adopting existing technologies (such as adoption rates, learning curves, and early adopters). What's been neglected, however, is managing the middle ground between creating something from scratch and installing something that comes preassembled. By now, I hope you'll agree that few projects actually fit either description; all new innovations build on elements of existing ones, and all new adoptions require tinkering to make them work. Innovations that recombine elements of established technologies succeed by (1) managing the process of bridging the distant worlds from which the elements are drawn, and (2) managing the construction of new networks around the new combination, networks made up of ties within the organization and to the outside community. So without detracting from the established literature on new-product development and on adoption, successfully managing one-time opportunities to broker technologies relies on managing the changing network in several ways.

These ways can be seen in General Motors's responses in developing its OnStar system, the wireless service that gives automobile drivers access to 911 dispatchers, directions, weather, sports, remote diagnostics, personal calls, and personal concierge services. OnStar will even unlock your door if you lock yourself out. OnStar combines technologies from GM's mobile communications and automotive markets, expertise that drew from Hughes Electronics, GM Locomotives, and Electronic Data Systems (EDS). OnStar began in May of 1995, when Harry Pearce, GM's vice chairman, approached Chet Huber, a long-time executive in GM's locomotive division, wanting to make use of GM's existing resources in a new way. As Huber described it, "Harry had this idea to bring together three big pieces of GM—technology, mobile communications, and the automobile—and leverage them into something that would connect us with our customers."[9] It's the dream of any president, CEO, or member of the board—anyone who sees every day the different parts of the organization, and the different technologies that could be brought together. But this time, Pearce chose the right person in Chet Huber to put this new venture together, and gave him the resources he needed to make it work. And so far, it seems to be working.

OnStar now has over 2 million subscribers and, besides being available in GM cars and trucks, is available in a range of Acura, Audi, Isuzu, Lexus, Subaru, and Volkswagen models. In the emerging world of vehicle communications and information services, it has a sizable head start over the competition. But what's most impressive about the OnStar system is that it is a bold new product from a tradition-bound company competing in an emerging industry where speed and flexibility are critical. OnStar's success rests in many ways upon GM's ability to bring together the new venture in ways that get the most out of the existing ideas, objects, and people while, at the same time, building critical new ties across GM and into the market. Keeping in mind that one-time opportunities for technology brokering arise when someone has already recognized the potential for combining elements from different worlds, much of the focus in management is on bringing these elements together and building a new network around them. Let's use this case and others to consider the three key tactics necessary to make one-time technology brokering work.

Building a Robust Internal Structure

Many stories of innovation in organizations tend to focus on the underground origins of the ideas—on the garage shops and weekend work that took place outside sanctioned organizational efforts. But even the best ideas must get organizational support eventually. Either that, or they leave with the people who developed them. It may not be possible to get the ear of the president for every new idea that bubbles up in the organization, but innovations require dramatic shifts in the allocation of organizational resources. Talented people need to be reassigned, dollars freed up, and space and capital equipment made available. In essence, a new network of ideas, objects, and people needs to be created within the organization that is focused on the new venture. For the development of PCR, it meant Cetus Corporation needed to commit other scientists, technicians, and lab space to the goal of making Mullis's original recombination into an efficient and reliable process.

These sudden changes in the organizational network, crystallizing around a new technology, can only be made by those in the organization with sufficient power, expertise, or connections of their own. That means finding the support of high-level executives who can manage, support, and protect new ventures. For new-product technologies, this may mean a heavyweight project manager; for changes in an assembly line, the plant manager. Changes in supply chains often require division-level authority. And for entering new markets, this need for support may rise to the level of the executive management team. This type of support shifts as a new venture matures and gains credibility. William Sims was able to introduce continuous aim firing on his ship, where he had the authority, but needed to find higher support to diffuse the technology throughout the fleet.

Building internal links also means recruiting people who have experience getting the work done—engineers who are veterans of the organization's development process or who have valuable experience with key technologies or suppliers. These are often the most influential people when it comes to getting acceptance from other divisions. At OnStar, Huber pulled in veteran GM executives to get the project off the ground. He hired Fred Cooke, from the Allison engine division, as vice president of commercial development. And he hired Dave Acton, now executive director of global telematics, but previously a GM electrical engineer in the car divisions. Acton was critical in getting the GM factories to go along with factory installation of the OnStar system. At GM, as elsewhere, factories depend on lean and efficient systems; they aren't rewarded for increasing the number of different parts customers *might* want in a car. To get the factories signed on, Acton put engineers in each of the fifteen assembly plants that would install the new system who were ready to answer questions, solve problems that came up, and generally build connections on the shop floors. Manufacturing is more likely to buy into a novel method or a new supplier when those changes are proposed by people with whom the division has worked before and trusts. The internal innovation process hinges on building connections to those in the organization who can support the next stage of growth in the new venture.

Building the External Community

While managers must respond to the need for resources within their own organization, they can't lose sight of the need to build similar communities in the marketplace. This entails, at the very least, developing products or services that the market values. But it also entails getting others to commit to the new venture. For GM's OnStar, that meant getting other car companies to accept and install GM's system; it meant getting the wireless manufacturers and networks, such as Motorola and Verizon, signed on; it meant signing up information providers such as Weather.com; and it meant getting key technologies developed, such as General Magic's voice recognition software. These additional players brought with them their own connections to ideas, objects, and other people.

Building the external community means cultivating ties to these many different organizations. For example, Chet Huber sits on the board of General Magic, where GM made a $15 million investment. But more important, it means building a team that draws from outside communities. In addition to the internal connections Huber pulled together, the OnStar team also pulled in Bruce Radloff (OnStar's CTO) from IBM, Walt Dorfstatter from a similar project under way at Ford, and Rod Egdorff from McCaw Cellular and Sprint PCS. Nearly 60 percent of OnStar's employees are from outside the auto industry. Finally, the OnStar venture strengthened its ties to users by investing heavily in live call centers, with operators who can come to the aid of drivers when they hit the blue "panic" button. While this looks like part of the service, it is also a valuable way to bring the user into the continued evolution of the system. Huber and the rest of the OnStar team recognize that their future depends on the networked world outside of GM. If they can build a community around their technology and services fast enough, other automakers will find it easier to use OnStar than to develop competing alternatives.

Creating an Independent Venture

The growing network that forms around an innovation signals that the early ideas are being adopted. But the community also ensures that the innovation continues to evolve from what was a recombination of old ideas into a new and cohesive whole. This is especially hard in organizations, where the old technologies often come with very strong ties to existing people and processes that are reluctant to let go of them. OnStar could only succeed in the new world of wireless if it was able to chart its own strategic course independent of GM's management. The original intent was for a three-way partnership between EDS, Hughes, and GM. But such a structure would have ensured disaster, as each of the different groups would have attempted to shape OnStar's evolution according to its own worldview. Huber recognized that the path to success lay in independence—where his team could be free to develop its own strategy and its own culture. Even more important, the team would have to move at the speed of consumer electronics projects, which are measured in months, and not at the speed of automobiles, which take up to five years to piece together. By developing external connections, OnStar was in a good position to exploit its independence. The people, the ideas, and the objects drew from a wide range of different domains.

A lot of ventures get past the initial approvals—both strategic and financial—by promising to be all things to all people. But the process of turning innovative ideas into real products and services is the process of shedding many of those initial promises. The Xbox, for example, started as an attempt to merge the work of the Windows operating system, DirectX, and WebTV, Microsoft's failing Internet TV appliance venture. Few products succeed in trying to please conflicting masters, and the process of turning the Xbox into something more than a combination of parts was also the process of deciding what stayed and what had to go. Those decisions are best left to the team—of insiders and outsiders—that makes up the new venture.

At the same time that a new venture is trying to establish its own ways, however, it becomes that much more critical to maintain the old ties that were its origins—particularly the people who were there at the beginning, saw the connections themselves, and made the early (and most risky) efforts to get the venture rolling. First, because these are the individuals around whom much of the later network formed. Lose them and you create gaping holes in networks, which can survive only to the extent they are densely connected. Second, because the desertion of key individuals can hurt morale in the group, since those who joined later often did so because they respected the early founders. Finally, because these original founders have already demonstrated they can move easily among worlds, they remain valuable in furthering the network.

When it comes time to build new ties to communities across the organization and in the market, these original founders are often the ones who know the outside worlds, who speak the different languages, and who have the credibility in those worlds to speak for the new product or process. In the Xbox case, for example, Seamus Blackley was instrumental in getting formal project status for the Xbox, but he lost de facto control to an already well-established project leader at Microsoft, Rick Thompson. Given his connections and experience, Thompson was the right person for the job, but losing Blackley would have meant losing one of the few critical connections to the gaming world. Instead, Blackley was given the role (and title) of Director of Advanced Technology, and one of his formal tasks was developing new ways to use the Xbox hardware and sharing them with game developers—basically, generating enthusiasm and support from the worlds from which he came in order to help build the new Xbox community.

· · ·

This chapter looked at the lessons technology brokers provide for taking advantage of one-time opportunities for recombinant innovation. Many organizations don't have the breadth of work to justify focused strategies for technology brokering. Often, however, people within firms come across technologies in one domain that might be revolutionary in another. In firms that are focused within a single or a few markets, where success depends on building competencies in what one is doing today and on building close relationships with a few key suppliers and customers, such accidental insights into potentially valuable technologies in other arenas usually go unnoticed or, if noticed, are dismissed within the organization by critical others.

Most firms won't have Teddy Roosevelt to turn to when valuable ideas get dismissed by those who are (often unwittingly) simply protecting their own expertise. Nor should they. Organizations need to develop the capabilities to recognize the value of technologies in other domains and to quickly build the bridges necessary to the ideas, objects, and people who make up those technologies. They also need to develop the ability to quickly build the network connections around these technologies to make them successful first within themselves and then in the market. Like the GM OnStar team, these innovative new ventures will require building webs of support and future development from across the small worlds of the organization and the outside.

The benefits of recombinant innovation are available to everyone. Technology brokers have simply developed strategies that routinely put them in the position of connecting the technologies of one world with the needs of another, and work practices that make it possible to bridge these worlds and to build new and innovative combinations from the elements they come across. These firms offer us specific lessons about a process that, in most firms, is too rare and fleeting to get a good look at. We can use these lessons, though, to see what it takes to prepare for those rare, but no less critical, opportunities for innovation in more traditional firms.

10

Looking Back, Moving Forward

The premise of this book is a simple one: that breakthrough innovations come by recombining the people, ideas, and objects of past technologies. The implication, recalling William Gibson, is that the future is already here—it's just unevenly distributed. Technology brokering provides organizations with the means to exploit the opportunities for recombinant innovation that this uneven distribution creates. The challenge for managers is to put in place the organizational capabilities to bridge distant worlds, in which lie potentially valuable resources, and to build the new worlds in which new combinations will thrive.

The difficulty lies in balancing the activities that bridge many small worlds and those that build new ones. Bridging activities pursue breadth over depth—preferring to gain broad access to and experience with the people, ideas, and objects of many different worlds rather than a deep expertise in any one set. In this way, bridging distant worlds involves loosening the ties that normally bind people, ideas, and objects into existing technologies and blind them to alternatives. Building activities, on the other hand, involve actively pursuing those ties—building links from the very beginning, when an innovation first emerges as a possible deviation from the status quo. And building new worlds involves encouraging commitment around a single set of people, ideas, and objects—the kind of commitment that sticks doggedly to an emerging technology in the face of more established alternatives.

So there you have it. The challenge for managers is to simultaneously encourage doubt and dedication. Doubt in the small worlds of today, and dedication to building new ones in their place. Managers need to find a way to embrace the past because it provides the raw materials for building the future and yet, at the same time, to see beyond the ties that bind together old and obsolete ways of doing things.

How might your company adopt an innovation strategy of technology brokering? Where might you bridge small worlds, recognizing and recombining ideas? And where might you build new ventures around those ideas? Consider your company strategy along the following dimensions.

Do your strengths lie in the close relationships your firm has developed with end users, competitors, retailers, regulators, and other key players in a particular market? In this case, key strategic advantages lie in the dense network the firm has already built within a single world. Such a position provides invaluable understanding of the existing problems and opportunities, as well as of the movements and thinking of the other players in that world. Abandoning this network in search of new markets would be foolhardy. Instead, the most promising opportunities for innovation may lie in bridging distant worlds in search of technologies, or pieces of technologies, that would become innovative again in your market when combined with your existing capabilities.

On the other hand, do your close relationships revolve around a particular set of product or process technologies, and the suppliers, scientists, and engineers who are part of this community? This is often the case in emerging markets, but also for those smaller firms within larger markets that contribute peripherally, such as the machine shops that serviced the textile industry of the early 1800s. These firms have less to lose by seeking market opportunities in other industries—where their expertise and connections surrounding a potentially valuable technology overcome their lack of ties within the new market.

Is your firm competing in a relatively stable market, with a set of core and mature technologies, or in a market where the technologies are still evolving rapidly and new generations emerge and are displaced within just a few years? In these cases, the opportunities for technology brokering are counterintuitive. In rapidly changing markets, firms must devote more resources to *building* coalitions around their particular innovations than to bridging distant worlds in search of the next breakthrough idea. The need to keep up will always be present, but often, *what* the next-generation technologies will be is already clear to everyone involved—the deciding factor will be *how* they are implemented. The battle between Microsoft's and Sony's game consoles will be won not because of how one or the other renders its games, but because of the communities these firms are able to build (inside the firm and out) around their systems—game developers, users, retailers, and the media. On the other hand, firms competing in stable markets will find few advantages in creating even more dense ties than they already have—though they can't ignore them. The pursuit of innovation will have to focus on bridging distant worlds, on finding the already well-developed people, ideas, and objects that would provide distinctive advantages.

Finally, does your firm produce a wide range of products—whether within a single market or across multiple industries—or relatively few? Does your firm have many different production sites or a relative few? Multiple products and multiple production sites create small worlds within organizations, worlds in which potentially valuable ideas can emerge and develop. Firms with such internal complexity will find it valuable to build technology brokering groups that bridge internal divisions, exploiting much of what the organization already knows. On the other hand, firms that have relatively few products or process technologies or that have few internal divisions may find it useful to seek out and draw upon the broad-ranging experiences of external technology brokers rather than attempting to create their own.

Parting Shots

This book has developed a network perspective to understand the competing dynamics in the innovation process. It used this perspective to revisit old and often oversimplified accounts of past innovations. And it has used it to consider how organizations today can manage the pursuit of similar breakthroughs. Eight rules emerge from this study as consistent and fundamental to the organized pursuit of innovation through technology brokering.

1. The Future Is Already Here

Nothing is more powerful than the recognition that our future already surrounds us: from the teenage crowds and electronic toys at the Akihabara in Japan to the student hackers and model railroads of MIT, from the meatpacking industry to wafer fabs. The pursuit of innovation should be directed outward—to other industries, to other cultures, perhaps to a rainforest somewhere—toward the distant worlds in which so many technologies have already emerged and developed. Most important, that search should be undertaken with an attitude of wisdom, an attitude that puts the same value on the people, ideas, and objects of other worlds as on those of your own. This attitude simply acknowledges that in moving through distant worlds, other people know something you don't, and you know something they don't. Nothing more and nothing less. The raw materials for the future are already here; they're just unevenly distributed.

2. Analogy Trumps Invention

The raw materials for the next breakthrough technology may already be here, but they are certainly not in a nice box with a big label, a plastic window, and assembly instructions. Those technologies do exist, but we see them coming for decades before they hit the market: the integrated cellphone/PDA/camera/MP3 player, the affordable flat-screen television, the downloadable movie, the flying car. No, the raw materials for breakthrough technologies will come in unexpected forms—the people, the ideas, and the objects will come dressed in other uses, other meanings, and other relationships.

Untangling these existing resources from their current context and putting them together in new ways requires thinking by analogy. It means constantly asking how things are the same. It's easy to point out how things are different; we do it every day in order to decide where to focus our attention and energy. Who we talk to and who we do not, which articles we read and which we ignore—these are difference-driven choices. And difference-driven choices are, by nature, defensive. It would take two hours to read the paper every morning (and why stop at just one paper?). But every time a manager dismisses an idea that works somewhere else because it's a different industry, a different customer, a different material—that's also a difference-driven choice. The best ideas won't come looking like they're just right. Fred Stratton, the CEO of Briggs & Stratton, once said that genius lay in the ability to see how two things that nobody else sees as related *are* related. This ability to make distant analogies unlocks a world of potential. And it's all a matter of looking for how things are the same, not for how they are different.

3. Find Your Discomfort Zone

An executive sat through one of my lectures on the network structure of technology brokers recently, and his eyes lit up. "I get it," he said, "Technology brokering is about being constantly uncomfortable. It's about never fitting in." He's right. The network position that sits across worlds rather than within any single one, enabling one to move easily among worlds, is inherently an uncomfortable place to be. We have already discussed the close ties, the certainty, and the stability that make sitting inside a small world so all-encompassing. Sitting *between* these worlds, on the other hand, means not being inside any one and hence not being fully accepted by any one. The benefit of this discomfort lies in freedom from the binding (and blinding) ties of any one small world. One foot on the platform, the other on the train. Such isolation is sometimes bitter, as Einstein said, but that is the cost of remaining independent of others' customs, opinions, and prejudices. Technology brokering entails finding your discomfort zone. Nolan Bushnell, founder of Atari (which commercialized—but did not invent—the video games Pong and Computer Space) once said, "The way to have an interesting life is to stay on the steep part of the learning curve."[1] Perhaps that's why it's inherently uncomfortable.

If the decisions you make, the budgets you sign, and the projects you initiate are easy—meaning your colleagues would agree with them—then chances are you're thinking within the same boxes they are. If, however, you find that your closest allies reside outside your traditional circles, chances are you're on to something good.

4. Divided We Innovate

The idea that the future is already here, that the potential for revolution lies in bringing together otherwise disconnected people, ideas, and objects, seems to point to a single solution: Bring everyone (and everything) together. That's the promise, after all, of today's information technology and knowledge management solutions. Capture the organization's knowledge and make it available to everyone. Flatten the organization, tear down the walls, build common spaces, and establish communities of practice to cut across the remaining borders. Then sit back and watch as breakthrough ideas come bubbling out of the resulting goulash. The primary role of most organizations, however, is *not* to develop breakthrough innovations but to focus on making the most of their existing technologies and markets. The more ties you build among different project teams, different manufacturing plants, and different divisions, the more time it takes to maintain these ties, and the more risk there is that a common set of people, ideas, and objects will come to dominate the larger community. It is better to embrace the boundaries in organizations: Those boundaries ensure both the focus needed within each and the variety of best practices that result from that focus. Then find and support the few people who will thrive by moving among these different worlds.

5. Bridge to Your Strengths

Nolan Bushnell had it half right—life's interesting on the steep part of the learning curve. But not many people will pay you to simply struggle along there. Technology brokering isn't about moving into worlds you know little about. It's about finding worlds you know little about *but where your own knowledge looks valuable*. There is an old joke about two friends out hiking. When a bear starts to chase them, one stops to change into running shoes. "You can't outrun the bear," his friend yells. "I don't have to," he yells back, "I just have to outrun you." IDEO got its start as a group of mechanical engineers who could design boxes for the electrical engineers in Silicon Valley. They weren't the most advanced mechanical engineers, but they could outrun the electrical engineers (who were busy with their own work anyway). Bridging to your strength means moving into those worlds where your past experiences will be valuable contributions, where you are a visitor bearing gifts. Without the ability to contribute in a new place, technology brokers will find it difficult, if not impossible, to work with the best people, the latest thinking, and the critical tools of that world. But from a position of strength, Edison, IDEO, Walter Flanders at Ford, and the Optics Technology Center at 3M were all able to hit the ground running, to quickly solve a few of the problems of another world and, in the process, to work with and learn about the existing technologies and demands of that world. IDEO has since become one of the most advanced mechanical engineering firms in the country—not in spite of, but rather *because* of, its strategy. Playing to their strengths allows the firm's engineers to seek out places where they can learn the most, like designing Apple's first mouse or Amtrak's high-speed rail cars, but at the same time give something in return.

But bridging to your strengths also means knowing your own limits. Just because you know something that others don't doesn't make you smarter than they are, and, more important, it doesn't make you right. Too many consultants spent the last decade dispensing advice as if they had all the answers, and then taking credit when their clients' capitalization went through the roof. For all its experiences, IDEO manages to keep its own limits in mind. In fact, it often treats its ignorance as an opportunity to learn something new. In a project on haircutting, the firm brought in hair stylists and a national expert on scissors, and the engineers hung out in barber shops. This kind of humility goes hand in hand with playing to your strengths, and applies equally to engineering or to asset management.

6. Build to Your Weaknesses

Samuel Goldwyn supposedly once said, "If two of you agree, then one of you is redundant." This is a good rule of thumb when it comes to bringing different perspectives and experiences to bear on a problem. When it comes to building on new ideas, however, it's an equally bad rule. Never underestimate the power of a group in turning emerging ideas, especially deviant ones, into new realities. Think different, together. Forget about the notion of the lone genius, even if that's what your organization rewards. Find one other person who complements your abilities, then another, and then another. The more ties you can build around you, the bigger the collective becomes and the more others become willing to join. Marc Ventresca, a professor at the Kellogg School of Business, once said that the smallest political unit in an organization (and in society) is the group. Individuals simply can't muster the needed resources to make a difference by themselves. Even Mother Theresa had her Sisterhood of Missionaries of Charity.

If you think you have a good idea, make the idea possible by making yourself redundant. If you think someone else has a good idea, build a network around him or her (or bring that individual into your network). Ken Kuturagi built Sony Corporation's video game business and the wildly successful PlayStation 2. Defying Sony's traditional Japanese culture of hierarchical deference, he once publicly told hundreds of Sony executives that "The old guys should step aside to make way for the young."[2] In a culture of conformists, he was a deviant advocating nothing short of revolution. And so Nobuyuki Idei, Sony's chairman, decided to do something about it. What he did was give Mr. Kuturagi access to Sony executives and board meetings, and he named Kuturagi to the committee charged with mapping Sony's future in the electronics business. Sony's leadership has always tended toward mavericks like Kuturagi, but without the necessary ties that link such individuals to the rest of the organization this would lead to disaster. Mavericks are invaluable, but only when they are tied to others and through others to the rest of the organization.

7. As Go the Individuals, So Goes the Organization

It's one thing to establish strategies that move a firm among worlds, or that build new project teams from across disparate divisions. It's another for the individuals involved to not only commit but also thrive in the new settings. One of the most striking features of the companies involved in this study—both the recent case studies and the business histories—is the environments in which the individuals worked. There were certainly many different environments, from the upstairs laboratory at Menlo Park to Ford's production floors, from the computer lab at MIT to the toy-filled hallways of IDEO's Palo Alto headquarters. But a common thread appears in each: People embraced technology brokering as a firm (or group, or project) strategy because their own path to success lay in brokering. An individual's value in these organizations came not from any fixed position or authority, but rather from the ability to see connections between what they had seen before and the problems others were facing now. Power, in these firms, didn't come from controlling a fixed resource—it came from making new resources out of old experiences. Bridging distant worlds and building new technologies from pieces of each was what good mechanics, engineers, program-mers, managers, and musicians did. Under these conditions, shining in a particular brainstorming session for one's creative insight and having the insight to call the brainstorming session are both the same talent. As go the individuals, so goes the organization.

8. Rip, Mix, Burn

The sources of invention range from ideas and objects in na-ture, such as spider silk, to the people, ideas, and objects of existing technologies, such as Edison's electric light or Ford's mass produc-tion. Apple's tag line "Rip. Mix. Burn." describes the ease with which its users can create their own CDs by ripping (uploading their old CDs), mixing (putting old songs together in new ways), and burn-ing a new disc. The tag line may as well be describing the process of innovation. There is no doubt that, at one extreme, this process steals the intellectual property of others: patent infringement, soft-ware piracy, bootlegging. And there's equally no doubt that, at the other extreme, it does not: muses, inspiration, and the Eureka mo-ment. Often, the courts must decide which existing people, ideas, and objects can be used and which cannot. Where can a valuable engineer work when he or she has signed a noncompete clause with his or her ex-employer?[3] Who controls Snow White and Mickey Mouse? Who owns the one-click checkout feature in online shop-ping? These decisions—whether made, anticipated, or avoided—determine the direction of innovation in a society because they determine which past ideas, which past objects, and which people can be used again and in which new ways.

Lawrence Lessig, writing in *The Future of Ideas*, does a marvelous job of laying out just how these decisions can open or close access to the past resources from which new technologies are built. The laws concerning intellectual property rights, from patents to copyrights to trademarks, do not encourage innovation. They encourage peo-ple to innovate in the ways that can be protected by those laws—or at least to say they did. Disney built its fortune animating childhood

classics already in the public domain such as *Snow White, Cin-
derella, The Jungle Book,* and *Beauty and the Beast.* And it has also
succeeded, with the Digital Millennium Copyright Act of 1998, in
extending its ownership of Mickey Mouse and friends for the fore-
seeable future. Microsoft, which got its start porting BASIC (free
software already in the public domain) to the Altair, now uses its
riches to ensure nobody else does the same.[4]

When our founding fathers established the first intellectual
property laws, there was no clear agreement on where to draw the
line or for how long. Benjamin Franklin and Thomas Jefferson, for
example, opposed patents and the government-mandated monopoly they provided to inventors.[5] Today, the same senators who fight
to keep federal lands open as public commons for private ranchers to
graze cattle also fight to keep the cultural and technological equiva-
lents closed to entrepreneurs and innovators. Rip, mix, and burn
may strike fear in the hearts of recording industry executives, but it
also describes the timeless dynamics of innovation. Aggressively
guarding the intellectual property of past innovations may reward
yesterday's risk takers, but it also chokes the flow of raw materials
from which tomorrow's innovations will be built.

· · ·

Common sense, it has been said, is genius in its dotage. We now un-
questioningly hold beliefs that, in their youth, were considered revolutionary and even heretical. And while it's easy to look back and
see their obvious value, it's more useful to try to understand why
that value was not obvious beforehand. Elements of the telegraph,
the telephone, mass production, the transistor, and the computer—
to name but a few—were in use long before the revolutions they
spawned. For these breakthroughs to happen, someone somewhere
had to make connections nobody else had made before. The very existence of these technologies made them revolutionary when they
were introduced elsewhere, but their very existence also made it
difficult for those most familiar with them to take them apart and

put them together in new ways. Completing the circle, Einstein once said, "Common sense is nothing more than a deposit of prejudices laid down before you reach eighteen."[6]

Just as genius turns to common sense, common sense turns to prejudice. The same people, ideas, and objects that spawned a generation of revolutions become the ones to suppress the next. Starting a new cycle requires building new combinations of people, ideas, and objects. And building those new combinations requires bridging distant worlds in order to find and exploit the existing resources within them. It may take genius to see the potential for breakthrough innovations across a fragmented landscape, but that genius depends more on the network of past wanderings that allows one to see across worlds than on any inherent talents.

Epilogue

One morning in the early fall of 1992, on the fifth floor of a building in Apple Computer's Cupertino campus, I got a phone call from an old mentor and friend, Jim Adams. Jim, a professor in the mechanical engineering department at Stanford's School of Engineering, knew me from way back and was my advisor in my days as a Master's student in product design. He knew I had always been interested in studying the innovation process, and he had called to tell me it was time. If I stayed with Apple any longer I would never be able to come back to academia. I would be too set in my ways—in my career, my family, and my mortgage—to become a graduate student again. He was joking, but only a little.

That phone call began a conversation that lasted through the fall and into the winter. We talked about what I might do for my doctoral research. Back then, the first portable computers were taking the market by storm. The Internet was just emerging, and Netscape had yet to appear. It felt like the revolution was growing every day, and I described my experiences as an engineer in the trenches of one of the more innovative companies of the time.

I had worked my way through graduate school in Stanford's product design program by moonlighting for IDEO (then called David Kelley Design) and, after graduating, had gotten a job at Apple, witnessing firsthand the successful introduction of Apple's first three portable computers. I'll be honest: I had a great time and we did great work. I can say that because I was part of several teams that did great work, part of which I got to take some of the credit for. And when the products shipped, the press praised their innovative form and features (these were, for example, the first laptop computers to place the keyboard in back to allow room for your wrists). And the public couldn't get enough: We were backordered for most of the first year. Inside the company, however, hidden from view of the press, the public, and even many of the top managers, we were scrambling to make it all work. Some careers were made and many others were broken in those days in a way that made me realize what little connection the outside story had to the events I had lived, sometimes night and day.

Several of the components I had designed were being built overseas, in Japan, Hong Kong, Taiwan, and China, and the twelve-hour flights to and from those factories gave me the chance to read the latest books on managing innovation. My schedule was as follows: work night and day designing new products, get on a plane and reflect for twelve hours, then go back and do it again. The companies and stories about innovation that I read about in those books seemed more culturally distant than the Chinese factories where my products were coming off the line. Who were these "Heavyweight Product Champions"? Where were these matrixed organizations? What cultures of creativity were those books talking about? Remember, I was working at Apple during (some of) its glory days. We lived the matrixed organization and we had the heavyweight project managers. We had the pinball machines in the break rooms, the free soda and the Friday afternoon beer-busts. Hey, Steve Jobs invented those perks.

We worked hard and those perks made our routinely twelve-hour days more enjoyable. But they didn't make us more creative. We would even joke about the folks in white labcoats who must be watching while we scurried around our cube farms playing Nerf football and pushing the lever for more diet Coke. Our very own Silicon Valley Habitrail. The connections those fun and games had

with the results of our work—what the press and others would ultimately label innovation—were not as clear to me as they seemed in
the books. Sure we were irreverent, we challenged authority, we designed first and asked questions later. But these perks didn't make us
that way. As you went higher in the organization, however, it seemed
as though people held these shared and popularized images of the
innovation process. To make innovation happen—these stories dic-
tated—you followed the recipe: Find the right people, feed them,
and get out of the way. Take the experience of Mark Leibovich, a reporter for the *Washington Post,* when he accidentally showed up
early to interview the CEO of a new Washington dot-com company.
"I got there just in time to see the CEO himself wheeling a foosball
table into the lobby." [1] Hoping to send the message that this firm was
every bit as wacky and innovative as its Silicon Valley competitors,
this CEO was only following the script: Mix some talented engineers
together, throw in a few toys, matrix them, collocate them, give them
stock options and, voilà, wait for the innovations to appear.

Jim listened to my stories. He had the patience to tolerate my
half-baked arguments, and after a while pointed me toward the
Organizations group of the Industrial Engineering department at
Stanford. There, he said, I could conduct my research on engineers,
engineering, and innovation. So it's possible that this book began
then, ten years ago, with my desire to describe what I was experiencing backstage at the revolution. While the story out front was
being constructed for investors, customers, and, someday, historians, we were scrambling around in the back to ship the next product and to stay one step ahead of everyone else. The press and
public like a clean story, a neat script with a clear cast of inventors
and inventions; typically, that's what they got. But the real story
was never that neat. There were no clear beginnings or endings; the
props on stage had wires running out the back; there was a lot of
smoke and mirrors.

Had I known then what I know now, I might have picked a different topic for my doctoral dissertation—one that had a clean storyline, easily identified actors, and well defined categories. But I was

young and had a bone to pick. I was interested in understanding how engineers solved problems in their everyday work and how, sometimes, they did so with surprising creativity. Most of the literature on innovation and creativity focused on particular companies and particular individuals—the geniuses, rebels, artists, and heroes who acted alone and, in so doing, created whole new worlds and overturned old ones. As a result, the workplace was seen as simply another environment in which individual inventors and heroes produced great works. Managing innovation meant recognizing these folks, giving them what they needed, and getting out of their way.

When I got to school, I met and started working with Professor Robert Sutton, and soon after began what would turn into an eighteen-month study of IDEO Product Development, where I had worked before.

Our intention was to hang around, in the tradition of anthropologists observing a distant culture, to try to understand what it was like to live in such a world. Bob and I turned out to be a good match. With his long and illustrious career as an organizational researcher, he could recognize the social and psychological dynamics at work in the company. On the other hand, with my design background and IDEO experience, I acted like Bob's seeing-eye dog, often explaining the engineering reasoning behind some particular problem, delighting in the elegance of a particular solution, or explaining the unique culture of the firm.

Together we studied the process of creativity at IDEO and soon began to recognize a more complex story at work than had been previously described. Each week, as our research unfolded, we would meet for an afternoon coffee or beer and try to make sense of what we had seen so far. Who were the creative geniuses we should watch more closely? What were the most creative solutions we had seen? At first, these answers came easily. But the closer we looked, the harder it became to single out individual efforts or recognize truly novel solutions.

Our evolving explanations made us feel like we were opening a Russian doll, where each time you looked at one doll you found another smaller one existed inside. Only in our case, we were going in reverse. Each time we looked at a creative act, we realized that it could only exist because it sat inside a larger set of social and technological dynamics that made it possible for that act to be creative.

For example, one team at IDEO had spun off to design and build special effects for movies. One of their early projects was a full-size mechanical whale that starred in the movie *Free Willy*. The robotic whale was a revolutionary product in movie productions. Typically, if a scene required a whale and the real one could not be trusted, a foam and latex model would be pulled across the set by divers or a cable. There was a right-side half for some scenes, a left-side half for others, and a head for when the creature popped out of the water. Time in movie productions can be measured in dollars, and each time a new model needed to be submerged and dragged through the set was costly. A robotic whale, on the other hand, was a complete replica except for a trailing "umbilical cord" that provided the power. It could swim to the right or to the left. It could climb. It could dive. Ultimately, it even let the kid ride on its back through the water.

What made the *Free Willy* whale so creative was that the movie industry had never seen such a large, versatile, and smart model before. But the designers at IDEO had—albeit in other ways and other places. Walt Conti, who led the group (now its own firm, called Edge Productions), had a history designing industrial robots, complete with the required hydraulic power plants and tubing. Other engineers in the group had worked with remote control cars and planes, and understood what could be done with the little servo motors and mechanisms that made up these toys. These diverse experiences, when blended together, produced a creative solution for an industry that had seen practically nothing like it before.

The creative act of designing and building the robotic whale was wrapped inside a larger set of social and technological circumstances, from the robotics and hydraulics of the industrial equipment to the tiny electric motors and hinges of remote control cars to a film industry that had little experience with either of these. The idea for the whale was creative. To the client (and to us the first time we saw it), it was new, nonobvious, and valuable. But the idea came from work in other IDEO projects done years before for other clients, and from the personal background and hobbies of the designers. So understanding what it meant to be creative at IDEO required understanding how the particular ideas involved in any one creative solution were drawn from the range of experiences held by the different designers.

When we looked at the creative process as it played out at IDEO, three central aspects of it began to emerge that suggested our study of IDEO's designers was not simply a study of a remote, if very creative, tribe of engineers. First, the creative solutions that IDEO's designers were providing their clients were not inventions but rather new combinations of old ideas that the designers had seen before in other places. These recombinations could be creative because IDEO's clients had not seen many of these ideas before, and yet these ideas had already been developed elsewhere (meaning they usually worked the first time in this new setting). Second, it was the nature of the technological landscape as much as the engineers at IDEO that made this recombinant innovation possible. By working together closely, but also working in a range of different industries, IDEO's engineers were in a good position to see ideas in one industry or market that were unknown in others. Third, and perhaps most important, we realized that this process of creativity both drove IDEO's business strategy and, at the same time, relied on that strategy. These three aspects of new product and process development are so tightly integrated that to appreciate the role of one it is necessary to understand its relationship to the others.

The implications of such a perspective were considerable. For one thing, it meant that there was more to creativity than designing the innovative organization, picking innovative people, and keeping them happy. All the structure or motivation in the world won't provide an engineer with a diverse set of ideas or with the ability to recognize how to combine those ideas in new ways. While we were studying IDEO, I was still reading. The history of technology is a hobby of mine, or perhaps more like a vice. As a mechanical engineer, I am simply more comfortable with the earthy descriptions of the Industrial Revolution, with its gears and pulleys, grease and coal smoke, than with the sterile Information Revolution with its integrated circuits, lines of code, and clean rooms. Visiting IDEO in the daytime and reading these books at night, I began to see parallels between the creative acts of IDEO engineers and the major technological innovations that, for example, Edison put forth in his career. And I began to see parallels between those innovations and others throughout the last several centuries—for example, those of Elmer Sperry, who developed the first automatic pilot for ships and planes, or of Thomas Fulton, who developed the first commercial steamship.

With both IDEO and the dramatic innovations of the Industrial Revolution in my head, I began a series of research projects that spanned the next five years and looked at a range of firms that created new products and processes in one industry by recombining old ideas they had seen in a range of relatively disconnected others. Some of these firms were large, multidivisional organizations like Hewlett-Packard and Boeing. Others were small engineering firms, like IDEO and Design Continuum in Boston; still others were consulting firms like McKinsey and Andersen Consulting. And finally, I looked back to some of the more profound cases of technological innovation in recent history—Henry Ford's Ford Motor Company of 1908 to 1914 and Thomas Edison's Menlo Park laboratory from 1876 to 1881, to name two. No company is innovative throughout its life—those of Ford and Edison are examples of this—yet few companies did more in so short a time to change the face of the world in which we live. The study of these firms provided the larger social and technological perspective that is only possible from the distance of time.

The more I learned in studying these firms, the more I realized that when I was watching the engineers at IDEO, I was watching the elemental process of technological innovation at work. A new theory of technological innovation began to emerge from what people in organizations are doing that leads them to design new products and processes that change their organizations and reshape the technological landscape. In this way, this book uses the examples from my research to describe how innovation unfolds at the ground level, in the minds and hands of the engineers and entrepreneurs who are doing the work.

In the spring of 1940, John Steinbeck and his friend Ed Ricketts rented a Monterey fishing boat, *The Western Flyer,* and collected specimens from the Sea of Cortez (the Gulf of California). He wrote about this trip in *The Log from the Sea of Cortez.* The book is a wonderful read because it places the fish and other marine specimens they collected in a rich context that includes not only the ecological system in which those specimens once lived, but also the social and technological world in which they were collected—from the negotiations with customs officials to the cranky outboard motor. Steinbeck described this perspective in the following passage:

> We knew that what we would see and record and construct would be warped, as all knowledge patterns are warped, first by the collective pressure and stream of our time and race, second by the thrust of our individual personalities. But knowing this, we might not fall into too many holes—we might maintain some balance between our warp and the separate things, the external reality. The oneness of these two might take its contribution from both. For example: the Mexican sierra has "XVII-15-IX" spines in the dorsal fin. These can easily be counted. But if the sierra strikes hard on the line so that our hands are burned, if the fish sounds and nearly escapes and finally comes in over the rail, his colors pulsing and his tail beating the air, a whole new relational externality has come into being—an entity which is more than the sum of the fish plus the fisherman. The only way to count the spines of the sierra unaffected by this second relational reality is to sit in a laboratory, open an evil-smelling jar, remove the stiff colorless fish from formalin solution, count

the spines, write the truth "D. XVII-15-IX." There you have recorded a reality which cannot be assailed—probably the least important reality concerning either the fish or yourself.

It is good to know what you are doing. The man with his pickled fish has set down one truth and has recorded in his experience many lies. The fish is not that color, that texture, that dead, nor does he smell that way.

It is in the spirit of Steinbeck that this book has attempted to similarly capture the texture and color of innovation—as it happened and as it happens—and by so doing forgo a simple recipe for innovation to provide a more nuanced understanding of the process.

As such, this book is not based on the kind of research that compares more and less innovative firms, measures the number of patents each has filed, accounts for their investments in research and development, monitors the percentage of new products they have on the market, and so on. In lieu of looking at many firms, I looked at only a few. In lieu of finding rules that applied to everyone, I looked for the actions and perspectives that drove particular behaviors in particular settings. I looked at some of the more famous inventors and innovators of our time, but only after looking at the people doing the work now in the trenches. If I could understand what they were doing, it wouldn't be much different from what the heroes of old were doing.

If the ideas of this book are any good, they have to explain not just new stories of successful innovation but also our old stories. It's too easy to say the rules have changed and that new theories should apply to new companies, but the innovation process doesn't change. The names and faces may change, but the game remains the same. So this book revisits our old cases of innovation to test their ability to explain why things happen the way they do. Historians have told us about Edison, about Ford, about the development of the transistor. But historians explain what happened. In this book I have tried to use history as a means to explain what happens.

Acknowledgments

The central arguments of this book are that new ideas are built from the pieces of old ones, and that nobody works alone. Nowhere in my research did I come face to face with these facts more than in the writing of this book. The central ideas of this book have been pieced together from across a range of intellectual disciplines. I draw heavily from work in social network theory and the ideas of Paul DiMaggio, Mark Granovetter, Ron Burt, and Wayne Baker. Similarly, my perspective on technologies and technological change was possible only by standing on the shoulders of giants such as historians David Hounshell, George Basalla, and Thomas P. Hughes, economist Nathan Rosenberg, and the community of scholars doing research in the sociology of technology: Wiebe Bijker, Michel Callon, Edward Constant, Bruno Latour, John Law, and Trevor Pinch. The value of this book, I hope, lies in connecting this extant research on technology and social change with the actions and understandings of those managers, engineers, and entrepreneurs who work at it every day. After all, technological innovations are the product of individuals and organizations, and they are significant only to the extent that they in turn shape the behavior of individuals and organizations. So I am equally indebted to the ideas of organizational scholars such as Karl Weick, Michael Tushman, Therese Amabile, Rosabeth Moss Kanter, Andrew Van de Ven, Raghu Garud, and Jean Lave, and to social and cognitive psychologists such as Dean Simonton, Mihalyi Csikszentmihalyi, and Diedre Gentner, all of whose work connects the larger concepts of technological change to its pursuit by individuals and teams in organizations.

As mentioned before, Robert Sutton's early contributions to the ideas of technology brokering are indistinguishable from my own (excepting, of course, any mistakes I have made). Indeed, our partnership blended my own engineering background with his expertise in understanding organizations—in our early days at IDEO, those different perspectives enabled us to see how the seemingly small but critical engineering details related to the equally subtle but crucial organizational factors. Moving from the field back to our offices, professors Kathleen Eisenhardt and Steve Barley helped transform our initial findings into useful theory. It was Steve Barley who captured a fifteen-minute explanation of my findings in the wonderfully concise term *technology brokering*. Indeed, the orginal ideas of this book first appeared as a term paper in his class on social network theory. I can think of no better place to have begun this work than Stanford's School of Engineering, where engineers mingle with social scientists on a daily basis. My colleagues there continually provided insights and encouragement, including Beth Bechky, Jim Bradley, Blake Johnson, Quintus Jett, Gerardo Ohkuysen, Mark Zbaracki, Lee Fleming, and Colin Kessinger. I am grateful also to the Stanford Alliance for Innovative Manufacturing (then know as SIMA) for its financial support and, more important, for the company of the people there and the exposure to so many different worlds of manufacturing. I would especially like to acknowledge Fred Stratton for his support and guidance. This research was funded in part with a grant from the Center for Innovation Management Studies.

As the research behind this book turned into academic articles and conference presentations, the minds of many helped to sharpen and clarify the ideas. Colleagues at Harvard, Kellogg, MIT, Carnegie-Mellon, Stanford, Berkeley, the University of Texas at Austin, and Queens all heard these ideas in various stages and provided helpful feedback and support. Martin Kenney, Yellowlees Douglas, Marc Ventresca, Eric von Hippel, Michael Tushman, Barry Staw, Christine Oliver, Rod Kramer, and Tina Dacin, in particular, lent their expertise to the project. Rodney Lacey was a constant source of insightful connections. Practioners were also essential to boiling down the research and resulting theories into practical findings: David Kelley, Bill Moggridge, Dennis Boyle, Sean Corcorran, Rickson Sun, Jim Yurchenco, and Chris Flink of IDEO; Carlo Pugnetti and Christian Else, then of Mercer Consulting; Corey Billington of Hewlett-Packard; Brook Manville of McKinsey; Harry West and Gian Zaccai of Design Continuum; William Pretzer of the Henry Ford Museum and Greenfield Village; engineers, consultants, and managers at Boeing's Operations Technology Center; 3M's Optical Technology Center; Accenture's Institute for Strategic Technology; McKinsey & Company; and countless informants from dozens of organizations.

As the ideas began to look like a book, Melinda Merino and everyone else at Harvard Business School Press provided the guidance, feedback, and encouragement to make it a reality. And Yellowlees Douglas and Martin Kenney were invaluable for reading (and rereading) the many drafts it took to move to a final manuscript.

Finally, Annie and Cody provided everything from advice to insight to sustenance to support to delight. I couldn't have done this without you.

Notes

Preface

1. The distinction between exploration and exploitation comes from the early organizations of the oil industry, which had to consider both the short-term realities and certainties of extracting oil from known wells and fields and the long-term risks and returns of exploring for new fields. The two pursuits conflicted in everything from goals to performance measures to cultures, and were often divided into two distinct divisions: exploitation and exploration. James March and colleagues have since developed this distinction between exploration and exploitation as an underlying tension within all organizations.

Chapter 1

1. The historical accounts of Thomas Edison and the doings at the Menlo Park laboratory have been culled from a number of excellent sources on Edison: Andre Millard, *Edison and the Business of Innovation* (Baltimore: John Hopkins University Press, 1990); Robert Conot, *Thomas A. Edison: A Streak of Luck* (New York: De Capo Press, 1979); Matthew Josephson, *Edison: A Biography* (New York: John Wiley & Sons, 1959); Thomas P. Hughes, *American Genesis: A Century of Invention and Technological Enthusiasm, 1870–1970* (New York: Viking, 1989); Paul B. Israel, Keith A. Nier, and Louis Carlat, *The Papers of Thomas A. Edison: The Wizard of Menlo Park, 1878* (Baltimore: Johns Hopkins University Press, 1998); and Paul Israel, *Edison: A Life of Invention* (New York: John Wiley & Sons, 1998).

2. Gary Hamel, *Leading the Revolution* (Boston: Harvard Business School Press, 2000), 27.

3. Two books stand out in a sea of biographies on Thomas Edison for their attempts to look at the mythmaking that Edison, journalists, and historians exploited to create the phenomenon that was Edison: Wyn Wachhorst, *Thomas Alva Edison: An American Myth* (Cambridge, MA: MIT Press, 1981), and David

E. Nye, *The Invented Self: An Anti-Biography, from Documents of Thomas A. Edison*, vol. 7 of *Odense University Studies in English* (Odense, Denmark: Odense University Press, 1983).

4. The myth also served journalists and historians, who, on the whole, need stories with a clear protagonist and plot. Magazines reported for years on the progress of Edison's "lieutenants" as they braved Amazonian wilds in their searches for the perfect material to "turn night into day."

5. Quoted in E. I. Schwarz, *The Last Lone Inventor: A Tale of Genius, Deceit, and the Birth of Television* (New York: HarperCollins, 2002), 6.

6. Millard, *Edison and the Business of Innovation*, 35–36.

7. Interestingly, Starr's original patent, in 1846, was rejected because it was not seen as anything new, and because the commercial production of such a design remained unfeasible. For a discussion of Farmer and Starr, see Conot, *Thomas A. Edison*, and for a more detailed consideration of Swan's influence on Edison's work, see Israel, Nier, and Carlat, *The Papers of Thomas A. Edison*. The history of the incandescent lightbulb is much more complex and interconnected than can be related here. A wonderful description was written by William J. Hammer, a colleague of Edison's, and can be found in the *Transactions of the New York Electrical Society*, New Series, No. 4, 1913, <http://www.bulb collector.com/William_Hammer. html> (accessed 27 November 2002).

8. John Law, "After ANT: Complexity, Naming, and Topology," in *Actor Network Theory and After*, ed. John Law and John Hassard (Malden, MA: Blackwell Publishers, 1999), 8.

9. Two enjoyable accounts of the evolution of the telegraph and the telegraph network (as a communication network and as a community) are found in Tom Standage, *The Victorian Internet* (New York: Walker & Company, 1998) and John Steele Gordon, *A Thread Across the Ocean: The Heroic Story of the Transatlantic Cable* (New York: Walker & Company, 2002).

10. Allan Newell and Herbert Simon, *Human Problem Solving* (New York: Prentice-Hall, 1972), 82.

11. Robert Merton, in *On the Shoulders of Giants: A Schandean Postscript* (Chicago: University of Chicago Press, 1993), does a wonderful job of tracing the lineage of this quote, which existed for centuries before Newton got the credit for coming up with it.

12. G. W. Downs and L. B. Mohr, "Conceptual Issues in the Study of Innovation," *Administrative Science Quarterly* 21 (1976): 700–714.

13. Edison also brought the artifacts of other industries into use with the telegraph. His automatic telegraph repeater and writing telegraphs, for example, used mechanisms pulled from watches and typewriters of the time. See Conot, *Thomas A. Edison*.

14. Conot, *Thomas A. Edison*, 80. Conot's biography of Edison, more so than the countless others, offers an unusually detailed description of the technical challenges and accomplishments that surrounded Edison and his work.

15. Millard, *Edison and the Business of Innovation*, 48.

16. Reese V. Jenkins, *The Papers of Thomas A. Edison,* vol. 3 (Baltimore: Johns Hopkins University, 1994); Josephson, *Edison: A Biography,* 87–90.

17. Conot, *Thomas A. Edison,* 43–44, 50, 86.

18. Quoted in Millard, *Edison and the Business of Innovation,* 32.

19. Many of his telegraph patents, for example, came at the same time he was under contract with Western Union, the Atlantic and Pacific Telegraph Company, the Automatic Telegraph Company, the Gold and Stock Company, and others. This often led to trouble, and Edison was almost perpetually involved in patent litigation with clients and between his own work and the work of his sponsors.

20. Conot, *Thomas A. Edison,* 128.

21. Millard, *Edison and the Business of Innovation,* 9.

22. Quoted in Dale Peskin, "Preparing for the Coming Era of Participatory News," <http://www.ojr.org/ojr/future/1017170352.php> (accessed 17 January 2003).

23. Gianfranco Zaccai, interview by author, 21 August 1996. All subsequent quotes from Design Continuum employees are from interviews by author, August 1996.

24. Usher quoted in Henry Petroski, *The Evolution of Useful Things* (New York: Knopf, 1992), 44.

25. Quote attributed to Albert Szent-Györgyi, reprinted at Epcot Center, Florida.

26. It was later in that decade, in 1929, that General Electric, Westinghouse, and even Henry Ford led a publicity campaign called "Light's Golden Jubilee" to crown Edison as the inventor of the lightbulb on the fiftieth anniversary (of sorts) of Edison's achievement.

Chapter 2

1. Alfred D. Chandler Jr., *Scale and Scope: The Dynamics of Industrial Capitalism* (Cambridge, MA: Harvard University Press, 1990), 729.

2. Richard Nelson and Sydney Winter, *An Evolutionary Theory of Economic Change* (Cambridge, MA: Harvard University Press, 1982), 130.

3. George Basalla, *The Evolution of Technology* (New York: Cambridge University Press, 1988).

4. Stephen Segaller, *Nerds 2.0.1: A Brief History of the Internet* (New York: TV Books, 1998).

5. Segaller, *Nerds 2.0.1;* Paul E. Ceruzzi, *A History of Modern Computing* (Cambridge, MA: MIT Press, 2002); Jacob Goldman, "Innovation Isn't the Microsoft Way," *New York Times,* 10 June 2000.

6. Ceruzzi, *A History of Modern Computing,* 234. The year after completing this program, Gates would write the now-famous "Open Letter to Hobbyists" complaining about the many illicit copies of his BASIC program. The original authors of BASIC, two professors at Dartmouth, John G. Kemeny and Thomas E. Kurtz, never made any money from their contribution.

7. The history of rock and roll, and the roots of this music, are meticulously documented in Robert Palmer, *The History of Rock and Roll* (New York: Harmony Books, 1995).

8. *History of Rock and Roll: Shakespeares in the Alley,* WGBH/PBS documentary, 1995.

9. Jonathon Keats, "Oliveira Stands Alone: The Heroic Originality of Our Great Figurative Artist," *San Francisco,* February 2002.

10. See, for example, Robert W. Weisberg, *Creativity: Genius and Other Myths* (New York: Freeman Company, 1986).

11. The history of the Ford Motor Company is primarily drawn from the excellent research of David Hounshell in *From the American System to Mass Production, 1800–1932: The Development of Manufacturing Technology in the United States,* vol. 4, *Studies of Industry and Society* (Baltimore: Johns Hopkins University Press, 1984). For those interested in this history, another useful compilation of the events and impact of Fordism is Thomas P. Hughes, *American Genesis: A Century of Invention and Technological Enthusiasm, 1870–1970* (New York: Viking, 1989). Data are also taken from David C. Mowery and Nathan Rosenberg, *Paths of Innovation: Technological Change in 20th Century America* (New York: Cambridge University Press, 1998).

12. Hounshell, *From the American System,* 218.

13. Ibid., 221.

14. Alfred D. Chandler Jr., "The Integration of Mass Production and Mass Distribution," Note 9-377-031, rev. ed., Harvard Business School, 1995; see also Chandler, *The Visible Hand* (Cambridge, MA: Belknap Press, 1977).

15. Chandler, "The Integration of Mass Production," 3.

16. Hounshell, *From the American System,* 229.

17. Ibid., 244–256.

18. Ibid., 241.

19. Ibid., 241.

20. Brent Goldfarb, "Adoption of General Purpose Technologies: Understanding Adoption Patterns in the Electrification of U.S. Manufacturing 1880–1930," working paper, University of Maryland, Robert H. Smith School of Business, 2002.

21. John Steele Gordon, *The Business of America: Tales from the Marketplace—American Enterprise from the Settling of New England to the Breakup of AT&T* (New York: Walker & Company, 2001).

22. Paul Rabinow, in *Making PCR: A Story of Biotechnology* (Chicago: University of Chicago Press, 1996), not only provides an explanation of the science behind PCR and the biotechnology revolution, but also offers a glimpse into the people and events that brought hitherto unrelated ideas together in new ways.

23. Rabinow, *Making PCR,* 6–7.

Chapter 3

1. Of course, Pasteur may have simply paraphrased Horace Walpole's 1754 term *serendipity*, used to describe those chance discoveries made by the three

princes of Serendip in the children's fable of that name. Walpole explains, in a letter to a friend, that these princes "were always making discoveries, by accident and sagacity, of things they were not in quest of." Sagacity, of course, refers to the *understanding* necessary to see and value the potential of any discovery. Richard Boyle, "The Three Princes of Serendip," 2000, <http://livingheritage.org/three_ princes.htm> (accessed 28 October 2002).

2. This story of chance discovery is one that Nobel himself refuted, arguing that he discovered the value of stabilizing nitroglycerin in a diatomaceous sand only after careful investigation and experimentation with a variety of materials.

3. Robertson Davies, *World of Wonder,* in *The Deptford Trilogy* (New York: Penguin Books, 1990), 534.

4. Robert Conot, *Thomas A. Edison: A Streak of Luck* (New York: De Capo Press, 1979), 162. The leading competitors in electric lighting declared that Edison's plans were "so manifestly absurd as to indicate a positive want of knowledge of the electrical circuit and the principle governing the construction and operation of electric machines."

5. Mark Granovetter, "The Strength of Weak Ties," *American Journal of Sociology* 78 (1973): 1360–1380.

6. Ronald S. Burt, "The Social Structure of Competition," in *Networks and Organizations: Structure, Form, and Action,* ed. N. Nohria and R. G. Eccles (Boston: Harvard Business School Press, 1992); Ronald S. Burt, *Structural Holes: The Social Structure of Competition* (Cambridge, MA: Harvard University Press, 1992).

7. Lawrence Lessig provides a wonderfully written, extensively researched, and cogent argument on Microsoft's tactics in his book *The Future of Ideas: The Fate of the Commons in a Wired World* (New York: Random House, 2001).

8. According to SEC filings for the first quarter of the fiscal year beginning 2002, Microsoft made $2.48 billion on sales of its Windows operating system, $1.88 billion in office software, and $0.5 billion in server operating systems. Those profits supported losses of $107 million in the "home and entertainment" category (read Xbox), $97 million in MSN Internet access and services, $33 million in handheld and cellular operating systems, and $68 million in small-office software. Joseph Menn, "Microsoft Discloses Its Winners, Losers," *Los Angeles Times,* 16 November 2002.

9. Paul DiMaggio, "Nadel's Paradox Revisited: Relational and Cultural Aspects of Organizational Structures," in *Networks and Organization: Structure, Form, and Action,* ed. Nitin Nohria and Robert Eccles (Boston: Harvard Business School Press, 1992), 118–142.

Chapter 4

1. Rob Sabin, "The Movies' Digital Future Is in Sight and It Works," *New York Times,* 26 November 2000.

2. Sally Kline, *George Lucas: Interviews* (Jackson: University Press of Mississippi, 1999), 170–171.

3. Ibid., 173.

4. Ibid., 178.

5. Sabin, "The Movies' Digital Future Is in Sight and It Works."

6. Ibid.

7. J. A. Chatman and K. A. Jehn, "Assessing the Relationship between Industry Characteristics and Organizational Culture: How Different Can You Be?" *Academy of Management Journal* 37 (1994): 522–553.

8. Lee Roy Beach, *The Psychology of Decision Making: People in Organizations* (Thousand Oaks, CA: Sage, 1997), 25.

9. The Battle of the Systems is described in great detail in Andre Millard, *Edison and the Business of Innovation* (Baltimore: John Hopkins University Press, 1990), as well as in Robert Conot, *Thomas A. Edison: A Streak of Luck* (New York: De Capo Press, 1979), and Thomas P. Hughes, *American Genesis: A Century of Invention and Technological Enthusiasm, 1870–1970* (New York: Viking, 1989). The quote from Harold Passer is cited in Millard, *Edison and the Business of Innovation*, 101.

10. "Edison and the Miracle of Light," *The American Experience*, WGBH Education Foundation, 1995.

11. Millard, *Edison and the Business of Innovation*, 3.

12. John Steele Gordon, *The Business of America: Tales from the Marketplace—American Enterprise from the Settling of New England to the Breakup of AT&T* (New York: Walker & Company, 2001).

13. Dean Keith Simonton, "Foresight in Insight? A Darwinian Answer," in *The Nature of Insight*, ed. Robert J. Sternberg and Janet E. Davidson (Cambridge, MA: MIT Press, 1996), 468.

14. Howard Gardner, *Creating Minds: An Anatomy of Creativity through the Lives of Freud, Einstein, Picasso, Stravinsky, Eliot, Graham, and Gandhi* (New York: HarperCollins, 1993), 114.

15. Ibid., 127.

16. Simonton, "Foresight in Insight?" 470.

17. Gardner, *Creating Minds*, 131.

18. Elting Morison, *Men, Machines, and Modern Times* (Cambridge, MA: MIT Press, 1966), 40.

Chapter 5

1. Thomas P. Hughes, *American Genesis: A Century of Invention and Technological Enthusiasm 1870–1970* (New York: Viking, 1989), 91.

2. Robert Conot, *Thomas A. Edison: A Streak of Luck* (New York: De Capo Press, 1979), 469.

3. Nathan Rosenberg, "Technological Interdependence in the American Economy," *Technology and Culture* 20 (1979): 25.

4. John H. Lienhard, "A Better Mousetrap," <http://www.uh.edu/engines/epi1163.htm> (accessed 7 November 2002).

5. J. A. Hope, "A Better Mousetrap," *American Heritage*, October 1996, 90–97.

6. De Forest's triode was an alteration of Fleming's diode rectifying tube. Adding a third electrode, in the form of a grid of wires surrounding the cathode,

De Forest found he could use an electric signal to increase or decrease the flow of electrons from the cathode to the anode. In this way, voice signals could be amplified using a variant of Fleming's diode, which was itself a variant of the incandescent lightbulb—making the vacuum tube triode the grandchild of Edison's lightbulb. In essence, the triode was by the 1940s based on a fifty-year-old technology meant originally to turn electricity into light. It never fully adapted to a purely electrical component, and J. R. Pierce, one of the researchers at AT&T's Bell Labs, summed the situation up once by saying "Nature abhors the vacuum tube."

7. See ScienCentral, Inc. and The American Institute of Physics, "John Bardeen," <http://www.pbs.org/transistor/album1/bardeen/bardeen2.html> (accessed 18 January 2003).

8. ScienCentral, Inc. and The American Institute of Physics, "Shockley, Brattain and Bardeen: Clashing Egos to the End," <http://www.pbs.org/transistor/album1/addlbios/egos.html> (accessed 2 May 2002).

9. T. R. Reid, in *The Chip: How Two Americans Invented the Microchip and Launched a Revolution* (New York: Random House, 2001), describes the links between Edison's experiences while perfecting the electric light for commercial use and the research of physicists just on the brink of quantum mechanics. For example, one of Edison's anonymous muckers, Francis Upton, would recognize within the problem of soot accumulating inside lightbulbs the phenomenon of thermionic emission, which became known, of course, as the Edison effect. Another, John A. Fleming, a physics professor consulting to Edison's London subsidiary, used this finding to develop the first cathode ray tube and, twenty years later, to build the first reliable radio receiver for Marconi's Wireless Telegraph Company. His contribution, the Fleming diode, was the child of Edison's lightbulb and, in turn, became the father of the vacuum tube. This connection has almost run its course, as we witness the big, bulky computer and television monitors made with cathode ray tubes—essentially big lightbulbs—being phased out in favor of the digital, transistorized LCDs. After 125 years, the lightbulb's broad diffusion into other uses has receded, and its last incarnation may very well be its first, the incandescent bulb.

10. This retelling of the story of the integrated circuit owes much to T. R. Reid's descriptions of the events at Fairchild and Texas Instruments, as well as his very useful explanations of the technologies and science that made the transistor and integrated circuit possible (see T. R. Reid, *The Chip*), and to Ernest Braun and Stuart McDonald, *Revolution in Miniature: The History and Impact of Semiconductor Electronics*, 2d rev. ed. (New York: Cambridge University Press, 1982).

11. The history of the Whiz Kids is documented in John A. Byrne, *The Whiz Kids* (New York: Doubleday, 1993), as well as in David Halberstam, *The Reckoning* (New York: Morrow, 1986).

12. Steven Levy, in *Hackers: Heroes of the Computer Revolution* (New York: Doubleday, 1984), provides a useful description of the role played by the MIT Tech Model Railroad Club in the early days of computing and of how the club's "hacker" values helped shape a generation of software programmers and helped launch the video game industry.

13. Michael P. Farrell, "Artists' Circles and the Development of Artists," *Journal of Small Group Behavior* 13 (1982): 451–474.

14. Ibid., 459.

15. Emile Zola, *The Masterpiece,* quoted in Farrell, "Artists' Circles and the Development of Artists."

16. Nathan Rosenberg's *Inside the Black Box: Technology and Economics* (New York: Cambridge University Press, 1982) does an excellent job of describing the improvements driven by learning-in-use as well as the impact that many such contributions have had on the productivity of technology. See also S. C. Gilfillan, *Inventing the Ship* (Chicago: Follett Publishing Company, 1935), for an in-depth description of such interdependent improvements to the steamship.

17. A small population of innovation scholars are recognizing the role played by the network of actors that crystallizes around an emerging technology. Prominent among them are Andrew Van de Ven and Raghu Garud, who laid out a framework in 1989 for understanding how new industries emerged around technological innovations. They argue, for example, that "the commercial success of a technological innovation is in great measure a reflection of the institutional innovations which embody the social, economic, and political infrastructure that any community needs to sustain its members." A. H. Van de Ven and R. Garud, "A Framework for Understanding the Emergence of New Industries," in *Research on Technological Innovation and Management Policy,* vol. 4, ed. R. Rosenbloom and R. Burgelman (Greenwich, CT: JAI Press, 1989), 195–226.

18. Evan Schwartz, *The Last Lone Inventor: A Tale of Genius, Deceit and the Birth of Television* (New York: HarperCollins, 2002), 2.

19. See ScienCentral, Inc. and The American Institute of Physics, "John Bardeen," <http://www.pbs.org/transistor/album1/bardeen/bardeen2.html> (accessed 18 January 2003).

20. Phil Harvey, "Alcatel Leads with a Suit," *Red Herring,* 9 August 2000; Ed Paulson, *Inside Cisco: The Real Story of Sustained M&A Growth* (New York: John Wiley & Sons, 2001); David Mayer and Martin Kenney, "Economic Action Does Not Take Place in a Vacuum: Understanding Cisco's Acquisition and Development Strategy," Berkeley Roundtable on the International Economy, University of California at Berkeley, September 2002.

21. Deborah Gladstein Ancona and David F. Caldwell, "Making Teamwork Work: Boundary Management in Product Development Teams," in *Managing Strategic Innovation and Change,* ed. Michael Tushman and Philip Anderson (New York: Oxford University Press, 1997).

22. Robert I. Sutton and Andrew Hargadon, "Brainstorming Groups in Context: Effectiveness in a Product Design Firm," *Administrative Science Quarterly* 41 (1996): 685–718.

23. Etienne Wenger, *Communities of Practice: Learning, Meaning, and Identity* (New York: Cambridge University Press, 1998). To see how these ideas have been applied to organizations, see also Julian Orr, *Talking about Machines: An Ethnography of a Modern Job* (Ithaca, NY: IRL Press, 1996); and John Seely Brown

and Paul Duguid, *The Social Life of Information* (Boston: Harvard Business School Press, 2000).

24. Michael Lamm, "The Earl of Detroit," *Invention & Technology,* Fall 1998.

25. Ralph Katz and Thomas J. Allen, "Investigating the Not Invented Here (NIH) Syndrome: A Look at Performance, Tenure, and Communication Patterns of 50 R&D Project Groups," *R&D Management* 12, no. 1 (1982): 7–19.

26. Michael Schrage, "What's that Bad Odor at Innovation Skunkworks?" *Fortune,* 20 December 1999.

27. Edward Baig, "Turn a Page on Twenty Years of Progress," *USA Today,* 8 August 2001.

28. David E. Nye, *The Invented Self: An Anti-Biography, from Documents of Thomas A. Edison.* vol. 7 of *Odense University Studies in English* (Odense, Denmark: Odense University Press, 1983), 126.

Chapter 6

1. Thomas P. Hughes documents much of Sperry's career and the details of his work in *Elmer Sperry: Inventor and Engineer* (Baltimore: Johns Hopkins Press, 1971) and *American Genesis: A Century of Invention and Technological Enthusiasm, 1870–1970* (New York: Viking, 1989). The quotes are from Hughes, *American Genesis,* 68, and Hughes, *Elmer Sperry,* xvi.

2. Hughes, *American Genesis,* 54.

3. Martin Kenney, ed., *Understanding Silicon Valley: The Anatomy of an Entrepreneurial Region* (Stanford, CA: Stanford University Press, 2000) provides a very informative set of studies undertaken to understand what made the Silicon Valley what it is today.

4. Mark C. Suchman, "Dealmakers and Counselors: Law Firms as Intermediaries in the Development of Silicon Valley," in Kenney, *Understanding Silicon Valley.*

5. Martin Kenney and Richard Florida, "Venture Capital in Silicon Valley: Fueling New Firm Formation," in Kenney, *Understanding Silicon Valley.*

6. To give a sense of the vantage point that suppliers have over changes in an industry, when I was working for Apple Computer, we would often find out from our suppliers what other groups in Apple were doing (e.g., what the state of the project was, what technical choices they were making)—information that was not readily shared by engineers across divisions.

7. For a brief but valuable description of the evolution of the machine tool industry, see Nathan Rosenberg, "Technological Change in the Machine Tool Industry, 1840–1910," *Journal of Economic History* 23 (1963): 414–443.

8. Eric von Hippel, *The Sources of Innovation* (New York: Oxford University Press, 1988); Eric von Hippel, Stefan Thomke, and Mary Sonnan, "Creating Breakthroughs at 3M," *Harvard Business Review,* September–October 1999, 47–57.

9. Willard Mueller, "The Origins of the Basic Innovations Underlying DuPont's Major Product and Process Innovations, 1920 to 1950," in *The Rate and Direction of Inventive Activity: Economic and Social Factors* (Princeton, NJ: National Bureau of Economics, 1962), 323–358.

Chapter 7

1. David Kelley, interview by author.

2. Tom Peters, *Liberation Management* (New York: Knopf, 1992).

3. Ibid., 167.

4. David Kelley interview.

5. Andre Millard, *Edison and The Business of Innovation* (Baltimore: Johns Hopkins University Press, 1990), 9.

6. Quote attributed to Thomas Edison, reprinted at Epcot Center, Florida.

7. Gian Zaccai, interview by author, 21 August 1996.

8. Millard, *Edison and The Business of Innovation*, 34–35.

9. Ibid., 40.

10. Research has begun to apply the concept of wisdom within organizational settings and within the innovative activities of new-product development teams. For the former, see John A. Meacham, "The Loss of Wisdom," in *Wisdom: Its Nature, Origins, and Development*, ed. R. Sternberg (New York: Cambridge University Press, 1990), 181–211; and Karl E. Weick, "The Collapse of Sensemaking in Organizations: The Mann Gulch Disaster," *Administrative Science Quarterly* 38 (1993): 628–652. For the latter, see Robert I. Sutton and Andrew Hargadon, "Brainstorming Groups in Context: Effectiveness in a Product Design Firm," *Administrative Science Quarterly* 41 (1996): 685–718.

11. W. B. Cannon, "The Role of Chance in Discovery," *Scientific Monthly* 50 (1940): 208.

Chapter 8

1. DuPont's history comes from DuPont's Web site, <http:www.dupont.com>, as well as Willard Mueller, "The Origins of the Basic Innovations Underlying DuPont's Major Product and Process Innovations, 1920 to 1950," in *The Rate and Direction of Inventive Activity: Economic and Social Factors* (Princeton, NJ: National Bureau of Economics, 1962), 323–358.

2. Hewlett-Packard, "HP Announces Strategic Realignment to Create Two Companies," press release, Palo Alto, California, 2 March 1999.

3. Frederick Brooks, Jr., *The Mythical Man-Month* (Reading, MA: Addison-Wesley, 1995), 18, 25.

4. The quoted phrase refers to the title of a study of Xerox by Douglas K. Smith and Robert C. Alexander, *Fumbling the Future: How Xerox Invented, Then Ignored, the First Personal Computer* (San Jose, CA: toExcel, 1999).

5. 3M Worldwide, "Roger Appeldorn and the Creation of Microreplication Technology," <http://www.3M.com/about3m/pioneers/appeldorn.jhtml> (accessed 28 March 2002).

6. The history of Augustin Jean Fresnel is another great story of innovation in an off-the-beaten-path and now obsolete technology. Fresnel improved upon the existing design of lighthouse lamps (which consisted of a lamp and rotating parabolic reflector) by designing a barrel-shaped set of lenses to fit around the gas lamp of a lighthouse, which redirected most of the available light into a horizontal beam. His innovation was not simply to put a magnifying lens in front of a lamp, but to

recognize that a giant magnifying lens could be broken into sections, each made considerably thinner because the angle of the outer surfaces and not the width of the glass changed the direction of the light. This modular form of focusing lens could be made and transported easily. The modular form also made it possible to build the same set of lenses for different-sized lamps. Further, it was possible to substitute colored panels and thus, for the first time, for lighthouses to signal their identity (as a unique sequence of alternating colored lights) as the lamps rotated. Ships coming close to shore could find their position exactly by triangulating between lighthouses. Fresnel's design was adopted immediately worldwide and was the dominant design until well into the twentieth century. A brief but interesting history can be found at <http://terrypepper.com/lights/fresnel/fresnel.htm> (accessed 28 March 2002).

7. 3M Worldwide, "Roger Appeldorn."

8. Thomas Stewart, "3M Fights Back," *Fortune,* 5 February 1996.

9. Corey Billington, interview by author, 3 October 1996.

10. Matthew Josephson, *Edison: A Biography* (New York: John Wiley & Sons, 1959), 431.

11. Fara Warner, "Creative Drive," *Fast Company*, September 2001; see also <http://www.designworksusa.com> (accessed 19 July 2002).

12. Fara Warner, "Creative Drive," *Fast Company*, September 2001, 43.

Chapter 9

1. Lawrence Osborn, "Got Silk?" *New York Times Magazine,* 16 June 2002.

2. Stephen Segaller, *Nerds 2.0.1: A Brief History of the Internet* (New York: TV Books, 1998).

3. Elting Morison, *Men, Machines, and Modern Times* (Cambridge, MA: MIT Press, 1966).

4. Ibid., 22.

5. When Theodore Roosevelt was 24, he wrote *The Naval War of 1812*, still considered one of the best historical accounts of the naval engagements of the war. In addition, he served briefly in 1897–1898 as Assistant Secretary of the Navy. He is widely considered the father of the modern navy for his insistence on installing the U.S. fleet as the dominant naval power in the world.

6. Steven L. Kent, *The Ultimate History of Video Games* (Roseville, CA: Prima Publishing, 2001), 574.

7. Dean Takahashi's *Opening the XBox* (Roseville, CA: Prima Publishing, 2002) provides a nice history of the development of Microsoft's game console.

8. Takahashi, *Opening the XBox* , 131.

9. Fara Warner, "Detroit Muscle," *Fast Company,* June 2002.

Chapter 10

1. Steven L. Kent, in *The Ultimate History of Video Games* (Roseville, CA: Prima Publishing, 2001), called Bushnell "an electrical engineer and inventor whose only invention was a $14 billion industry" (p. 28).

2. Robert A. Guth, "Sony Is Grooming Games Maverick for the Next Level," *Wall Street Journal,* 18 November 2002.

3. Phil Harvey, "Alcatel Leads with a Suit," *Red Herring*, 9 August 2000.

4. David Pogue, "Profit and Innovation at Microsoft," *New York Times*, 21 November 2002; Joseph Menn, "Microsoft Discloses Its Winners, Losers," *Los Angeles Times*, 16 November 2002; Lawrence Lessig, *The Future of Ideas: The Fate of the Commons in a Wired World* (New York: Random House, 2001), 61–68.

5. Reuven Brenner, "Reforming the Idea Race," *Wall Street Journal*, 19 November 2002.

6. Quote attributed to Albert Einstein.

Epilogue

1. John Schwarz, "Dot-Com Is Dot-Gone, and the Dream with It," *New York Times*, 25 November 2001.

Further Reading

General Reading on Innovation and Organizations

Brown, Shona L., and Kathleen M. Eisenhardt. *Competing on the Edge: Strategy as Structured Chaos*. Boston: Harvard Business School Press, 1998.

Leonard-Barton, Dorothy. *Wellsprings of Knowledge: Building and Sustaining the Sources of Innovation*. Boston: Harvard Business School Press, 1995.

Nonaka, Ikujiro, and Hiro Takeuchi. *The Knowledge-Creating Company: How Japanese Companies Create the Dynamics of Innovation*. New York: Oxford University Press, 1995.

Sutton, Robert I. *Weird Ideas That Work: 11-1/2 Practices for Promoting, Managing, and Sustaining Innovation*. New York: Free Press, 2002.

Tushman, Michael, and Charles A. O'Reilly. *Winning through Innovation: A Practical Guide to Leading Organizational Change and Renewal*. Boston: Harvard Business School Press, 1997.

von Hippel, Eric. *The Sources of Innovation*. New York: Oxford University Press, 1988.

Chapter 1

Thomas A. Edison

Conot, Robert E. *Thomas A. Edison: A Streak of Luck*. New York: De Capo Press, 1979.

Israel, Paul. *Edison: A Life of Invention*. New York: John Wiley, 1998.

Millard, Andre. *Edison and the Business of Innovation*. Baltimore: Johns Hopkins University Press, 1990.

Nye, David E. *The Invented Self: An Anti-Biography, from Documents of Thomas A. Edison*, vol. 7 of *Odense University Studies in English*. Odense, Denmark: Odense University Press, 1983.

Social Studies of Technology and Innovation

Bijker, Wiebe E. *Of Bicycles, Bakelites, and Bulbs: Toward a Theory of Sociotechnical Change.* Cambridge, MA: MIT Press, 1995.

Bijker, Wiebe E., Thomas P. Hughes, and Trevor J. Pinch, eds. *The Social Construction of Technological Systems: New Directions in the Sociology and History of Technology.* Cambridge, MA: MIT Press, 1989.

Hughes, Thomas Parke. *American Genesis: A Century of Invention and Technological Enthusiasm, 1870–1970.* New York: Viking, 1989.

Law, John, and John Hassard. *Actor Network Theory and After.* Oxford, UK: Blackwell Publishers, 1999.

Westney, D. Eleanor. *Imitation and Innovation: The Transfer of Western Organizational Patterns to Meiji Japan.* Cambridge, MA: Harvard University Press, 1987.

PCR and the Biotech Revolution

Judson, Horace Freeland. *The Eighth Day of Creation: Makers of the Revolution in Biology.* Expanded ed. Plainview, NY: CSHL Press, 1996.

Rabinow, Paul. *Making PCR: A Story of Biotechnology.* Chicago: University of Chicago Press, 1996.

The Telegraph

Gordon, John Steele. *The Business of America: Tales from the Marketplace—American Enterprise from the Settling of New England to the Breakup of AT&T.* New York: Walker and Company, 2001.

Standage, Tom. *The Victorian Internet: The Remarkable Story of the Telegraph and the Nineteenth Century's On-line Pioneers.* New York: Walker and Company, 1998.

Chapter 2

Histories of Innovation

Basalla, George. *The Evolution of Technology.* New York: Cambridge University Press, 1988.

Ceruzzi, Paul E. *A History of Modern Computing.* Cambridge, MA: MIT Press, 1998.

Gilfillan, S. C. *Inventing the Ship.* Chicago: Follet, 1935.

Hounshell, David A. *From the American System to Mass Production, 1800–1932: The Development of Manufacturing Technology in the United States,* vol. 4, *Studies in Industry and Society.* Baltimore: Johns Hopkins University Press, 1984.

Hughes, Thomas Parke. *American Genesis: A Century of Invention and Technological Enthusiasm, 1870–1970.* New York: Viking, 1989.

Palmer, Robert. *Rock & Roll: An Unruly History.* New York: Harmony Books, 1995.

Petroski, Henry. *The Evolution of Useful Things.* New York: Alfred A. Knopf, 1992.

Rosenberg, Nathan. *Inside the Black Box*. New York: Cambridge University Press, 1982.
Usher, Abbott Payson. *History of Mechanical Invention*. Cambridge, MA: Harvard University Press, 1929.

History of Ford Motor Company
Chandler, Alfred D. *Scale and Scope: The Dynamics of Industrial Capitalism*. Cambridge, MA: Belknap Press, 1990.
Hounshell, David A. *From the American System to Mass Production, 1800–1932: The Development of Manufacturing Technology in the United States*, vol. 4, *Studies in Industry and Society*. Baltimore: Johns Hopkins University Press, 1984.
Hughes, Thomas Parke. *American Genesis: A Century of Invention and Technological Enthusiasm, 1870–1970*. New York: Viking, 1989.

Chapter 3
Social Network Theory
Burt, R. S. *Structural Holes: The Social Structure of Competition*. Cambridge, MA: Harvard University Press, 1992.
Granovetter, Mark. *Getting a Job*. Cambridge, MA: Harvard University Press, 1974.

Chapter 4
Small Worlds—A Network Perspective
Barabási, Albert-Laszló. *Linked: The New Science of Networks*. Cambridge, MA: Perseus Publishing, 2002.
Gladwell, Malcolm. *The Tipping Point: How Little Things Can Make a Big Difference*. New York: Little, Brown, 2000.
Watts, Duncan J. *Small Worlds: The Dynamics of Networks Between Order and Randomness*. Princeton, NJ: Princeton University Press, 1999.

Small Worlds—In Organizations and Industries
Davenport, Thomas H., and Laurence Prusak. *Working Knowledge: How Organizations Manage What They Know*. Boston: Harvard Business School Press, 1998.
Saxenian, AnnaLee. *Regional Advantage: Culture and Competition in Silicon Valley and Route 128*. Cambridge, MA: Harvard University Press, 1994.
Weick, Karl E. *Sensemaking in Organizations*. Thousand Oaks, CA: Sage Publications, 1995.

Creative Insight
Gardner, Howard. *Creating Minds: An Anatomy of Creativity Seen Through the Lives of Freud, Einstein, Picasso, Stravinsky, Eliot, Graham, and Gandhi*. New York: Basic Books, 1993.

Koestler, Arthur. *The Act of Creation*. New York: Dell, 1964.

Simonton, Dean Keith. *Origins of Genius: Darwinian Perspectives on Creativity*. New York: Oxford University Press, 1999.

Sternberg, Robert J., ed. *Handbook of Creativity*. New York: Cambridge University Press, 1999.

Chapter 5

Collectives

Bennis, Warren G., and Patricia Ward Biederman. *Organizing Genius: The Secret of Creative Collaboration*. Reading, MA: Addison-Wesley, 1997.

Farrell, Michael P. "Artists' Circles and the Development of Artists." *Small Group Behavior* 13, no. 4 (1982): 451–474.

History of the Transistor and Early Computing

Braun, Ernest, and Stuart Macdonald. *Revolution in Miniature: The History and Impact of Semiconductor Electronics*. 2d ed. New York: Cambridge University Press, 1982.

Ceruzzi, Paul E. *A History of Modern Computing*. Cambridge, MA: MIT Press, 1998.

Reid, T. R. *The Chip: How Two Americans Invented the Microchip and Launched a Revolution*. Rev. ed. New York: Random House, 2001.

Riordan, Michael, and Lillian Hoddeson. *Crystal Fire: The Birth of the Information Age*. New York: W. W. Norton, 1997.

Building Communities in Organizations

Brown, John Seely, and Paul Duguid. *The Social Life of Information*. Boston: Harvard Business School Press, 2000.

Cohen, Don, and Laurence Prusak. *In Good Company: How Social Capital Makes Organizations Work*. Boston: Harvard Business School Press, 2001.

Lave, Jean, and Etienne Wenger. *Situated Learning: Legitimate Peripheral Participation, Learning in Doing*. New York: Cambridge University Press, 1991.

Wenger, Etienne, Richard A. McDermott, and William Snyder. *Cultivating Communities of Practice: A Guide to Managing Knowledge*. Boston: Harvard Business School Press, 2002.

Building Communities in Industries

Gladwell, Malcolm. *The Tipping Point: How Little Things Can Make a Big Difference*. New York: Little, Brown, 2000.

Hughes, Thomas Parke. *Networks of Power*. Baltimore: Johns Hopkins University Press, 1983.

Kenney, Martin. *Understanding Silicon Valley: The Anatomy of an Entrepreneurial Region*. Stanford, CA: Stanford University Press, 2000.

Saxenian, AnnaLee. *Regional Advantage: Culture and Competition in Silicon Valley and Route 128*. Cambridge, MA: Harvard University Press, 1994.

Segaller, Stephen. *Nerds 2.0.1: A Brief History of the Internet*. New York: TV Books, 1998.

Shapiro, Carl, and Hal R. Varian. *Information Rules: A Strategic Guide to the Network Economy*. Boston: Harvard Business School Press, 1998.

Chapter 6
Elmer Sperry
Hughes, Thomas Parke. *Elmer Sperry: Inventor and Engineer*. Baltimore: Johns Hopkins University Press, 1971.

Chapter 7
IDEO
Kelley, Thomas, and Jonathan Littman. *The Art of Innovation: Lessons in Creativity from IDEO, America's Leading Design Firm*. New York: Currency, 2001.

Chapter 8
Xerox PARC
Hiltzik, Michael A. *Dealers of Lightning: Xerox PARC and the Dawn of the Computer Age*. New York: HarperBusiness, 1999.

Segaller, Stephen. *Nerds 2.0.1: A Brief History of the Internet*. New York: TV Books, 1998.

Smith, Douglas K., and Robert C. Alexander. *Fumbling the Future: How Xerox Invented, Then Ignored, the First Personal Computer*. New York: William Morrow, 1988.

3M
Gundling, Ernest, and Jerry I. Porras. *The 3M Way to Innovation: Balancing People and Profit*. New York: Kodansha International, 2000.

Kanter, Rosabeth Moss, John J. Kao, and Frederik D. Wiersema. *Innovation: Breakthrough Ideas at 3M, Dupont, GE, Pfizer, and Rubbermaid*. New York: HarperBusiness, 1997.

Chapter 9
Continuous Aim Firing
Morison, Elting Elmore. *Men, Machines, and Modern Times*. Cambridge, MA: MIT Press, 1966.

The Xbox and the Video Game Industry
Kent, Steve L. *The Ultimate History of Video Games: From Pong to Pokémon and Beyond: The Story Behind the Craze That Touched Our Lives and Changed the World*. Roseville, CA: Prima Publishing, 2001.

Takahashi, Dean. *Opening the Xbox: Inside Microsoft's Plan to Unleash an Entertainment Revolution*. Roseville, CA: Prima Publishing, 2002.

Chapter 10

Intellectual Property

Lessig, Lawrence. *The Future of Ideas: The Fate of the Commons in a Connected World*. New York: Random House, 2001.

Index

About the Author

ANDREW HARGADON is Assistant Professor of Technology Management at the Graduate School of Management at the University of California, Davis, where his work focuses on the management of technology and innovation. He has previously worked as an engineer and designer for IDEO and Apple Computer and has consulted for firms including Hewlett-Packard, Nike, and SabreLabs.

Hargadon has written more than thirty articles in scholarly and applied publications on the management of technology and innovation, including the role of knowledge management in new product development, creativity and innovation among engineers, speed and quality in new product development, and the role of design in the diffusion of innovation. He serves on the editorial boards of numerous scholarly publications.

Hargadon received his Ph.D. in management science and engineering from Stanford University's School of Engineering, where he was the Boeing Fellow in Stanford's Alliance for Innovative Manufacturing. He received his B.S. and M.S. in product design from the Mechanical Engineering Department in Stanford University's School of Engineering.